DEVELOPMENTAL PSYCHOLOGY & YOU

Julia C. Berryman
David Hargreaves   Martin Herbert
& Ann Taylor

and Routledge

THE AUTHORS

Julia C. Berryman: Department of Adult Education, University of Leicester
David Hargreaves: Department of Psychology, University of Leicester
Martin Herbert: Child Health Directorate, Plymouth Health Authority
Ann Taylor: Department of Psychology, University of Leicester

First published in 1991 by BPS Books (The British Psychological Society),
St Andrews House, 48 Princess Road East, Leicester LE1 7DR, in association with
Routledge Ltd, 11 New-Fetter Lane, London EC4 4EE.

Reprinted 1992, 1994

A catalogue record for this book is available from the British Library.

Library of Congress Cataloguing-in-Publication Data is available.

ISBN 1 85433 068 3 paperback
ISBN 1 85433 069 1 hardback

Typeset by Bookman Ltd, Bristol BS31DX
Printed and bound in Great Britain
Whilst every effort has been made to ensure the accuracy of the contents of this publication,
the publishers and authors expressly disclaim responsibilty in law for negligence or any other
cause of action whatsoever.

CONTENTS

Start reading this book at the point, chapter or subheading that interests you most. Each chapter is relatively self-contained but refers you to other related chapters as appropriate. A glossary at the end defines all the technical terms. We hope that by dipping in here and there you will soon find that you have read the whole book.

LIST OF EXERCISES

LIST OF FIGURES AND TABLES

PREFACE AND ACKNOWLEDGEMENTS

Developmental Psychology & You is written for those with no previous knowledge of this subject. We have assumed that our readers will have only a small acquaintance with psychology – perhaps familiarity with an introductory text such as *Psychology & You*, but no more than this. Our aim is to whet the reader's appetite for this subject and to stimulate interest so that readers will want to follow-up and extend their knowledge of the topics discussed here. Space does not permit our book to be a comprehensive introduction to developmental psychology; we have had to be selective in the areas that we have chosen and making such choices is always an invidious task. Our selection of topics has been based on our experience as teachers: we have taken those areas that we have found to be exciting and intriguing to our students and have presented the material in ways that we feel make the topics particularly relevant to everyday life. With this in mind we have included many exercises that we hope will stimulate interest in a very practical way. We have not adopted a uniform 'ages and stages' approach in each chapter because we have tried to present each topic so that it is most accessible to new students. Psychological research within each area has not produced a uniform picture of development across the life span and for this reason we have sometimes focused on a particular stage in life – the early years for example – whereas at other times a longer view has been explored or some particularly interesting research studies within a given area have been considered. Naturally much has been left out, but we trust that what we have included will open mental doors and windows. If this is achieved then our aims have been fulfilled. The rest is up to you. Annotated recommended reading and references will enable you to pursue your interests, in what we hope will be a life-long enthusiasm for this subject.

Many people have played a vital part in the preparation of this book: Philip Drew, Linda Hargreaves and D.R. Davies, who have given much support and many helpful comments on drafts of the manuscript; Jonathan and Thomas Hargreaves, who gave permission for their drawings, songs and writing to be reproduced; and the many students whose questions and comments have been a major stimulus for producing this book. Our thanks to them all.

1. *What is Developmental Psychology?*

▽ *What is normal development?*
▽ *Methods in the study of development*
▽ *Experiments in psychology*
▽ *Asking questions and forming hypotheses*
▽ *Ethical issues*

Developmental psychology is concerned with exploring all aspects of human psychological development and change. In essence it is about all the sorts of psychological changes – changes in human behaviour, thoughts and feelings – that can occur between cradle and grave. If you pick up a psychology book with the word 'developmental' in the title you will find that the bulk of the book is concerned with childhood, indeed at one time developmental psychology and child psychology were one and the same. The notion of development in adult life was, until recently, hardly considered and it is only in the last four decades that there has been an outbreak of books on adult development and life-span psychology. If you counted all the research studies that deal with development you would still find that most of them focus on the first 15 to 20 years of life and this simple observation is very revealing about when most of us expect to be shaped or formed into the person we are as adults. These ideas are encapsulated in many well-known thoughts, proverbs and sayings about development.

❝ *And the first step, as you know, is always what matters most, particularly when we are dealing with those who are young and tender.* ❞

(Plato 428–348 BC)

❝ *Train up a child in the way he should go: and when he is old, he will not depart from it.* ❞

(Bible, Proverbs 26.22)

❝ *Give me a child for the first seven years and you may do what you like with him afterwards.* **❞**

(Attributed to the Jesuits; see Vincent Lean)

❝ *The Child is father of the Man* **❞**

(William Wordsworth, 1770–1850)

The essence of all of these sayings is that the early years not only lay the foundations of the person, they shape every aspect of that person, making him or her what he or she will become. There's a sense in which this is irrevocable – it may be difficult or impossible to alter the individual who has been formed in a particular way:

❝ *But once a child's character has been spoiled by bad handling, which can be done in a few days, who can say that the damage is ever repaired?* **❞**

(John B. Watson, 1878–1958)

❝ *. . . As the twig is bent the tree's inclined.* **❞**

(Alexander Pope, 1688–1744)

❝ *You cannot teach an old dog new tricks.* **❞**

(Old proverb)

Whether or not you agree with these words they have been influential in shaping popular views of the crucial stages in life – the formative years. Developmental psychologists have tended to concentrate their research efforts on the early years of life, but psychologists are now much more aware of the potential for development and change in adulthood as we shall see in the two final chapters of this book. Before going further let us consider why it is important to study psychological development.

Why study psychological development?

Interest in human development is a rather recent phenomenon. Historians such as Philippe Aries claim that the idea that childhood is an important and valuable period is probably only 200 or so years old. He argued that children were regarded either as miniature and rather inferior adults or were viewed with indifference. They were reared strictly and were often severely punished. Infant mortality was so high that it was felt to be futile to grieve over the death of a child. A scientific interest in the study of childhood is inconsistent with this lack of concern.

Charles Darwin was amongst the first to keep a detailed diary of one of his sons, Doddy, from birth. In his *Biographical Sketch of an Infant* (1877) he reflected on the causation of his child's behaviour, noting when emotions such as fear or anger were first shown and discussing whether this behaviour showed signs of reason. Not long after this, Stanley Hall, considered by some to be the 'father' of child psychology, published in 1891 his 'Notes on the Study of Infants' and he recorded 'the contents of children's minds . . . ' by asking children numerous questions. Thus began the more systematic study of infancy and childhood. But what are the particular advantages of studying psychological development?

Perhaps one of the most useful results of this field of psychology is that for the first time normal behaviour, thought and emotion for a given age group were documented. There is a tendency for each of us to view ourselves as normal, average, or typical of humans in general; that how we think, feel and behave is how most people do, and every now and again when we encounter someone who seems to be very different from us it can come as a surprise, or even a shock. Developmental psychology has provided data which shows the range of behaviour, thoughts and feelings typical for any particular population, at any particular time. Thus it may show that thumb sucking, temper tantrums, nightmares, or nail biting are all 'pretty normal' at a certain age, because a high proportion of children show these patterns. So what might be viewed as problematic by a new parent encountering these in their first child is seen quite differently once put in the context of children's behaviour in general. Recording in detail the course of human development also enables us to see how events may change or shape the individual. Thus we are able to compare, for example, children reared in the nuclear family with those who are reared in extended families or by just one parent, or orphans who are brought up in institutions. Observing how individuals in these groups develop may give us clues to the importance of parents (or figures fulfilling a parental role) in children's lives, and the importance of love in fostering psychological growth and well-being. Developmental psychology enables us to assess the truth of a whole range of other common assertions about humans:

66 *Leave her to cry – if you pick her up you'll only spoil her.* **99**

66 *Babies and children need their mothers more than anyone; fathers are not so important early on.* **99**

66 *There is no substitute for stable family life, children from broken homes are bound to suffer.* **99**

66 *Little girls are more sensitive and caring towards others than little boys.* **99**

66 *Boys are more boisterous and aggressive: it's in their nature.* **99**

" A good smack for being naughty never did anyone any harm. "

" He's always been bad-tempered, you'll never change him. "

" Second children are always more competitive. "

" Children grow up too quickly these days, it's not good for them. "

" Childhood is the happiest time of life. Children don't have problems. "

Developmental psychologists have devised methods which enable us to investigate the truth of the above statements. This also means that we have a much better idea today of the conditions which foster optimum psychological growth and well-being, and if these are not present we also know what to do to compensate.

If we are to understand ourselves and others better developmental psychology has a key role to play. Understanding the course of human life and the factors which shape the developing person is a cornerstone of psychology, but studying human development is not quite as straightforward as it may, at first, appear to be.

What is normal development?

We all have our own ideas about what people are like at different ages. Two year olds have a reputation for being 'terrible', young teenagers troublesome, and students in their late teens are idealistic, politically active and so on. If one observes people at different ages it is easy to begin to link physical growth to various types of psychological change. Thus one can derive a picture of *age-related norms*, of what is normal for a given age. However, it has become apparent from research over the last century that the 'normal' course of growth has changed dramatically in a matter of decades.

When is puberty? Research on puberty and adolescence provides an interesting example. As boys and girls reach *puberty* (physical maturity) we generally expect that psychological changes accompany the physical changes that take place over some years: the period of adolescence. A growing interest in the opposite sex is the one obvious change, but we also expect a greater maturity of outlook to be linked to this stage. In the 1860s records show that girls in the UK were on average aged 16 or more at menarche (the start of menstruation). For anyone studying development the natural conclusion might be that girls take about 16 years to reach physical maturity: the age when they can become mothers. However in the last 130 years the age at menarche has dropped and today it occurs on average at about twelve and a half. So what has happened? How can a biological timetable speed up so rapidly in such a short period? After all if this rate continued for just a few more centuries the ludicrous outcome would be menstruating newborns! It is not just the age of puberty that has changed: growth rates in two to five year olds are markedly faster today, and full adult height is achieved much earlier than in previous decades and centuries.

The explanation that has been put forward is that greatly improved nutrition, general health and living conditions have accelerated the rate of growth. James Tanner argues that there is always a biological limit for accelerated development, and he believes that we are unlikely to see a continued decline in the age at menarche. Perhaps social conditions of today are so much better than they were a century ago that it may be easier to explain by saying that poor diet and health impede and slow down growth, and that much of the Western world now has optimum conditions for children's growth and development.

But what are the implications of this for developmental psychologists? If physical and psychological development are linked then our concept of what the 12-year-old girl of today is like is quite different from that of only a century ago. The same applies to boys. In medieval Europe the adult male was the size of the average 10 to 12-year-old American boy of today – we know this from the size of knights' armour. Yet although our notion of the age of 'adulthood' has altered, it has certainly not kept pace with the accelerated growth rates discussed here. We might be shocked at the idea of a 12-year-old girl marrying and having a child, yet a hundred years ago it is likely that a 16 year old who did so did not differ so greatly either physically or psychologically from a 12 year old today.

To return to one of the functions of developmental psychology – to define age-related norms – we can see that age *per se* may not necessarily be a helpful guide. In underdeveloped countries of today age at menarche is much later than in developed countries, so we need to take into account social conditions in order to explain human development. Let us now briefly explore how psychological research into development is carried out.

METHODS IN THE STUDY OF DEVELOPMENT

Longitudinal and cross-sectional studies

The quickest way of trying to answer the question 'how do people change as they get older?' is to do a *cross-sectional study*. To investigate how learning ability changes with age, for example, we might devise a series of learning tests and, in a controlled setting, invite groups of 10, 20, 30, 40, 50, 60 and 70 year olds to take the tests, allowing a specified time only. Our participants would be selected so that education, socioeconomic status, and health would be matched across the age groups. The result of this study is quite likely to show that people in their twenties have the greatest learning ability, and that as age increases a slight decline occurs initially and then more markedly in the upper age groups. So can we conclude from this that learning abilities decline past the age of 20? Let us leave this question unanswered whilst we contrast the cross-sectional study with the longitudinal study.

A *longitudinal study* is designed so that individuals are tested or assessed in some way at regular intervals over a period of their lives. In order to study learning ability a sample of individuals would be tested at, for instance, age 20, then tested again 10 years later at 30, and then again after a further 10 years in the final test at 40 years. Thus each participant would be tested three times over 20 years. In this study the three tests given to the participant would have to be similar, but they could not be identical or the experimenter might be accused of simply observing the *practice effect* (an improvement due merely to repeating the same task).

What results might be recorded after 20 years? Would they be the same as those found for the cross-sectional study? It might reveal a decline in the two latter tests, but it is more likely to show little change with age, or an increase in ability. So two procedures, apparently designed to answer the same question, give us quite different answers. Which one is right?

To put it simply: neither test is measuring age alone and thus each has quite specific problems. Historical events affecting some or all participants, as well as individual life experiences unique to each participant, may have a greater impact on the characteristic being measured by the psychologist than age itself. Resolving these and other problems is complex and the final chapter of this book considers Warner Schaie's solution.

Although developmental psychology is concerned with people throughout their lives, many of the research studies discussed in this book concentrate on explaining behaviour within a relatively limited time period. For example, Chapter 2 on perception describes work that has looked at changes in olfactory or visual perception over a matter of days, weeks or months within the first year of life. Often when studying in detail one such age group psychologists use the experimental method.

Experiments in psychology

The essence of the *experimental method* is that the psychologists can investigate how some aspect of behaviour is changed by a given factor which is thought to influence it. To take an example, in 1960 Orvis Irwin investigated what effect reading to children had on their language development. He devised a simple experiment in which 24 children aged 13 months were read to by their mothers for 15–20 minutes a day until up to the age of 30 months. A second group of 10 children, matched on the basis of their fathers' occupational status, received no instructions about special reading, but were treated otherwise exactly as the experimental group.

The first group, the *experimental group*, is the group exposed to the variable which the psychologist believes may influence language development. This variable here is 'being read to' and the psychologist thus varies the amount of 'being read to' in the two groups. We call the variable that is being manipulated by the psychologists the *independent variable*, and the behaviour which it is thought to affect is the *dependent variable* – in this case language development. Language development was measured by recording the children's spontaneous speech (the types of sound made and their frequency) assessed at two-monthly intervals throughout the study. The children who were not exposed to the independent variable (being read to) form what is called the *control group*. They provide a baseline against which the experimental group's language development can be compared.

In this study the researcher did find that being read to accelerated language development because the experimental group were soon ahead of the controls when measures of language development were compared. Consistent differences became evident from about 17 months. (See Chapter 6 for further discussion of language development.)

Asking questions and forming hypotheses

Before embarking on a rigorously controlled experiment it is necessary to make sure that the questions asked are sensible ones not wildly at odds with common-sense views. It would be unwise not to do preliminary observations on the behaviour you are interested in and observe children or adults in situations relevant to the type of question posed. For example, in the above example young children would need to be observed in the first months and years and some knowledge of how much exposure they had to books and being read to would have to be gleaned before an experiment is devised.

However 'common sense' varies. For instance:

❝ *Rushing to pick up baby when she cries just encourages her to fuss more.* **❞**

OR

❝ *Responding quickly to your baby's cries makes for a happier baby who cries less.* **❞**

At different points in the last four decades both these views have been forcefully propounded to the confusion of new parents. Psychologists interested in investigating the role of picking up in encouraging or discouraging crying would start by *observing* parents and infants to see if clues could be found to the truth of either statement. From these observations a *hypothesis* would be generated:

RESPONDING QUICKLY TO INFANTS' CRIES BY PICKING THEM UP REDUCES THE OVERALL NUMBER OF CRYING BOUTS IN A GIVEN PERIOD COMPARED WITH INFANTS WHO ARE LEFT FOR SOME MOMENTS BEFORE BEING PICKED UP.

This hypothesis is a prediction of what the psychologists think may happen.

The psychologists are now in a position to plan a controlled experiment in which babies, matched on a variety of variables such as age, socioeconomic factors and so on are exposed to different treatment regimes varying in the interval between the onset of crying and being picked up.

If the research shows that babies picked up quickly over a given period start crying less often then our hypothesis could be accepted. But, if the babies picked up after a longer period start crying less overall then the hypothesis would have to be rejected. However if there is no consistent pattern of results, or if some babies cried more often and some cried less often, the psychologists might conclude that their approach had been too simplistic. A different sort of hypothesis might be required which could, for instance, take into account temperamental factors in the infant, or the parents' style of picking up.

On reading about this hypothetical experiment you might find yourself thinking 'I wouldn't dream of leaving a baby of mine to cry for ten minutes just for the sake of a psychological experiment' – this raises the important and very difficult question of ethics in research.

Ethical issues in research

Just because a psychologist comes up with an interesting hypothesis does not mean he or she is entitled to test it.

There are many areas of human development which, for ethical reasons, we could not investigate experimentally. The British Psychological Society has detailed guidelines for researchers to assist them in planning their investigations which recognize that the rights of the human participants, and their welfare, are paramount. Even if the degree of distress, pain, inconvenience or whatever is considered to be minimal in relation to the benefits which would accrue if a given experiment could be carried out, people who volunteer to participate in a study must always be free to drop out if they wish to, even if the ethical guidelines permit a particular area of study.

A number of topics that are not investigated in humans on ethical grounds have been explored in non-human animals. The importance of parents, and in particular the mother, has been a question continually probed by psychologists, and yet no experiment would be contemplated which involved taking a child from its mother for a prolonged period solely for experimental purposes. We have to rely for our data on this from naturally occurring situations where children and parents are parted. Nevertheless amongst non-human animals Harry Harlow did empirically investigate how baby rhesus monkeys cope without their mothers. Guidelines for animal experimentation are also available: the Society for the Study of Animal Behaviour issues guidelines for researchers, and the Home Office is the ultimate control for research in this area in the UK. Regulations are being tightened up continually and many psychologists of today feel revulsion at some of the studies carried out in the past.

Thus in some important areas in human life we may never be able to be truly 'scientific' in our methods of investigation.

Other research methods

The experimental method is not always appropriate as a means of answering questions about behaviour. We cannot always manipulate the independent variable so that two groups of participants differ only in the presence or absence of this variable (or the amount of this variable).

The study of sex and gender is a case in point. Suppose we think that maleness is associated with certain characteristics and femaleness with others, and we believe that 'sex' hormones may be responsible for the differences observed, we cannot run an experiment in which male or female sex hormones are used as the independent variable on two otherwise identical groups. We all have a biological sex of one sort or the other – no one is neutral – so hormones have, from before birth, influenced our development. All that is possible is to *correlate* behaviour patterns with each sex (i.e. show an association between them) but this tells us nothing about *causal* differences. An example may explain this better. In Britain males are traditionally encouraged not to cry when they are hurt, upset or distressed. Observers, ignorant of this British characteristic, might thus correlate crying with femaleness and not crying with maleness. If they believed that biological sex played a causal role in this difference they might suggest that the adult human male is unable to cry – his hormones make crying impossible!

Used and interpreted correctly, *correlational studies* have an important place amongst the methods available to psychologists, and there are many other methods and techniques which are explained in the final chapter. Methodology is often described by those new to psychology as uninteresting and, although its place is fundamental in exploring developmental psychology, we propose to postpone further discussion until later and start by examples. Each chapter describes one particular area of interest and concern to developmental psychologists. Just how questions about behaviour, thoughts and feelings have been investigated will become clear. The importance of the methods available is often lost until we try to answer a particular question within psychology and so we shall now turn to some of those questions.

What next?

Let's start at the beginning. Our earlier years are widely viewed as laying the foundations of who and what we are, and experiences in the first few years may have long-lasting influence. So how do the foetus and newborn experience the world through their senses? Can they hear, see and smell like we as adults can, and if not what sense can they make of the world? How soon does a baby recognize its mother? Do babies prefer some sorts of visual, olfactory, auditory stimulation over others? Psychologists are beginning to find some of the answers.

Recommended reading

Berryman, J.C., Hargreaves, D.J., Hollin, C.R. & Howells, K. (1987) *Psychology and You: An informal introduction.* Leicester: BPS Books and Routledge. [See the introduction and chapter 12 for a discussion of 'what is psychology?' and methodology.]

Colman, A.M. (1981) *What is Psychology?* London: Kogan Page. [An excellent book: chapters 1 and 2 introduce psychology in a most lively way.]

McGurk, H. (1978) *Growing and Changing.* London: Methuen. [A very readable book.]

References

Aries, P. (1962) *Centuries of Childhood.* London: Jonathan Cape. [Historical attitudes to children.]

Darwin, C.R. (1877) A biographical sketch of an infant. *Mind, 2,* 285–294. [A description of Doddy's behaviour.]

Code of Conduct, Ethical Principles and Guidelines (1991) The British Psychological Society. [Guidelines for research in psychology.]

Guidelines for the use of animals in research. (1986) *Animal Behaviour, 34,* 315–318. [Guidelines for animal research.]

Hall, G.S. (1891) Notes on the study of infants. *The Pedagogical Seminary, 1,* 127–138. [One of the first systematic studies of children.]

Harlow, H.F. (1958) The nature of love. *American Psychologist, 13,* 673–685. [Infant monkeys reared without mothers.]

Irwin, O.C. (1960) Infant speech: Effect of systematic reading of stories. *Journal of Speech and Hearing Research, 3(2),* 187–190. [Experiments on reading to babies.]

Lean, V.S. (1903) *Lean's Collectanea, Vol 3.* Bristol: J.W. Arrowsmith. [Quotation attributed to the Jesuits.]

Muuss, R.E. (1970) Adolescence development and the secular trend. *Adolescence, 5,* 267–286. [Medieval men's armour fits boys of 10–12 today.]

Schaie, K.W. (1975) Age changes in adult intelligence. In D.S. Woodruff & J.E. Birren (Eds) *Aging: Scientific perspects and social issues.* New York: Van Nostrand. [Longitudinal and cross-sectional studies compared.]

Tanner, J.M. (1978) *Foetus into Man.* London: Open Books. [Age at menarche.]

2. First Views of the World

Babies are so small and defenceless at birth that parents may wonder to what extent they can make sense of their world. Certainly compared with the young of precocial species, such as lambs, ducklings and calves babies lag far behind, but they are not as immature as those of altricial species such as mice and rats, whose young are born naked and have eyes closed and ears sealed. Human infants are at an intermediate level between these two extremes: they are immature in terms of motor development and are highly dependent on the mother for food, but they are precocious in sensory development and can make surprisingly good sense of their world at birth and even before.

It is often said by those who care for the new baby – usually the mother, in our society – that a baby knows its own mother very early on, can distinguish her from others and prefers her. Indeed, many mothers comment that their babies can distinguish between different sounds even before birth, and anecdotes about the noises, or tunes, that babies like in the womb are common.

All of us know that the premature (or pre-term) baby born just three or four weeks early is not a totally different creature from the full-term baby. The baby's eyes are open and in many ways it does not seem much less mature in terms of its awareness of the world than one born on time. Does this mean that the foetus can experience sensations inside the womb, and, if so, in what way can it make sense of that dark and watery world before birth? Studies of pre-term babies and babies in utero have provided some of the answers as we shall see.

Philosophers and psychologists have long been intrigued by the question 'Are babies born with some built-in abilities to organize or make sense of the stimuli impinging on their sense organs, or must they learn to make sense of their world by trial and error?'. The two opposing views come from the *nativists* and the *empiricists*. Nativists argue that the baby's senses work like the adult's, and once the baby opens its eyes it can see much as we adults do – perceiving objects, space, distance and so on. Empiricists would argue that only through experience of the world can the baby really perceive it as adults do and that at birth the notion that a baby can distinguish an object from the background, or recognize the object as close by rather than at a distance, is meaningless. As we shall see, research has thrown considerable light on this debate, and like so many situations where views are polarized, both views are in fact right to some extent. The baby is pre-programmed to a degree, but experience also plays a vital role in perception too.

Let us start at the very beginning – with the baby inside the womb.

WHEN DOES PERCEPTION START?

In 1960 Lee Salk suggested that the baby *imprints* on (becomes strongly attached to) the sound of its mother's heartbeat in utero and this led to much discussion of the use of heartbeat sounds to calm the crying baby postnatally. In fact, tape recordings of the heartbeat, and bodily sounds as they would be heard in utero, are widely available as calming aids. The notion of 'imprinting' in this context has now been abandoned but research on auditory sensitivity in utero continues with some intriguing findings.

The auditory system of the human foetus is functional at about 30 weeks conceptual age, or ten weeks before the birth of the full-term baby, but sound may be experienced by the foetus (in the womb) or the pre-term baby at less than 30 weeks in the form of vibrations. As Elizabeth Ockleford points out, if rhythmical stimuli, such as the heartbeat as heard by the foetus between 30 and 40 weeks, can have a calming effect, this is due to experience in the last ten weeks of the mother's pregnancy. Premature babies born before 30 weeks will have no auditory experience of these sounds because they have no aural perception of sound.

Ockleford showed that infants born at least ten weeks before term differed from normal full-term neonates in their response to rhythmical sounds. In the presence of a metronome beat of 144 beats per minute, full-term crying babies were pacified, whilst the pre-term babies were not. One curious feature of this study is that 144 beats per minute resembles the *foetus's* heart rate. The mother's heart rate of 72 beats per minute which Salk and other researchers believed to be calming did not in fact pacify the babies. Recent work has shown that the sounds of the maternal heart are not always audible in utero so this may explain why the above findings arise.

Does the baby 'know' its mother's voice before birth?

If babies can become used to sounds such as heartbeats before birth, and show quite specific responses to more familiar sounds, then we may ask whether familiarity with other sounds before birth have similar effects. The foetus can (as recent studies by Elizabeth Ockleford and others show) hear a variety of louder sounds in its mother's environment, so will her voice, or even her choice of music, affect it? Finding newborn babies who have no auditory experience is virtually impossible since even in the delivery room there will be a wide range of sounds, but with this limitation in mind Ockleford found a sample of newborns and she showed that they could discriminate between their own mothers' and other voices when *under* 24 hours old. She measured changes in heart rate and found deceleration (or what is called an 'orienting response') to the mother's voice. Since the baby has had about ten weeks' experience of the mother's voice, it is probable that this response is not due to immediate experience in the first day of life. Evidence in support of this conclusion comes from studies of newborn lambs who, within a few hours of birth, respond to their *mother's* first bleat by a drop in heart rate. Bleats from other sheep are responded to by an increase in heart rate.

Thus the human newborn appears to show selective responses to certain sounds within its environment as a result of its experience of these sounds when it was in the mother's womb.

Smelling the world

Although as adults most of us would rate vision as our major sense – the one we would miss most – in recent years the importance of smells in our lives has become clearer as a result of some surprising research findings. The role of olfaction in sexual behaviour is widely known, but psychologists are now able to show that we are very much aware of the odour of others in all sorts of contexts, and olfactory recognition of family and friends is clearly demonstrable.

Research on other mammals, such as rats and mice, has shown that infants may learn odours associated with their mothers long before their eyes open and visual recognition is even possible. Whilst human babies are hardly comparable with the infant rat, their olfactory sense is functional at birth and thus its role in infant perception has intrigued a number of researchers.

Mother's milk – in breastfed babies – is a vitally important part of the newborn's world, and a hungry baby will respond by sucking movements to a milky smell even when asleep. In 1976, Michael Russell decided to use this response in his experiments designed to explore olfactory recognition of mother's milk.

Babies, preferably sleeping, were exposed to a pad held 1–2 cm from the baby's nose for 30 seconds. These pads had different olfactory characteristics: the 'mother's' pad had been placed for three hours before the test inside her bra; the 'strange mother's' pad had been placed in another breastfeeding mother's bra for three hours, and a 'control' pad was simply left clean but moist.

The sucking reflex was shown in response to both mothers' pads in babies tested at two days, two weeks and six weeks after birth, but by six weeks almost all babies tested showed a more marked sucking response to their own mother's pad – indicating a preference for her familiar odour. One baby even cried and jerked away from the strange mother's pad. Recognition of the mother's pad was evidently established by this stage, and another similar study by Aidan Macfarlane demonstrated a differential response as early as six days after birth.

Exploring this topic further, Richard Porter and his colleagues studied babies' responses to other odours associated with mothers. Not all babies are breastfed, so mothers' milk is not always appropriate as a stimulus. In one study these researchers decided to look at responses to underarm (or axillary) odours. Odour pads were made by adult participants, who wore a small gauze pad in their armpits for eight hours on the night prior to the test. The sucking response was inappropriate for this odour, so babies were tested by having two pads placed one to the left of the infant's head and one to the right, so that if the baby moved its head its nose would be 1–2 cm from the pad. Movement of the baby's head from the midline, towards either pad, was recorded in the test and babies were tested in their cribs at 12–18 days old (see *Figure 2.1*).

A whole range of stimulus odours was explored, including:

- mother versus a non-parturient female (one who has not recently given birth and is not breastfeeding);
- mother versus a 'strange', non-lactating female;
- father versus a 'strange' adult male.

The first two pairs were given to samples of either breastfed or bottlefed babies. Only breastfed babies showed a preference for their own mother's axillary odour in the first two pairs described; fathers were not preferred, and bottlefed babies showed no preferences. Richard Porter's team considered two possible explanations for this

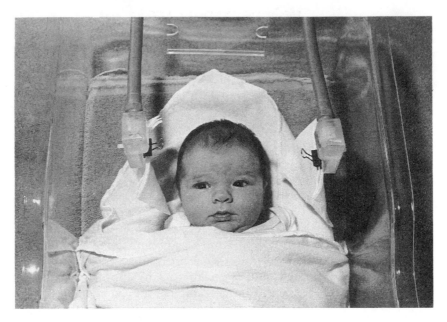

FIGURE 2.1: *A baby being tested in the odour preference experiment by Richard Porter and colleagues*

result. Breastfeeding mothers may have a stronger axillary odour than non-lactating mothers and thus babies might be responding to intensity of odour rather than individual odours. Alternatively, breastfed babies receive much closer, skin-to-skin contact with their mothers than bottlefed babies and thus they are exposed to more maternal body odours.

Whatever the explanation, babies can, in appropriate circumstances, show a preferential response to odours from their own mother's milk and her underarm odours. This suggests that very early in life they learn the distinctive odours of those to whom they are physically close and that smell may play an important role in recognition of their mother.

We know that humans in general are surprisingly adept at recognizing close relatives by olfactory cues alone: parents can recognize their newborn baby and their older children just by smelling their clothes. Why not try your own skill at recognizing family members or friends by completing *Exercise 2.1* on page 32.

VISION IN INFANTS

No parents would doubt that their newborn infant can see something of the world, but exactly how well he or she sees has been a matter of debate for many decades. William James wrote at the beginning of the twentieth century that the infant's world was all 'one great blooming, buzzing confusion'. Recent research, however, shows us that this is far from the reality. Babies do not see just as adults do, but psychologists are continually being surprised as evidence accumulates about the newborn and young infant's abilities and this has led to the notion of the 'competent infant' in relation to perceptual abilities.

The baby's eye is, of course, smaller than the adult's, and the immaturity of their whole nervous system affects the optic nerve and hence the efficiency with which visual information is transmitted. The retina, and the rods and cones, are fairly well developed at birth so there is no obvious area where we might expect major deficits. The

newborn's natural focal length is about 17 cm so we would expect that stimuli close to the baby are likely to be seen more easily than those at some distance.

Alan Slater has compared the newborn's visual acuity to that of the adult cat – it is between 10 and 30 times poorer than adult humans, which means that fine lines are much harder for babies to perceive and appear as a blurred grey. The infant's field of view is also more restricted. Objects are most likely to be looked at by a baby from 0–5 months if they fall within the range 25–30° to the left or right of centre, 10° above or below the line of sight, and within 90 cm of the baby. Babies also require stimuli of high contrast for their attention to be gained. If this sounds as if the baby is likely to be rather unresponsive, this is not the case, as every mother knows. Babies seem particularly interested in faces, as we shall see, and it is argued that they may have an in-built predisposition to respond to faces.

Seeing colour

Since we as adults see in colour, it is likely that most of us assume that babies also do. Is this true? Alan Slater tells us that infants of two months often are able to distinguish colour and thus are using cone receptors (the receptors on which colour vision depends), although it is not certain whether infants are using all three cone types. There is a suggestion that information from the cone type sensitive to 'blue' may be lacking in babies aged under three months. Slater concludes that infants probably are trichromatic from an early age but that information from 'blue' cones may not be used as effectively in the first months. So perhaps newborn boys who are traditionally dressed in blue are less sensitive to this colour than are newborn girls dressed in their traditional pink!

Marc Bornstein and his colleagues have carried out research to see if infants distinguish hue categories and the boundaries between them in the way that adults do. They studied four-month-old infants' responses to different light wavelengths. Pairs of stimuli were chosen whose wavelengths either fell within a single colour-naming boundary (blue, green, yellow, red), or straddled a boundary (e.g. blue–green, green–yellow, yellow–red): thus a colour might either fall within the 'blue' range for instance, or across the boundary 'blue–green'. Each of the four basic colour categories and their boundaries were investigated and pairs of stimuli used differed by equal physical distances. The researchers found that infants showed by their behaviour that they made a greater distinction between members of a pair when the second hue was taken from an adjacent hue category than to one selected from the same hue category, indicating that babies see the spectrum divided into the familiar four colour categories – and not as a continuous slightly changing sequence in which pairs separated by the same physical distance all differ to the same degree.

STUDIES OF INFANT PERCEPTION

Researching the visual world of the infant has particular problems. Babies have few well co-ordinated movements, so responses used in experiments with chicks or ducklings for example, such as approach or following a particular stimulus, are impossible in newborns, and language, of course, is even slower to develop. Researchers have devised some intriguing techniques to get over this.

Patterns of attention

Babies do not just look around at random but look at some parts of their environment for longer periods than others. Researchers realized that by recording patterns of attention they might be able to find out more about just how the infant sees the world. One method that has been used is to record the *direction* and *duration* of the infant's looking, and typically experimenters present two sorts of visual stimuli side by side and observe whether these two measures vary in relation to each stimulus. If the baby views one target much more than the other it is argued that the baby can distinguish them. Another successful technique makes use of the observation that when we become very familiar with a stimulus we pay it less attention. Researchers have found that by varying the degree of novelty or familiarity of the stimulus, they can learn about the infant's abilities to discriminate. One way of doing this is to give the baby many repeated exposures to a single stimulus until a decline in looking is observed. The infant seems to have become 'bored' with looking at the same old thing. If at this point a new stimulus is presented, one that the infant can perceive as different, they then perk up and their attention score goes up. This procedure, called the *habituation method*, enables psychologists to compare a whole variety of stimuli, differing in different ways, and through recording the baby's attention we can gain some insight into the degree of difference that a given baby can perceive.

Perception of pattern

Robert Fantz, in a now famous series of experiments, found that infants showed preferences for some stimulus configurations over others.

By recording the amount of time the baby spent fixating (looking at) various stimuli, he was able to see if fixation times varied when a baby was presented with two stimuli. Using a 'looking chamber', in which it was possible to see reflected in the baby's eye exactly what was being observed, Robert Fantz carried out a series of intriguing studies published in 1961. Thirty infants, aged from 1–15 weeks old, were tested and he recorded the time they spent looking at a series of pairs of stimuli differing in complexity. These were two identical triangles, a cross and a circle, a checkerboard, two sizes of a plain square, horizontal stripes and a bull's-eye design. The babies spent more time looking at the pairs of the more complex kinds of stimulus, and within each of the pairs the stimulus which was more patterned was fixated most. In his paper, Fantz also noted that even younger infants (aged from 1–14 days) were found, by another researcher, to show this preference for patterns.

Robert Fantz also explored the baby's ability to perceive stripes of

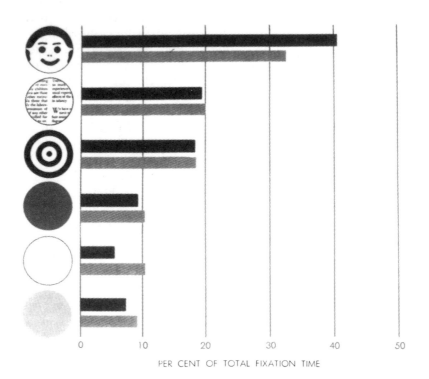

PER CENT OF TOTAL FIXATION TIME

On the left of the picture are stimuli used in one of Fantz's studies. The upper bar of each pair indicates fixation time for two to three month olds, the lower bar for babies of four months.

FIGURE 2.2:   *Babies' fixation times for six stimuli*

varying widths. He showed that under one-month-old infants could perceive 3 mm stripes (at 25 cm distance from the baby), and by six months they could distinguish stripes of less than half 0.5 mm. Although this level of visual acuity is much less than that of adults, it is very different from the earlier idea of a world full of confusion and lacking in definition.

In two further experiments Fantz included face-like stimuli and patterns. In one he compared three plain coloured discs (red, yellow and white), a bull's-eye pattern, a disc of newsprint, and a stylized face in black and white (see *Figure 2.2*). Each stimulus was presented singly and in varied sequences, but again patterns were fixated more than plain discs, and the face was preferred most of all. The other study used three face or egg-shaped stimuli – one was a stylized face, one had the same features but they were 'scrambled' into a non-face like pattern, and the third (the control pattern) had simply a patch of black at the wide end of the face – covering an area equivalent to that covered by all the features in the other two. Each stimulus was black on a pink background (see *Figure 2.3*). Perhaps by now you can predict the result? In *Exercise 2.2* on page 34 you can try out a version of this study on young babies.

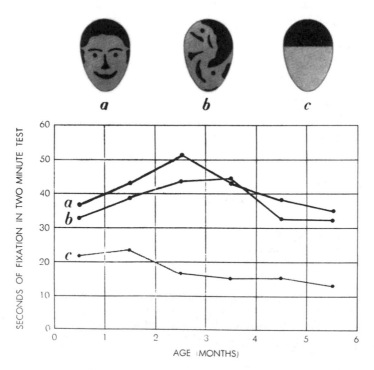

FIGURE 2.3: *Babies' fixation times for three face-like stimuli*

Babies aged between four days to six months were tested, and preferred the face, with the scrambled face next and the control face last. Fantz argued that this interest in patterns and faces did not seem to be acquired, and he believed his work provided evidence against the views of the empiricists that infants must learn to see 'from scratch'.

Smiling by babies in response to various face-like and true face stimuli has been studied by other researchers. Infants from about six weeks of age (when the social smile first becomes evident) were used and it was found such infants would smile at two eyes on a black background. The contours of the face become more important as babies get older and by six months of age smiling is only elicited by the whole face.

Perception and recognition of faces

Smiling at a face is not the same as showing recognition of that face. Recognition requires that the elements within the face are seen as being related to each other in a particular manner. Smiling at mother therefore does not tell us that mother's features are recognized and distinguished from those of other women. Several studies have suggested that facial *recognition* occurs between the sixth and ninth week of life (for example those by Robert Haaf and Cheryl Brown, and Daphne Maurer and Philip Salapatek), but a recent study by Ian Bushnell and others reported in 1989 claims to have shown that *neonates* can recognize and show a preference for their mothers 'on the basis of visual clues alone'. *Figure 2.4* shows what the human face may look like to the newborn and to us.

Bushnell and colleagues recorded fixation times shown by alert newborns placed in an upright position in front of two faces that were behind a screen. These were the faces of the mother and a strange mother, matched for hair colour and complexion. The procedure controlled for the possible influences of a directional bias in looking by the baby, the influence of olfactory cues from the mother, and actions on the part of the mothers which might make them try to gain the attention of their infant (since they could see them during the procedure). The authors concluded that infants can learn rapidly the visual features of their mother's face within a few hours of birth.

Clearly visual experience of the mother cannot be acquired prenatally and so this research inevitably poses problems for those who believe recognition takes some time to develop. Whilst some researchers have argued that it is possible that the 'infant's nervous system is especially

FIGURE 2.4:   *The face as it might appear to the newborn, and to us*

equipped to respond to face-like configurations' – and thus this may produce the preferential responding noted by Bushnell – this is not the same as saying that babies actually know the 'meaning' of the face and recognize that it belongs to the person from whom they receive love and care.

Perception of depth and distance

Can babies judge distances and perceive depth? This question was pondered by Eleanor Gibson as she picnicked at the Grand Canyon. She decided to try and find out. The apparatus she devised for testing this was the 'visual cliff'. This is an apparatus which is divided into two halves. The top or shallow side of the cliff is covered in a checkerboard pattern and covered with a piece of glass which extends horizontally out above the deep side of the cliff. The floor of the deep side of the cliff, about a metre below the shallow side, is also covered in the checkered pattern. If the infant stays on the checkered part of the shallow side it can look over to the deep side, but it cannot fall because the glass extends across the whole apparatus – hence the name 'visual' cliff. The lighting of the apparatus is arranged such that the reflection in the glass is minimized and hence retains the illusion of a steep drop. The infant is placed on the shallow side of the cliff and is encouraged to cross the cliff by the mother who stands on the other side. In 1960, Eleanor Gibson and Richard Walk found that human infants tested as soon as they could crawl – from about six months of age – showed apprehension at the edge of the cliff and showed a clear tendency to stay on the shallow side. Only eight per cent of one group tested ventured over the cliff. Studies of other animals showed that chickens, turtles, rats, goats, lambs, pigs, cats, dogs and monkeys also perceived depth as soon as they could be tested in infancy – in the case of chicks this could be on the first day of life. These researchers concluded that the infant can probably perceive the drop because they could see the change in size of the checkered pattern over the one metre drop, and also through motion parallax – the distant side of the cliff would be seen to move more when they moved their head relative to the near or shallow side of the cliff.

The essential problem with the cliff experiment for human infants is that, unlike newly hatched chicks, all infants have had considerable experience of the environment prior to the test, so the study tells us little about the extent to which depth perception may be in-built. A number of other researchers have devised experiments for younger infants and in particular infants' responses to approaching objects has been explored. Tom Bower and his colleagues designed an experiment using a real object moving towards the infant. Two-week-old babies were placed in an upright position and their behaviour was recorded. Bower noted three types of defensive behaviour in this situation: eye widening, head retraction, and moving of the hands up between the face and the approaching object (blinking was not observed and indeed does not occur in this situation until about eight weeks).

A variety of cues could play a part in eliciting this behaviour: the object is perceived as expanding (increasing in size on the retina) as it approaches, and it would also produce a rush or displacement of air which might also indicate movement to the baby. Bower was able to show that air movement alone did not produce the head and hand movements described above, and that responses to the optical expansion pattern alone were less intense than in the natural situation.

Bower argued, however, that at one week old infants can perceive distance as specified by the optical expansion pattern and probably therefore have a built-in capacity for perceiving distance. He suggested that in breastfeeding the 'over-enthusiastic application of the breast' to the baby may elicit the same defensive pattern (as the breast moves towards the baby's face) as he found in his experiment, and thus he joked somewhat facetiously that even at birth babies are at risk of being struck in the face by rapidly approaching objects, and hence the need to judge distances and take evasive action are present very early in life.

Perceptual organization

Why does the baby see things or objects rather than the spaces between them? This may seem to be just a silly question until we realize that even adults can make errors – as examples of the reversible figure (see *Figure 2.5*) remind us. Do you see faces or a vase? You probably alternate between the two – so that the object versus the space also alternates.

FIGURE 2.5:   *An example of a reversible figure; do you see faces or a vase?*

Since the world for the newborn is all new in visual terms, is it realistic to expect the newborn to make the object/space definition? *Gestalt* psychologists (who emphasize that 'the whole is greater than the sum of its parts') worked out some rules that adults seem to use to define an object. These are first, *common fate* (elements moving together may be seen as a single moving object); second, *good continuation* (contours that seem to be related may be seen as contours of a single object), and third, *proximity* (when a range of contours are seen those that are closer than average are viewed as belonging to the same unit). *Figure 2.6* illustrates the latter two rules.

If these rules apply to adults, do they also apply in infant perception? Emile Brunswick argued that infants may have to learn them by trial and error, and hence would not respond as adults do. Tom

This figure is not seen as a triangle by adults unless a pencil or similar object is placed in front of the gaps. The pencil conceals from the eye information that the triangle is not complete, allowing good continuation to operate.

FIGURE 2.6a: *The rule of good continuation.*

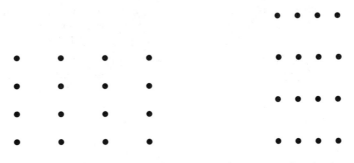

This is seen as four vertical columns.

This is seen as four horizontal rows.

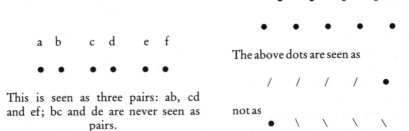

a b   c d   e f

• •   • •   • •

This is seen as three pairs: ab, cd and ef; bc and de are never seen as pairs.

The above dots are seen as

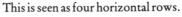

not as

FIGURE 2.6b: *The rule of proximity.*

Bower set out to explore this. He showed that at six weeks infants use the rule of good continuation, common fate also is evident in very young infants, but proximity develops very slowly and was not evident until around one year of age. Thus there does seem to be support for Brunswick's view in the case for proximity.

Object perception and size constancy

Another aspect of object perception is whether infants show *size*, *shape* and *brightness constancies*. Essentially these mean that we perceive an object as being the same regardless of how these three elements change it in relation to us. As your friend walks away from you, you don't perceive her as shrinking even though on your retina she is rapidly occupying less and less space (size constancy). Similarly, you still recognize her as your friend, whether she is in profile or at a whole variety of different angles in relation to you (shape constancy), and in changes of illumination (brightness constancy) she is still the person that you know as having a particular skin and hair colour whatever the level of light at a given time.

Size constancy in infants was first demonstrated by Tom Bower in the 1960s using two-month-old infants. However his research could not reveal whether learning was involved. More recently Alan Slater and colleagues have been able to do this. They familiarized newborn babies with a single cube which was presented at different distances from their eyes. When, subsequently, a different-sized cube was paired with the familiar one, but placed at a different distance in order that the retinal sizes of both objects were the same, it was found that babies looked *more* at the novel cube.

Alan Slater and Victoria Morison also looked at shape constancy in newborns. In this experiment babies were given a period of familiarization with either a square or a trapezium (see *Figure 2.7*), with the stimulus being shown at different slants from one trial to the next. After this the square and the trapezium were shown for two paired test trials (i.e. two stimuli per trial). In these trials only one stimulus was familiar for each infant and this was shown at a *different* slant from any of those used during familiarization.

All the babies spent more time looking at the novel shape in the test trials – showing that they display shape constancy because even when the familiar object is displayed at a *novel* slant, it is evidently recognized as familiar relative to a truly novel (but one similarly shaped) stimulus.

Alan Slater and Gavin Bremner have also explored other 'constancies' and the reader is referred to their work (see Recommended Reading section) for a full review of these topics.

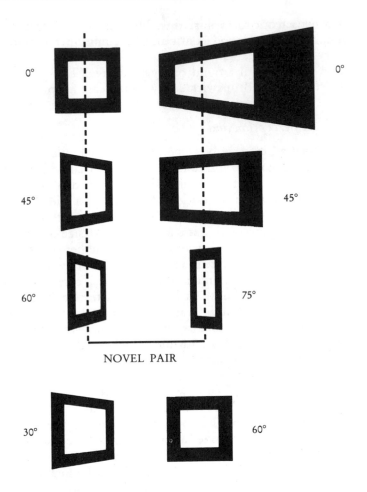

FIGURE 2.7: *The stimulus slants presented during familiarization and post-familiarization (test) trials by Slater and Morison (1985). The familiarization stimulus (for half the infants the square, for half the trapezium) was shown in six slants: the ones shown here and their mirror images.*

CRITICAL PERIODS
IN PERCEPTUAL DEVELOPMENT

It is easy to assume that our eyes and brain are programmed in such a way that they respond automatically to visual stimuli. Although the infant does not see as adults do at birth, it is probable that many people assume that maturation sorts out any deficiencies and *what* we see makes no difference to this process. In fact there is now evidence that certain sorts of visual experience, or lack of it, may be crucial in shaping the development of vision and visual perception.

Binocular vision

Research on kittens, by Torsten Weisel and David Hubel, has shown that the development of *binocular vision* (the ability to perceive an object with both eyes simultaneously so that the two images fuse) is shaped by early visual experience. Many cells in the part of our brain dealing with visual input (the visual cortex) will respond to a visual stimulus shown to either eye, but if one eye is covered early on subsequently it is found that cortical cells will only respond to a stimulus presented to the other eye.

Martin Banks and colleagues noted that children who are born with a squint may be affected in a similar way. If the eyes look in different directions this is bound to affect the degree to which cortical cells, which respond binocularly, receive input from both eyes simultaneously. If such children are operated on under three years of age then subsequently their binocular vision is very like that of normal children; however if surgery is delayed binocular vision is adversely affected. The first three years are the *critical period* for the development of binocular vision in humans.

Seeing horizontals and verticals

Another area where early visual experience appears to be important and possibly crucial for the development of visual perception is in the ability to recognize horizontal and vertical stimuli. Colin Blakemore and Grahame Cooper reported an experiment in 1970 which explored the effect of limited early visual experience on kittens.

Kittens were raised in the dark from birth and at about two weeks of age they were placed in special apparatus for five hours a day. Each kitten was exposed to either a totally horizontal world, or a vertical world, where the walls were totally striped. The kittens were placed in large Elizabethan-like collars so that they could not even see their own bodies. After five months of this experience, tests showed that when kittens were placed in a normal environment they were effectively blind to the type of stimulus (either vertical or horizontal) that they had not experienced. Evidence suggested that the kittens lacked cells in the visual cortex which could respond to the stimuli that they had been reared without. Again, it seems that there is a critical period for the development of appropriately responding cortical cells and these kittens had missed the period during which their brain could develop a response to either the vertical or horizontal stimuli which had been denied them. The findings of this experiment have not been fully replicated but the result is generally accepted as revealing the crucial role of early experience in the development of normal visual perception.

In conclusion

In this chapter we have only been able to consider a few aspects of early perceptual development. To some extent the topics covered reflect the areas that have been well researched. This is certainly true of visual perception, but nothing has been said about hearing and it would be wrong to conclude that we are quite ignorant of this area, though it is less widely discussed in most developmental textbooks. Our main aim has been to show, in selected areas only, that the human infant, even before full-term, is amazingly sensitive to its environment and that researchers are being continually surprised by its abilities.

Recommended reading

Bower, T.G.R. (1982) *Development in Infancy.* San Francisco: W.H. Freeman & Co. [An excellent introduction to the topic – chapters 1–5 are particularly relevant to perceptual development.]

Goldberg, S. & Di Vitto, B.A. (1983) *Born Too Soon.* San Francisco: W.H. Freeman & Co. [A most readable account of the capabilities of pre-term babies – perceptual development is covered in chapters 2 and 3.]

Gregory, R.L. (1979) *The Eye and Brain.* London: Weidenfeld & Nicholson. [A very lively and readable book on the eye and visual perception.]

Slater, A. & Bremner, G. (1989) *Infant Development.* Hove & London: Lawrence Erlbaum Associates. [Chapters 1–3, 5 and 6 are particularly relevant to this chapter – this is in fairly technical language and Bower or Gregory above should be tackled first.]

References

Ahrens, R. (1954) Beitrage zur Entwicklung des Physiognomie und Mimikerkennens. In H. Gardner (1982), *Developmental Psychology.* Boston: Little, Brown & Co. [Babies' interest in faces.]

Banks, M.S., Aslin, R.N. & Letson, R.D. (1975) Sensitive period for the development of human binocular vision. *Science, 190,* 675–677. [Children with squints and the development of binocular vision.]

Blakemore, C. & Cooper, G.R. (1970) Development of the brain depends on the visual environment. *Nature, 228,* 477–478. [Research on perception of horizontals and verticals.]

Bornstein, M.H., Kessen, W. & Weiskopf, S. (1976) The categories of hue in infancy. *Science, 191,* 201–202. [Infants' ability to distinguish hue categories.]

Bosher, S.K. (1975) Morphological and functional changes in the cochlea associated with the inception of hearing. *Symposium of the Zoological Society of London, 37,* 11–22. [Function of the foetal auditory system.]

Bower, T.G.R. (1965) The determinants of perceptual unity in infancy. *Psychonomic Science, 3,* 323–324. [Experiments on the use of 'proximity' in infants.]

Bower, T.G.R. (1966) The visual world of infants. *Scientific American, 215,* 80–92. [Size constancy in infants.]

Bower, T.G.R. (1982) *Development in Infancy*. San Francisco: W.H. Freeman & Co. [Babies and the need to judge distances of a rapidly approaching breast.]

Bower, T.G.R., Broughton, U.M. & Moore, M.K. (1970) Infant responses to approaching objects: An indicator of response to distal variables. *Perception and Psychophysics, 9,* 193–196. [Infant perception of distance.]

Brunswick, E. (1956) *Perception and the representative design of psychology experiments*. Berkeley: University of California Press. In T.G.R. Bower (1982) *Development in Infancy*. San Francisco: W.H. Freeman & Co. [How do infants learn rules to define an object?]

Bushnell, I.W.R., Sal, F. & Mullin, J.T. (1989) Neonatal recognition of the mother's face. *British Journal of Developmental Psychology, 7,* 3–15. [Neonatal recognition of mother's face.]

Cernoch, J. & Porter, R.H. (1985) Recognition of maternal axillary odours by infants. *Child Development, 56(6),* 1593–1598. [Infants' recognition of underarm odours in mothers and other adults.]

Fantz, R.L. (1961) The origin of form perception. *Scientific American, 204,* 1097–1104. [Perception of various patterned stimuli.]

Gibson, E.J. & Walk, R.D. (1960) The visual cliff. *Scientific American, 202,* 64–71. [The visual cliff experiment.]

Haaf, R.A. & Brown, C.J. (1976) Infants' responses to face-like patterns: Developmental changes between 10 and 15 weeks of age. *Journal of Experimental Child Psychology, 22,* 155–160. [Facial recognition in infants.]

James, W. (1890) *The Principles of Psychology*. New York: Holt, Rinehart & Winston. [Quotation on infant perception.]

Macfarlane, A. (1975) Olfaction in the development of social preferences in the human neonate. In *Parent–Infant Interaction Ciba Foundation Symposium, 33*. New York: Elsevier. [Studies of smell recognition.]

Maurer, D. & Salapatek, P. (1976) Developmental changes in the scanning of faces by young infants. *Child Development, 47,* 523–527. [Facial recognition in infants.]

Ockleford, E. (1984) Response to rhythmical sound in pre-term infants and term neonates. *Journal of Reproductive and Infant Psychology, 2,* 92–96. [Pre-term and full-term babies' responses to rhythmic sounds.]

Ockleford, E.M., Vince, M.A., Layton, C. & Reader, M.R. (1988) Responses of neonates to parents' and others' voices. *Early Human Development, 18,* 27–36. [Newborns' responses to mothers' and others' voices.]

Porter, R.H., Cernoch, J.M. & McLaughlin, F.H. (1983) Maternal recognition of neonates through olfactory cues. *Physiology and Behaviour, 30,* 151–154. [Mother's recognition of infant's odour.]

Russell, M.J. (1976) Human olfactory communication. *Nature, 260,* 520–522. [Olfactory recognition of mother's milk.]

Salk, L. (1960) The effects of the maternal heartbeat sound on the behaviour of the newborn infant: Implications for mental health. *World Mental Health, 12,* 168–175. [Mother's heart beat and its effects on baby.]

Salter, A. (1989) Visual memory and perception in early infancy. In A. Slater & G. Bremner (Eds) *Infant Development*. Hove & London: Lawrence Erlbaum Associates. [Newborn's visual acuity.]

Slater, A. (1990) Infant development: The origins of competence. *The Psychologist, 3,* 109–113. [The face as it might appear to the newborn.]

Slater, A.M. & Morison, V. (1985) Shape constancy and slant perception at birth. *Perception, 14,* 337–344. [Shape constancy in newborns.]

Walk, R.D. (1981) *Perceptual Development*. Monterey: Brooks Cole. [Visual cliff experiments.]

Walker, D., Grimwade, J. & Wood, C. (1971) Intrauterine noise: A component of the fetal environment. *American Journal of Obstetrics and Gynaecology, 109,* 91–95. [Lambs' responses to the first bleat that they hear.]

Weisel, T.N. & Hubel, D.H. (1963) Single-cell responses to striate cortex of kittens deprived of vision in one eye. *Journal of Neurophysiology, 26,* 1003–1017. [Binocular vision in kittens.]

Odour Recognition of Family and Friends

This exercise is a simplified version of the kinds of experiment carried out by Michael Russell, Richard Porter and others discussed earlier in this chapter. Read the instructions carefully before attempting the exercise.

▶ Procedure

Select three people, preferably relatives or people who know each other well and who preferably live in the same house. They can be adults or adolescents, but do not use children in this initial test. You may include yourself but note the proviso at the end of the exercise.

Each participant will need a pure cotton T-shirt (ideally this should be new, or as new as possible), or if one is not available two clean cotton handkerchiefs may be used, but these will have to be sewn into the armholes of a close-fitting T-shirt or jumper. You will also need three envelopes or paper bags large enough to contain a single T-shirt, or, if handkerchiefs are used, a single handkerchief. Avoid using envelopes with strong smelling adhesive as this may mask the odours to be tested.

Participants should be advised to use their normal hygiene procedures prior to the experiment but they should not use perfume, deodorant or antiperspirant. On the same day ask each person to wear the T-shirt (or handkerchief sewn to a similar garment – hereafter also referred to as a T-shirt) for a minimum of 12 hours, but preferably for 24 hours prior to the odour recognition test. Everyone should wear the item for the same length of time. Then place each T-shirt in a clean envelope, folding it so that the underarm portion is uppermost in the envelope, seal the latter and mark it with the number 1, 2 or 3 (rather than the participants' names) to indicate whose garment it contains.

Explain to the participants that they will be making paired comparisons of odours, and test each of them as follows:

- A: Test T-shirts 1 and 2 for 6 trials
- B: Test T-shirts 1 and 3 for 6 trials
- C: Test T-shirts 2 and 3 for 6 trials

Blindfold the first of the participants and tell him or her the names of the two people whose T-shirts are to be identified in the first text. Then choose one of the two envelopes at random (i.e. in Test A you could toss a coin to choose between envelopes 1 and 2), undo it, and invite the participant to sniff into the top. Place the envelope close to (but not touching) his or her

continued . . .

Odour Recognition of Family and Friends cont.

nose, and ask whose T-shirt is in the envelope. After 30 seconds close the envelope and repeat the procedure with the second envelope. If the participant cannot identify the T-shirt note a zero response, then after a minute or so go on to the next trial.

When all six trials have been completed repeat the whole procedure with the second and then the third participants. If you included yourself in the test, you must ask someone else to test you on the odours. Remember to keep envelopes well sealed between trials – use pegs or masking tape so that they can easily be reopened.

▶ Comment

It will become immediately clear that some people are very good at this exercise and others are not. Results need to be clear cut because on a chance basis a score of 50 per cent correct across the six trials could occur. Participants who achieved 5 or 6 out of 6 can be accepted as accurate. For those who are very accurate, the tests can be repeated with T-shirts from a range of other friends or relatives. Observe in your results whether errors occur only between same sex pairs for instance. If you have preadolescent children in your family you may like to try a test using children only. As children's body odours are not as strong as adults', it is best not to mix children and adults in a paired comparison test.

Visual Preferences in Infants

This experiment is a simplified version of that by Robert Fantz described earlier in this chapter. The participants are babies aged 0–6 months.

▶ **Procedure**

Draw three circles with a 10 cm diameter on a piece of white card.

- On the first circle draw in black a simple stylized face such as that shown in *Figure 2.8a.*
- On the second circle a scrambled version of this face is required: this can be produced either by tracing the features on the first circle and reproducing them rearranged approximately as shown in (b) or by photocopying, cutting out each feature and sticking these onto the second circle.
- On the third circle draw a solid black area in one part of the circle so that the area covered is equivalent to that occupied by all the features of the face in (a) or (b) (see (c)).

Cut the stimulus circles out.

Test as many infants as you can, giving each infant three tests, (for example ab, ac, bc), randomly pairing the stimuli in all combinations. Each pair of stimuli should be presented to the baby simultaneously for 60 seconds. Stimuli may be attached to each end of a 30 cm rule and the ruler should be held about 30 cm from the baby's face so that the centre of the ruler is directly in front of the baby's eyes. For infants under about one month the stimuli may need to be held slightly closer to the head (18 cm away). Record the amount of time the baby fixates each stimulus over a 60-second test; it may be helpful to ask the baby's care giver to hold the stimuli whilst you record the fixation times on two cumulative stopwatches. If you do not have access to stopwatches simply record the stimulus which appears to be preferred most. Repeat this procedure with each combination of stimuli, allowing a rest period between tests.

Record fixation times (or preference scores) for each stimulus in its pair. Repeat the whole procedure with the other infants.

▶ **Comment**

Do your results correspond with those of Fantz? What problems did you find in testing babies? You can extend this study by preparing other types of stimuli – for example a checkerboard pattern, plain black, plain white, plain colours, stripes, a bull's-eye pattern, newsprint, and repeat the procedure.

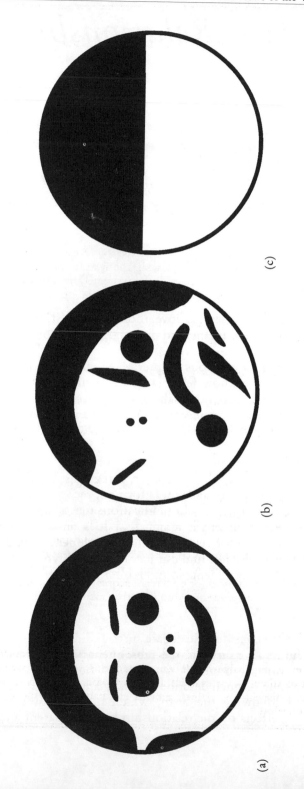

(c)

(b)

(a)

FIGURE 2.8:   *Sample figures for use in Exercise 2.2*

3. *First Relationships*

∇ *The growth of love*
∇ *Sisters and brothers*
∇ *Short-term separations*
∇ *Long-term separations and substitute care*
∇ *Can peer relationships replace mothering?*
∇ *Recovery from early deprivation*

How does a baby come to love those around it? Does love grow rapidly between an infant and its caregivers – or is it a gradual process?

As we saw in the previous chapter, even within the mother's uterus the baby comes to know features of its environment. The mother's voice is familiar, the sounds of the home environment are also known, and very soon after birth the baby can show a preferential response to its mother – her smell and that of her milk, her voice and possibly her face.

Does this preferential responding constitute evidence of early attachment to the mother or other caregiver? Psychologists agree that before a specific attachment is formed, recognition of individuals is an obvious prerequisite. Thus indications that a baby can distinguish those in its environment is a sign that it is on course for the next stage – but it does not reveal whether attachment is evident. Before reading further why not find out just how much you know about the development of attachments in *Exercise 3.1* on page 38.

Bonding at birth?

There has been considerable debate surrounding the importance of the first few hours after birth for the subsequent bonding between mother and baby. In their book, *Parent–Infant Bonding* (1982), Marshall Klaus and John Kennell describe a rapidly appearing mother-to-infant attachment following the birth, which not only was said to have long-lasting effects on the relationship between parent and child, but also to affect the child's subsequent development.

As a result of research studies on the amount of contact permitted in hospitals between premature or full-term babies and their parents, Klaus and Kennell argued that early mother–infant contact was crucial for the mother's relationship with her child. It was even suggested that early contact with the baby, together with the hormonal changes associated with giving birth, may release innate species–specific maternal behaviour. The publication of these ideas led to further research by other researchers. Wladek Sluckin and his colleagues reviewed the literature on this topic extensively but found no evidence for the *crucial* nature of this early contact. Researchers such as Klaus Minde have concluded that, while early mother–infant contact does seem to increase parental confidence, and the establishment of nursing by the mother, in the long term it has no effect on the subsequent relationship established between mother and her infant. Nevertheless, because parents enjoy such contacts – and feel benefit from them – such contact is now encouraged. What is important from this debate is that for parents and children who are, by force of circumstances (illness, for instance), unable to have early contact, there is no reason to feel that their relationship will be permanently damaged. It may take a bit longer to establish, but there need be no difference in the end.

The research discussed so far has primarily centred around the role of the mother in the early days and weeks of her baby's life, and her importance to the baby has been the focus of much concern over the last 40 or so years.

The importance of mother love

That a mother is vitally important to her baby may seem so obvious that it is not worthy of closer investigation – yet in the 1990s the assumption that mother must be the primary caregiver is not universally acknowledged. John Bowlby has been particularly influential in shaping our ideas.

Bowlby was a psychiatrist who worked with 'separated' children and adolescents living in hospitals and orphanages. He was influenced by Sigmund Freud and by research on non-human animals by Konrad Lorenz and Harry Harlow. Lorenz became famous for his studies on imprinting in various bird species. He showed that ducklings and goslings become strongly attached to one specific individual soon after hatching. This rapidly formed bond with a single individual was termed *imprinting*, and Lorenz believed that it had major and long-term effects on the young animal's later social and sexual behaviour.

In his research on rhesus monkeys Harry Harlow found that monkeys reared without their mothers, but given a choice between

Exploring Infant Social Relationships

Explore your knowledge of infant social relationships by answering the following questions:

(1) Does bonding between mother and baby occur shortly after birth?
YES/NO

(2) At what age does an infant smile in response to other people?
(a) 3 weeks
(b) 6 weeks
(c) 3 months
(d) 5 months

(3) What is the likely response of babies at the following ages to a 'peek-a-boo' from a stranger?
(a) at 4 months
(b) at 7 months
(c) at 9 months

(4) How would you expect an infant to behave at the following ages if left with a stranger?
(a) at 5 months
(b) at 15 months

(5) At what age do children show specific attachments to particular individuals?

(6) At what age do infants show the first signs of a preference for their caregiver(s)?

(7) If your 18-month-old child was ill and had to go into hospital without you, how do you think he or she would react?

(8) Do you think that a child *always* loves one person more than any other?

(9) Do you think that a father can look after a baby (excluding breast-feeding) just as well as a mother can?

Exploring Infant Social Relationships cont.

(10) Do you think that brothers and sisters in general get on worse or better or no different from same sex siblings?

(11) Do you think that adopted children are likely to have identity problems at any stage?

(12) If children are deprived of any form of attachment in the first few years what do you think is the likely outcome?

(13) If children lose their parents and are orphaned at the age of two (or thereabouts) can they ever make up for their loss and learn to love others?

Chapter 3 provides all the answers to these questions insofar as they are answerable with our present psychological knowledge.

a wire surrogate mother providing milk, or a towelling-covered surrogate mother not providing milk, preferred the 'contact comfort' of the latter, rather than the mother who was just a source of food. This work was evidence, until then not recognized, that mother love isn't just cupboard love (based on the association of food and mother), but is something more. Infants are, it seems, biologically designed to become attached to a mother figure – independently of the satisfaction of basic physiological needs, such as hunger (see *Figure 3.1*).

Bowlby argued that, to the infant, becoming attached to the individual who can attend to its needs is adaptive – without this the vulnerable infant would die. Thus the infant is biologically prepared to elicit caregiving and to become attached to its caregiver.

Bowlby described attachment behaviour as 'any form of behaviour that results in a person attaining or retaining proximity', and attachment as a bond that is developed with 'some other differentiated and preferred individual, who is usually . . . stronger and/or wiser'.

The absence of attachment by the infant towards the mother shortly after birth was not viewed as essential because, unlike Lorenz's goslings, the infant cannot crawl and get away. However, once crawling is established, in the latter half of the first year, an exclusive

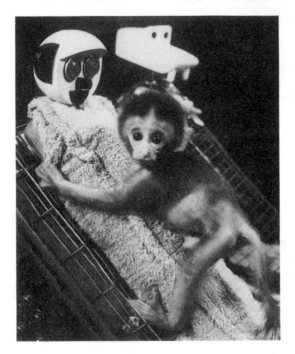

FIGURE 3.1: *The cloth and wire surrogate monkeys in Harlow's research*

relationship with mother (or other major caregiver) is formed. Now the baby can keep close to the mother and continue to elicit her caregiving behaviour.

For John Bowlby, the mother's place in infant care was crucial. She was viewed as the primary attachment figure, and Bowlby emphasized the need for the infant to have her above all others as the source of care and love because he believed that initially infants are unable to form attachments to more than one person (this is his concept of 'monotropism'). He recognized that children become attached to others but believed that their mothers usually remained their 'primary' attachment figures.

Bowlby's first writings on this topic were published shortly after the Second World War, when women who had played an active role in the labour force were being taken out of it, so that their menfolk, returning from war, could return to their civilian jobs. The roles of women and men in postwar Britain were seen as quite distinct – the male as provider, the female as caregiver – and Bowlby's 'findings' coincided nicely with the political needs of the time which were to return women to the home. The father's role in relation to his children was hardly considered.

The father's role in infant care

Traditionally, fathers have had a very minor role in the direct care of the infant in its first few years – indeed, for many children in the UK and other parts of the Western world their fathers were distant figures in childhood as the following quotation shows:

❝ *We had a conventional upbringing. My father didn't believe in seeing much of the children until we reached the age of reason, about 16, so we saw little of him as children.* **❞**

(Lord Dacre, 1989)

Father's job was to provide for the family – 'to go to work' – and single fathers who had to take over the care of children in families split by death or divorce were pitied. The man in an apron cooking and washing for his family was seen as a poor thing. Because it had for so long been accepted that women have special and distinct qualities that uniquely fit them for infant and child care, it was felt that children *ought* to be cared for by mothers, or if they were not, a man could not adequately provide the necessary care. Something was bound to be missing – he had no 'maternal instinct', after all.

A number of studies have shown that this conclusion is not borne out by the facts.

In the 1960s, Rudolph Schaffer and Peggy Emerson were studying children in and around Glasgow, Scotland. In a series of studies on attachment, they found that a considerable number of children did not love their mother most. Nearly a third of 18-month-old children in one study were most strongly attached to their father; some were equally attached to both parents or to three or more figures; and about half were most strongly attached to their mother. Infants direct their love to those who are sensitive to their needs and attend to them quickly. It is the quality of care given that is important in eliciting love.

Maternal instinct as a concept is now questionable. Harry and Margaret Harlows' work on female rhesus monkeys reared with surrogate mothers revealed that such females made very poor mothers. They did not know what to do with their babies. If they had possessed some in-built package enabling them to provide appropriate care for their babies, surely this would have been evident? Whilst no one denies that mothers carry babies for nine months, give birth and lactate – and thus can do things males cannot – all other aspects of infant care can be provided by others just as effectively. In the traditional family – where mother has the role of primary caregiver – fathers interact with their offspring rather differently from mothers.

Fathers play with children in a more physical 'rough and tumble' way, whilst mother's games are more 'intellectual' in approach, involving more talking, reading and watching games. However, the difference is linked to the father's traditional role as secondary caretaker because Tiffany Field has found that if father takes on the role of primary caregiver, he is much more likely to relate to his child as does the traditional mother. Role reversal is not complete, however, since fathers who are primary caretakers still tend to be more physical in games with their children.

It seems clear that parents may have complementary functions in relation to their children, but these functions are in part determined by the role of each parent in the family rather than the sex of the parent *per se*.

THE GROWTH OF LOVE

How does love develop in infants? When do babies begin to show love, and what types of love can they reveal?

Psychologists distinguish between vertical and horizontal relationships; the former are attachments to individuals who have greater knowledge and social power, such as parents or older siblings, and the latter are relationships where the individual has the same amount of social power – for children these will involve relationships with other children. These relationships emerge at different times in development. Vertical relationships typically emerge in the first year of life, whilst the others take longer, and it is not until the third year of life that they are clearly formed.

Signs of love

The newborn soon shows preferences for salient features of those who care for him or her. Once social smiling emerges at six weeks, this behaviour is a most potent reinforcer of caretaking behaviour, encouraging its repetition. But although infants show some preferential responses to certain individuals over others, in general for their first six months they are highly sociable creatures, enjoying the smiles and coos of anyone who cares to interact with them. Rudolf Schaffer was one of the researchers who clearly identified the changes that take place at around six to seven months. Studies of the effects of both brief and longer term separations on infants show that the period between six to eight or nine months is the time when attachment(s) become focused. By their behaviour, babies show clearly who they want to be with, and who by their absence causes distress.

Under six months, separation from the caregiver typically produces only a temporary upset, the baby can be comforted by others; after this time, separation distress is much harder to relieve – indeed, comfort from strangers may cause even more distress. In 1967 Mary Ainsworth described 16 types of behaviour that reveal evidence of an infant's love or attachment for another person; these include: differential smiling, differential crying and differential vocalization. In each of these infants display these patterns at different frequencies in the presence and absence of the attachment figure – thus they might smile and vocalize more towards the mother than others, and cry in her absence. Other patterns include: greeting responses, followings, clinging, embracing, hugging and kissing, and flight to the caregiver as a haven of safety.

Becoming attached to a person or persons has always been recognized – certainly since Freud – as vital for the normal development of the human baby. Freud believed that later psychological problems could be attributed to problems in the first, and for him, the primary relationship – that with the mother. Bowlby followed in this tradition and whether or not psychologists agree over who should be the attachment figure, or whether several will do equally well, all agree that children suffer if deprived of the opportunity to form attachments. Measuring attachments has thus become important for those assessing infant development.

The 'strange situation'

Mary Ainsworth devised a standard procedure for assessing 12–24-month-old infants' relationships to their mother or other caregiver(s). She described it in 1982 as follows:

An infant and mother are brought into a comfortable laboratory room; a stranger enters and sits talking to the mother and then to the infant; the mother leaves the room unobtrusively; the mother returns and the stranger leaves them together; the mother leaves the infant alone in the room; the stranger returns; the mother returns once more. Each of these seven episodes lasts three minutes unless the infant is more than mildly distressed.

Each stage in the above procedure is increasingly more stressful for the infant and, by videotaping the session, attachment in the infant is assessed. Measures of proximity and contact seeking, contact maintaining, resistance, avoidance, search and interaction at a distance are all made, and the infant's responses when reunited with its mother (or caregiver) are regarded as a particularly important indicator of the relationship.

Mary Ainsworth classified infants in three ways. Securely attached infants are classified as Type B, infants showing avoidance are Type A, and those resistant or ambivalent in relationship to the caretaker are classified Type C. Both A and C are said to be *anxiously attached*. A further category has been proposed more recently and this is the insecure-disorganized/disorientated or Type D infant. This infant appears to show confusion and disorientation on reunion with the mother or caretaker. Because it is a fairly recent category, it is most common to hear an infant described simply as securely versus anxiously attached (i.e. B versus A or C).

Although measured only in the second year, the behaviour shown has been found to be a stable indicator of the relationship studied (see Randolph Paterson and Grey Moran) and is felt to be primarily an indicator of the interaction between mother (or caregiver) and baby rather than of the infant's temperament alone. If family life is relatively stable, then so is attachment status – but in more stressful environments secure infants may become insecure or anxiously attached. The 'strange situation' has been used very extensively in recent years in research on attachment, yet it does have problems.

The situation is contrived and artificial, and it does not take into account the mother's or caregiver's behaviour. It is always limited by the time during which such an assessment can be made, as for infants over two years it becomes inappropriate as a measure of attachment.

Attachment status and temperament

The 'strange situation' test can be used to assess attachments to a variety of individuals, and when used in this way, it is generally seen as showing that children can have quite different relationships amongst family and friends, thus indicating that temperament is not the determining factor in the infant's relationship. Indeed, even between mother and father there can be a zero correlation between attachment security towards each parent, showing that a strong attachment to one parent may tell us nothing about the level of attachment to the other. Temperament, and the constitutional influences on it, are discussed in Chapter 4.

SISTERS AND BROTHERS

So far in this chapter, we have considered relationships between children and adults, but let us now turn to children's relationships with other children in the family – their siblings.

For a first-born child, the arrival of a new baby is a very deeply emotional experience. The new baby is a great source of interest, but it is also likely to cause feelings of distress and ambivalence. Judy Dunn describes how the first-born's initial responses may include crying and sleep disturbance, plus deliberate naughtiness and aggression towards the mother. Nevertheless, for many, but not all, children a friendly bond does develop and Judy Dunn and Carol Kendrick noted that this can be described as an 'attachment' in the sense that Bowlby or Ainsworth used it. In their study some babies as young as eight months old missed the older sibling when he or she was not there, and by 14 months half of the babies in Dunn and Kendrick's research clearly missed their older sibling.

In laboratory studies where a situation like the 'strange situation' was used, babies, when left by their mothers, were calmed if their older sibling was present and went to reassure them. Similarly, if a stranger entered, the baby moved towards the older sibling – treating it as a 'secure base'.

Dunn notes that by the end of their first year, many babies

are attached to their older sibling and this has a great impact on their behaviour. Much imitation takes place and this is greater when the older sibling is of the same sex. Of course, not all siblings love each other, and even when an attachment is evident interactions may be aggressive and hostile at times, or show a mismatch, with one child being friendly whilst the other is indifferent or hostile.

Sibling rivalry

Hostility is more common amongst siblings of the opposite sex, and this may be linked to at least two factors. Children seem to copy those who they see as more 'like me', thus same sex siblings are more likely to act together. This is mutually reinforcing for both children and this may promote an easier relationship. Mothers' behaviour may also play a role since some research suggests that mothers show more intense and playful attention towards the second-born if he or she is not the same sex as the first-born. The arrival of the second-born is always associated with a reduction of attention by the mother toward the first-born, and this enhanced interest in the opposite sex newborn may increase sibling hostility and jealousy.

Dunn notes that the rivalry aspect of sibling relationships has been greatly stressed in much of the literature, but her own view is that siblings also play a vitally important role to each other as 'friends, supporters, comforters, and as playmates' and that children's behaviour to their siblings 'reflects both a striking depth of understanding and of emotion'. Judy Dunn argues that it 'really matters' to a child that they should understand each other – after all, siblings are together from the earliest days and have shared a familiar world. They know how to comfort and support, and how to tease and annoy. This is a most powerful relationship and one from which children learn to understand a great deal about others.

SHORT-TERM SEPARATIONS

Once a relationship is established, short-term separations – even for a few minutes – will in many cases lead to great distress in the infant. Ainsworth's 'strange situation' is, as we have seen, one way in which reactions to such separations can be measured. If the mother (or other caregiver) leaves her baby, the separation anxiety exhibited commonly takes the form of screaming, shouting, crying, and searching behaviour. The following paragraphs will discuss separation anxiety in relation to separation from the mother, but it should be noted that the attachment figure could be father or any other caregiver towards whom the baby has formed a strong attachment.

Protest and despair

The distress of the separated infant is self-evident to anyone hearing this response, and there can be few parents who do not feel the searing feelings that such responses evoke. This first reaction to separation is known as the phase of 'protest' and it is clear that the infant is trying desperately to get its mother back. If the separation continues, perhaps because it is caused through illness or death, the child then moves into the phase of 'despair'. This phase resembles the response of a bereaved person who feels sad, hopeless and apathetic. The despair phase also includes anger directed towards the lost loved one and should the mother return, or any sign of her be found, the infant may well fly into rage. Anger may seem to be an unexpected aspect of despair, but the angry cry 'how could you leave me' is a natural reaction to loss and is also common in adults who mourn a loved one. The similarity to the situation of the bereaved can be explained because the young infant cannot comprehend the notion that mother will return. After the age of six months, the infant knows that objects out of sight are still there; it is this knowledge that adds to the pain – mother is there somewhere but not with me. Mother cannot explain to a nine- or twelve-month-old child that she'll only be gone for a short time, nor can the child hold in mind an image of the absent mother, and unless the child can be left with someone to whom it is also attached, the separation will be exactly like a loss through death.

Detachment

If the separation continues for weeks or months, the child moves into the phase of 'detachment'. Now the child seems to be coping well, has recovered its vitality and is getting on with life, but in fact this phase is really the sign that all hope has gone. The child is friendly with everyone but may not risk forming a relationship with anyone for fear of losing them too. Should mother now return, she will be hardly noticed; indeed, the child may seem almost not to know her.

Because John Bowlby stressed the tendency of a child to attach to *one* figure, typically the mother, from this it naturally follows that she is indispensable to the child. Separation from her, even for short periods, was viewed as damaging and leading to long-term ill effects on the child. The full-time employment of the mother was seen as something that would cause suffering to the family, and Bowlby stressed that it 'must be regarded as a potential source of a deprived child'. This view of Bowlby's was, and continues to be, a source of great controversy. Nowadays it is expected that women will form a significant part of the paid workforce and yet many, perhaps most, mothers are dogged by the view that they, and only they, can care for their child adequately. Despite the work of Rudolf Schaffer and others, who have shown that mother is not necessarily the most loved person in a child's life, and also that the notion of a primary attachment figure is not upheld, the effect of Bowlby's opinion is not lightly shaken off. Women's place is still seen by many as being in the home, and if she is not there, dire consequences for her children are predicted.

Infants in daycare

Research in recent years has addressed this problem; countless papers have been published on this thorny issue, as Alison Clarke-Stewart's (1989) paper 'Infant Day Care: Maligned or malignant' indicates. The answer is not a simple one but it may be summarized thus. The effect of daycare provision depends in great part on the quality of the care offered, and providing that the child is not moved from one arrangement to another, research suggests that there may be no differences between daycare and home-reared children. Indeed some studies suggest that infants with daycare experience may be more socially skilled than home-reared infants.

In her review of this topic, Clarke-Stewart records that one year olds whose mothers work full-time are more likely to avoid their mothers, are less compliant with their mothers, and are more aggressive with peers. She also notes that seven per cent more, or 36 per cent of daycare children whose mothers work full-time, are classed as insecurely attached, whereas only 29 per cent of infants whose mothers have either no employment or only part-time occupations are classified in this way. Although this difference is significant, its meaning is not entirely clear. Clarke-Stewart notes that this finding does not necessarily mean that children are *insecure* in general. Indeed, she argues that daycare children may be less compliant because they 'think for themselves and they want their own way', and she also notes that there is evidence that children in daycare are more advanced in terms of intellectual development. Clarke-Stewart concludes that further research is needed to clarify the position and it should also be emphasized that as nearly one third of children whose mothers do not work full-time are insecurely attached whilst many children of full-time working mothers are, despite this, securely attached, the reasons for insecure attachment are clearly complex. Clarke-Stewart stresses that as employment in mothers is now a fact of life, the issue is not whether infants should be in daycare, but how to make their experiences there and at home supportive of their development and of their parents' peace of mind!

LONG-TERM SEPARATIONS AND SUBSTITUTE CARE

Whilst most children are brought up with their natural (biological) parents, a few will be separated from their parents on a long-term basis, in foster homes, in care, or as adopted children permanently based in new homes. Death, divorce or separation of parents are just some of the ways that may give rise to long-term separation, and it is obvious that this potentially may cause problems for such children.

There are four important elements in the success of substitute parenting. These are:

- the child's age when substitute parenting begins;
- the continuity of care;
- the quality of care;
- society's attitude towards both the situation giving rise to the care and the type of care selected.

This final point is important because the success of the substitute care for the child will be harder to achieve if society views the situation as inferior to the natural situation. In the past, illegitimacy was something that people were ashamed of, and it was often felt to be preferable for a child to be reared by adopters rather than in its natural home with a single 'biological' parent. Today, this situation is viewed rather differently; many more children are born outside marriage, and attitudes towards this situation are far less critical.

Once fostering or adoption has occurred, what is the likely success of this 'substitute parenting?'

Fostered children

In reviewing this subject, Martin Shaw has considered some advantages and disadvantages. For the fostered child, there may be a continued relationship with the biological parents – thus the task of parenting is 'shared'. Sadly this does not necessarily make life easier for the foster child because there is evidence that the biological parents often feel a sense of guilt, resentment and powerlessness in relation to the new 'parents'. One potential advantage of a foster mother is that she is generally more experienced in mothering than are most biological parents. Foster mothers are, according to research (which incidently concentrates on mothers much more than fathers), most likely to be older women whose own children have left home – thus the child is less likely to be 'practised on' in the way that inevitably occurs for most first-borns. This positive aspect of fostering is often neglected and as Shaw points out, foster parents are traditionally viewed as wishing to foster in order to resolve some underlying personal or family problem rather than as offering a skill. Thus social workers are more likely to view them as clients rather than as colleagues sharing a common aim: to provide satisfactory care for the foster child. For the child, the success of his or her placement again depends on the factors listed above, and providing that the placement does not 'fail' and the parents give up their task (which most often occurs within the first year if at all), then there is a good chance of a positive outcome. Indeed, for many foster parents, the children are treated just as their own and the label 'foster child' is a distinction that is only made by other people outside the family.

Adopted children

For children who are adopted, the situation is rather different, for whilst both foster parents' and adopters' task is to rear someone else's child or children, the adoptive parents are able, once the legal formalities are completed, to get on with the job without continued scrutiny by the professionals.

However, there is a common tendency to assume that the outcome of adoption can never be quite as good as that for children reared by their biological parents. Is this borne out by the research?

In a longitudinal study of adopted children, Barbara Tizard and others found that by the age of eight, children who had been adopted between the ages of two and four showed, on average, no more problems than were found in 'home-reared' controls. However, they were more likely to be described as overfriendly and more attention-seeking in their behaviour. Indeed by eight the great majority of all the adopted children studied, including those adopted later, were viewed as successful although more problems were evident amongst the later adopted group.

Other research has indicated that puberty may be a time when problems become evident. In 1963, Michael Humphrey and Christopher Ounsted reported that adopted children are more likely to be referred for psychiatric consultation after the age of eleven. It has been suggested that at the onset of puberty, when questions such as 'Who am I?' arise (discussed more fully in Chapter 12), the adopted adolescent may have more difficulty establishing a stable self-concept. The notion of 'genealogical anxiety' has been put forward to explain this problem. However, a more recent research study on 50 white, mainly middle-class adoptees, all of whom had been placed for adoption before the age of two, found no evidence that the adoptees had any more identity problems when compared with carefully matched controls. Whilst there can be little doubt that adoptees will, at some time, show concern about the nature of their biological parents, this is not the same as saying that they will have an identity crisis that cannot be satisfactorily resolved, nor does it necessarily mean that psychological problems will follow if this phase is more than usually bumpy. Michael and Heather Humphrey conclude this debate by saying:

In the final analysis it is surely life experience that contributes most to self-awareness; and until we can add to our store of facts we may be in danger of over-estimating the handicap of ancestral ignorance to children cut off from their roots.

FAILURE TO BOND

There can be few children who lack an opportunity to form bonds early in life, but occasionally this does occur and it is possible to see what the effect of a total lack of love can have. Research on non-human animals has been more systematic in studying the effects of privation and deprivation, and such work has given us some insights into the likely outcome for humans.

Research on monkeys

Gary Griffin and Harry Harlow found that monkeys raised in total isolation for three months, who were subsequently placed with other juveniles, soon began to behave appropriately. Peers seemed to play an important role in their rehabilitation. However, in other studies monkeys isolated for six months with a cloth-covered surrogate mother showed marked alterations in their social behaviour when they were later placed with other monkeys. Such monkeys are either aggressive or indifferent to others, and their sexual behaviour is so disrupted that normal reproduction was impossible. These infants missed the sensitive period for the development of attachments and their rehabilitation seemed unlikely.

A different approach was taken by Melinda Novak and Harry Harlow in some research exploring the effects of gradual rehabilitation of isolated monkeys. At the start monkeys were only allowed to look at another at a distance and then the isolate was gradually introduced to a 'therapist monkey' – one who had been normally reared and who was younger than the isolate. Therapists played with their isolate 'patients' and gradually recovery took place, and it was found that such rehabilitated monkeys could eventually become adequate parents. Thus monkeys who have missed the sensitive period for the development of attachment can, given the right treatment, recover. These studies are intriguing, but how far can we hope to relate their findings to the equivalent human situation?

'Wild' children and 'wolf' children

Children who have had a period of total isolation from other normal humans may help us understand better the effect of others on a child's development. 'Wild' children and 'wolf' children have been discussed in this context, and in 1801 one of the first of these to be documented in detail was Jean-Marc-Gaspard Itard's work in trying to raise the 'Wild Boy of Aveyron'. This young boy was found living in the woods around Aveyron, and he appeared to have been totally without human contact for some years (sighting of him had occurred over a long period). After his capture, Itard took over his care in the belief that he could provide the treatment that would 'civilize' him. His success was limited, and though the boy who had trotted and grunted like an animal came to live like a human being, he never became a normal human being. So-called 'wolf' children – such as Romulus and Remus – cannot, in the view of Ann and Alan Clarke be taken seriously as evidence, and in general stories of 'wild' children must be viewed with some sceptism. Bruno Bettleheim has suggested that they may not be 'wild' at all, but children who may have been abandoned – in some cases for only a short period before being found – by parents because they were autistic, psychotic or retarded. Since the origins of such children are unknown, we cannot make any guesses about how a period of isolation, of unknown length, has affected their development.

44 thieves

If we look at cases that are less extreme, more insights can be gained. John Bowlby suggested that the failure to form bonds may lead to the 'affectionless character' (affectionless psychopath). Such a person is without feelings for others and is unable to form relationships. In a study of 44 thieves, Bowlby claimed that he had evidence that separation experiences in early childhood had produced an inability to form relationships. However, separation was not the only factor linked with affectionless psychopathy in this study. A number of the thieves had experienced many different mother figures in early life, and this may also have impaired these children's ability to form bonds.

Michael Rutter believes that bond disruption (the breaking of a bond that has been formed) is not linked to affectionless psychopathy; what is important is the *failure* to form bonds in early childhood.

Peer bonding: a compensation for lack of 'mothering'?

The monkey research by the Harlows and others has shown that bonding to peers can offset, to a very great extent, the potentially damaging effects of being reared without a mother, or mother figure (of either sex). Does this also apply to humans?

Few studies are available, but the experiences of young children whose parents were taken and persecuted by the Nazis, has been documented. Anna Freud and Sophie Dann reported on six pre-school children who had undergone such an experience and had stayed together whilst in various concentration camps. These children formed very strong bonds with each other, and although they suffered extremes of deprivation (having been initially taken from their parents in the first weeks of life), the presence of peers enabled them to cope with their lack of mothering.

RECOVERY FROM EARLY DEPRIVATION

It has long been thought that early experiences are crucial in determining the course of subsequent development. Psychoanalysts stress that many problems have their roots in early childhood experience. John Bowlby, following in this tradition, has stressed that children should experience a warm, intimate and continuous relationship with their mother (or permanent mother substitute) and that without this their mental health will suffer. Today, however, views on this matter are far more flexible. In 1976 Ann and Alan Clarke reviewed a wide range of studies on the influence of early experience, and concluded that: 'it appears that there is virtually no psychosocial adversity to which some children have not been subjected, yet later recovered'. They consider a wide range of studies and whilst noting that, for instance, later adoptions may be less satisfactory than early ones, or that children in institutions may fare less well than those who are adopted, they point out that there are many exceptions. Institutions vary enormously and young children certainly can develop normally when living in these circumstances. Similarly, late adoptions may have very satisfactory outcomes. Even in the most extreme circumstances, amazing success has been achieved.

One, now famous, example is that of a small girl of six, known as Isabelle (a pseudonym), who was 'rescued' from life-long isolation with a deaf-mute mother. Because she was an illegitimate child, born in 1932, she had been kept in seclusion with her mother in a dark room, shut off from the rest of the family. When found, she had no speech and was severely subnormal in ability, having a score of nineteen months on an intelligence test (the Stanford-Binet scale). She also had rickets as a result of a very inadequate diet. Her improvement was dramatic, and by the age of eight she had reached the normal level educationally, and, according to Kingsley Davis, in 1947 she gave the impression of being 'a very bright, cheerful, energetic little girl'. After this time she continued to make excellent progress. Although Isabelle had some human contact, her early life was lived in appalling conditions, yet her recovery was rapid. Later experiences of a much more positive type enabled her to recover from six years of adversity.

Ann and Alan Clarke conclude that all of development is important, not just the early years. This is not a justification for not bothering too much about the circumstances in which our children are reared. What is important is the quality at each stage in development. Infancy is important but experiences at this early stage do not invariably set the stage for what is to follow. Later experiences can offset early difficulties.

Now go back to *Exercise 3.1* on page 38 and see if you know all the answers.

Recommended reading

*Dunn, J. (1984) *Sisters and Brothers*. Glasgow: Fontana. [A most readable book.]
*Parke, R.D. (1981) *Fathering*. Glasgow: Fontana. [A readable account of research comparing mothers and fathers.]
Rutter, M. (1989) *Maternal Deprivation Reassessed*. Harmondsworth: Penguin. [A most comprehensive account of research on maternal deprivation.]
Schaffer, R. (1985) *Mothering*. Glasgow: Fontana. [A lively account of research on attachment and mothering.]

[*Out of print, so only available through libraries.]

References

Ainsworth, M.D.S. (1967) *Infancy in Uganda*. Baltimore: Johns Hopkins University Press. [Patterns of attachment behaviour.]
Ainsworth, M.D.S. (1982) Attachment: Retrospective and prospect. In C.M. Parkes & J. Stevenson-Hinds (Eds), *The Place of Attachment in Human Behaviour*. New York: Basic Books. [Quotation on the 'strange situation'.]
Bettleheim, B. (1959) Feral children and autistic children. *American Journal of Sociology, 64*, 455–467. ['Wild' children may have been abandoned because of various problems.]
Bowlby, J. (1944) Fourty-four juvenile thieves: Their characters and homelife. *International Journal of Psychoanalysis, 24*, 19–52 & 107–127. [The study of 44 thieves.]
Bowlby, J. (1952) *Maternal Care and Mental Health*. Geneva: World Health Organization. [Includes comment on nature of relationship which child needs with mother.]
Bowlby, J. (1977) The making and breaking of affectional bonds. I. Aetiology and psychopathology in the light of attachment theory. *British Journal of Psychiatry, 130*, 201–210. [Quotation concerning attachment behaviour.]
Clarke, A.M. & Clarke, A.D.B. (Eds) (1976) *Early Experience: Myth and evidence*. London: Open Books. [Comment on 'wild children'; review of the effects of early experience.]
Clarke-Stewart, K.A. (1989). Infant day care? Maligned or malignant? Special issue: children and their development: knowledge base, research agenda, and social policy application. *American Psychologist, 44(2)*, 266–273. [Review of studies of infants in daycare.]
Dacre, Lord (1989) Relative values. *Sunday Times Magazine, 21 May*, 11–14. [The quotation on fathers.]
Davis, K. (1976) Final note on a case of extreme isolation. In A.M. Clarke and A.D.B. Clarke (Eds) *Early Experience: Myth and evidence*. London: Open Books. [The case of 'Isabelle'.]
Dunn, J. (1984) *Sisters and Brothers*. London: Fontana. [Sibling relationships.]
Dunn, J. & Kendrick, C. (1982) *Siblings: Love, envy and understanding*. Cambridge, Mass.: Harvard University Press. [Studies of siblings.]
Field, T. (1978) Interaction behaviours of primary versus secondary caretaker fathers. *Developmental Psychology, 14*, 183–185. [Father's role in childcare.]
Freud, A. & Dann, S. (1951) An experiment in group upbringing. *Psychoanalytic Study of the Child, 6*, 127–168. [A study of six children whose parents had been taken by the Nazis.]
Griffin, G.A. and Harlow, F. (1966) Effects of three months of total social deprivation on social adjustment and learning in the rhesus monkey. *Child Development, 37(3)*, 533–547. [Monkeys reared for three months in isolation, then exposed to others.]
Harlow, H.F. (1958) The nature of love. *American Psychologist, 13*, 673–685. [Infant monkeys reared without mothers.]
Harlow, H.F. & Harlow, M.K. (1962) Social deprivation in monkeys. *Scientific American, November*, Reprint No 473. [The inability of female monkeys reared in isolation to care for offspring.]

Humphrey, M. & Humphrey, H. (1988) *Families with a Difference: Varieties of surrogate parenthood*. London: Routledge. [The dangers of overstressing the handicap of ancestral ignorance in adoptees.]

Humphrey, M. & Ounsted, C. (1963) Adoptive families referred for psychological advice: (1) The children. *British Journal of Psychiatry*, *109*, 599–608. [Adoption and psychiatric problems.]

Itard, J.M.G. (1962) *The Wild Boy of Aveyron*. New York: Appleton-Century-Crofts. [The 'civilization' of an isolated boy.]

Klaus, M.H. & Kennell, J.H. (1982) *Parent–Infant Bonding*. St Louis, MO: Mosby. [Maternal bonding.]

Lorenz, K. (1952) *King Solomon's Ring*. London: Methuen. [Studies of imprinting.]

Main, M., Kaplan, N. & Cassidy, J. (1985) Security in infancy, childhood, and adulthood: A move to the level of representation. *Monographs of the Society for Research in Child Development*, *50*, 66–104. [Insecure-disorganized/disorientated attachment.]

Minde, K. (1986) Bonding and attachment: Its relevance for the present day clinician. *Developmental Medicine & Child Neurology*, *28(6)*, 803–806. [Early mother–infant contact increases mothers' confidence.]

Novak, M.A. & Harlow, H.F. (1975) Social recovery of monkeys isolated for the first years of life. I. Rehabilitation and therapy. *Development Psychology*, *11*, 453–465. [Recovery of isolated infant monkeys.]

Paterson, R.J. & Moran, G. (1988) Attachment theory, personality development, and psychotherapy. *Clinical Psychology Review*, *8*, 611–636. [Review of attachment.]

Robertson, J. & Bowlby, J. (1952) Responses of young children to separation from their mothers. *Courrier de la Centre Internationale de l'Enfance*, *2*, 131–142. [Effects of separation on children.]

Ruppenthal, G.C., Arling, G.L., Harlow, H.G., Sackett, G.P. & Suome, S.J. (1976) A 1-year perspective of motherless-mother monkey-behaviour. *Journal of Abnormal Psychology*, *85*, 341–349. [Motherless monkeys can be rehabilitated.]

Rutter, M. (1981) *Maternal Deprivation Reassessed*, 2nd ed. Harmondsworth: Penguin. [Effects of separation from caregiver.]

Schaffer, R. (1977) *Mothering*. London: Fontana. [Covers many studies of attachment behaviour.]

Schaffer, H.R. & Emerson, P.E. (1964) The development of social attachments in infancy. *Monographs of Social Research in Child Development*, *29*, Serial No 94. [Attachment to mothers, fathers and others.]

Shaw, M. (1986) Substitute parenting. In W. Sluckin & M. Herbert (Eds) *Parental Behaviour*. Oxford: Basil Blackwell. [Review of substitute parenting.]

Stein, L.M. & Hoopes, J.L. (1985) *Identity Formation in the Adopted Adolescent: The Delaware family study*. New York: Child Welfare League of America. [Identity problems in adopted children.]

Tizard, B. (1977) *Adoption: A second chance*. London: Open Books. [Discusses a longitudinal

4. *Early Influences and Personality*

*Come listen now to the good old days when children,
  strange to tell,
Were seen not heard, led a simple life, in short,
  were brought up well.*

(Aristophanes, fifth century BC)

PERSONALITY AND SELF-AWARENESS

Personality development has long been a major preoccupation of psychology. Although there is general agreement that the concept of personality is useful, psychologists have not been able to agree on an acceptable definition. However, the idea that underlies different theoretical perspectives is that each individual has a relatively unique and enduring set of psychological tendencies and reveals them in the course of his or her transactions with various social environments such as home, school and playground. It is assumed that inherited biological influences interact with environmental influences as children grow up with the consequence that they gradually develop characteristic patterns of behaviour – the outward and visible signs of inner moral values, traits, habits, cognitive structures and needs – which become progressively resistant to change with maturity. It has been said of personality that in some ways we are like *all* other persons, like *some* other persons, and like *no* other person. Each of us is, in many respects, unique.

Of all the qualities that we possess, self-awareness is a very special characteristic of humans. But there can be no self-image until there is an awareness of others – social awareness. Who we are, and what we are, is socially defined; that is to say that the way we see ourselves is influenced, in large part, by the terms in which others see us, or the ways in which we *think* others judge us. One of the consequences of being human is that a person becomes an object to him or herself. Indeed, the *self* (or ego, as it is referred to in the psychoanalytic literature) is usually the aspect of personality that people are most concerned about. Most of the goals which motivate us, such as love, security, prestige, adequacy, status and power, are related to so-called ego needs – matters that have their impact on how we feel about and judge ourselves. So are many of the causes of frustration and conflict. For those who value themselves in terms of what they own, money and material things are likely to be highly motivating; for those who measure themselves in other non-material terms, income and goods will be less influential.

From an evolutionary point of view, this self-awareness is something of a novelty. Among the millions of species that live on earth, humans are the only one who have this characteristic to a well-developed degree. The closest that our nearest relatives – primates such as chimpanzees or gorillas – come to this is an ability to recognize their own reflections in a mirror. This ability represents the first step towards a sense of self. Self-awareness as we know it has far-reaching consequences for human experience, leading as it does to a yearning for love and a feeling of relatedness to other persons. It is these yearnings which are among the most important driving forces in the shaping of personality – the focus of so much of our attention in considering the psychology of children.

The bond of love

It is generally agreed that the infant's first human relationships form the foundation stones of his or her developing personality. Healthy adjustment depends upon the adequate satisfaction of the infant's need for certain actions (such as nurturant care, warm and affectionate communication, attention, play and other stimulation) which flow from the feeling and attitude of love.

In order to win their parents' love and approval, children generally try to please them. They imitate attitudes and behaviours they observe in the home; they try to master difficult skills, and they endeavour (much of the time) to be obedient. After all, it is often made quite explicit that approval is contingent upon obedience: 'Mummy loves you when you're good' or, 'Daddy doesn't like you any more because you're naughty'. And, of course, more tangible sanctions

may follow non-compliance. Social training, or *socialization* as it is
called, requires a reasonable level of compliance from children, hence
the serious implications for extremely disobedient youngsters such as
those with conduct disorders (see Chapter 11).

The writer François Mauriac observed that 'we are moulded and
remoulded by those who have loved us; and though the love may
pass, we are nevertheless their work, for good or ill'. Psychologists
confirm this view. Erik Erikson, a psychologist and psychoanalyst,
believes that during the period of infancy a baby learns whether the
world is a good and satisfying place to live in or a source of pain,
misery, frustration and uncertainty. These contrasting points of view,
which he calls 'basic trust' and 'basic mistrust', are very like our adult
attitudes of optimism and pessimism. *Exercise 4.1* on page 60 looks
at Erikson's ideas in greater detail.

Neglect and its effects

Neglect, abuse and indifference are all major obstacles to the development of a perception of a benign and predictable world in which
children feel secure enough to initiate independence-seeking and
perceive their own actions as having meaningful consequences. Such
influences are likely to produce a child who behaves in a very troubled
and troublesome manner.

Martin Seligman says of the earliest caregiver–infant relationship
that the infant begins a 'dance' – a complex interaction – with the
environment that will last throughout childhood; it is the outcome of
this dance that determines the infant's helplessness or mastery. When a
response (an all-purpose psychological term for behavioural reactions
to stimuli) is made by the infant – perhaps crying due to some distress
– it can either produce a change in the environment (mother comforts
her baby) or be independent of what changes occur (the cry has no
predictable effect). At some primitive level, Seligman speculates, the
infant 'calculates' the association (correlation) between his or her
behaviour and its consequence. If the correlation is zero (i.e. there
is no association) then helplessness develops. If there is a correlation
(either positive or negative) the response is working and the infant
learns either to perform that action more frequently or to refrain from
performing it, depending on whether the correlated outcome is good
(positive) or bad (negative). However, over and above this, children
learn that *responding works*, and that in general there is synchrony
– a smooth meshing – between actions and outcomes. When there is
an absence of synchrony leading to helplessness – a feature of severely
neglectful homes – children stop performing the response; they also
learn that in general responding doesn't matter. Such learning has the

Erikson's Developmental Tasks and the Influences which may Hinder Children's Progress

The table below contains an account of what Erik Erikson considers to be the main developmental tasks for each stage of development from birth to adolescence. Taking each task (goal) in turn, use the righthand column to write down which main hazards or influences you think may hinder children's progress towards maturity.

Stages of Development Towards Maturity

Age Period	Characteristics to be achieved	Major hazards to achieve
Birth to 1 year	SENSE OF TRUST OR SECURITY – derived from affection and gratification of needs.	[*Example*: parental neglect, abuse . . .]
1–4 years	SENSE OF AUTONOMY – child viewing self as an individual in their own right, apart from parents although dependent on them.	
4–5 years	SENSE OF INITIATIVE – period of vigorous reality testing, imagination, and imitation of adult behaviour.	
6–11 years	SENSE OF DUTY AND ACCOMPLISHMENT – laying aside of fantasy and play and undertaking real tasks, developing academic and social competencies.	
12–15 years	SENSE OF IDENTITY – clarification in adolescence of who one is and what one's role is.	
15 to adulthood	SENSE OF INTIMACY – ability to establish close personal relationships with members of both sexes.	

ANSWERS on page 73.

same consequences that helplessness has in adults: lack of response initiation, negative thoughts, and anxiety and depression. But this may be more disastrous for the infant since at this sensitive stage learning about the self and one's importance in the world is the foundation on which confidence and personality are built (see Chapter 11).

Security of attachment

Jay Belsky argues that the past decade has witnessed a 'virtual revolution' in our understanding of early development, and in particular a recognition that certain attributes that indicate differences between individuals, measured within the first year of life, are capable of anticipating or predicting later developments in the child. For example when it is a matter of social and emotional development, the measurement of the child's sense of security in its relationship to its mother (referred to as 'security of infant-to-mother attachment') at the end of the first year of life, predicts the infant's likely *competence* when it is old enough to go to school.

The basic assumption is not that the relationship between mother and baby inevitably or comprehensively influences later development, but rather that the infant's initial (and foundational) experience of his or her relationship with the mother anticipates much that is of significance in later social development. This occurs because the experience affects the infant's expectations and ideas about cause and effect (what psychologists call 'attributions') with regard to other relationships, as well as his or her feelings about the self and social skills, which arise in other social contexts.

BIOSOCIAL ASPECTS OF PERSONALITY

While it is quite true that such early experiences are crucial because they are the building bricks for the foundations of personality development, we have to go even further back in time in order to uncover significant influences. These consist of both environmental and biological (e.g. genetic, endocrinal) factors. For example, the child's very first home is in the mother's womb; and while it usually provides a benign environment for the developing embryo and foetus, this is not always the case.

The uterine environment

Courts of law have given recognition to the fact that the foetus, developing and growing inside the mother, is always a distinct individual.

The unborn baby is never actually a part of the mother's body despite its tenancy of her womb. It has its own unique pattern of genes, and possesses its own nervous system and blood stream. There is no direct nerve connection between the mother and infant. Their bloodstreams are separated by a semipermeable barrier, the placenta. The mother's blood, which carries the nourishment, stops on one side of the barrier and the blood elements are broken down and strained through it. There is therefore no more direct blood tie between a mother and a child than between a father and child. Nevertheless, there are several physical and psychological factors which, by severely distressing the mother, can have a disruptive effect on the embryo or foetus. The mother's distress is transmitted to the foetus through effects on the chemical composition of her blood brought about by stress-related changes in her endocrine system.

Active substances (such as nutrients but also toxic agents and viruses) are transmitted to the foetus across the placenta. These may be capable of affecting its neural, endocrinal or other structures. Those physical agents that are capable of altering the design or morphology of the organism have their most disruptive effect during the germinal period (the first two weeks after conception) and the embryonic phase (weeks two to eight) when the organ systems are first emerging. Most damaging are diseases in the mother such as german measles (rubella), AIDS and syphilis, and drugs such as alcohol, nicotine, thalidomide and barbiturates. All can impair the child-to-be to different degrees. Incidentally, handicapped children are found disproportionately often (i.e. are statistically over-represented) in the population of youngsters with *behaviour* problems.

It remains a debatable question as to whether, and to what extent, maternal stress can convey itself to the unborn child to a degree that has long-term adverse consequences. In the short term, at least, there *is* suggestive evidence that severe maternal distress during pregnancy makes for a restless fretful baby. However, much of the work on the relationship between maternal attitudes and emotions and *significant* effects on the unborn child is beset by serious methodological problems which make it difficult to arrive at confident generalizations.

INTERACTIONS OF HEREDITY AND ENVIRONMENT

A normal set of *genes* (the basic chemical units of heredity) and an appropriate, encouraging environment are each needed for satisfactory personality development and the acquisition of flexible and effective (adaptive) behaviour for dealing with life. Environmental factors can set limits on (or enhance) the individual's achievement of all his or her genetic potential. A youngster well endowed with intellectual potential (for example) may well be cognitively 'stunted' if starved of stimulation and the opportunity to learn.

Phenotypes

The term *phenotype* is used to describe all the observable features or characteristics of an individual at any given time. Personality is an example of a phenotype. It is the end product of an inter-action between all that the individual has inherited and all the environmental influences which have made their mark. The same sort of interaction – but on a more restricted basis – is thought to occur in the evolution of the so-called personality problems. Specific problems acquired by parents through their life experi-ences can only be transmitted to their offspring via psychosocial mechanisms, that is to say by example, teaching and experience; their germ cells (the ones passed on from generation to generation) are not affected by what they learn with their brain cells. Thus, a father cannot transmit his fear of confined spaces to his daughter through genetic mechanisms. What the individual may inherit is the *potential* for behaving in certain ways. This is referred to as a *predisposition*. For example, the individual might inherit a predisposition (in the form of a volatile (over-reactive) autonomic nervous system and an introverted personality type) to acquire neurotic fears. More seriously for the efficient functioning and well-being of the personality, there is a well-established genetic component in the susceptibility to develop depressive illness and schizophrenia.

Many characteristics in which there are quantitative variations (i.e. differences of degree), particularly complex ones like intelli-gence and temperament, depend upon the action of many genes. This is called *polygenic* inheritance. Polygenic inheritance is of much greater significance in those children with a neurotic per-sonality, with behaviour problems, learning difficulties and devel-opmental problems than are abnormalities of chromosomes or single genes.

In psychiatric or psychological disorders, what is inherited is usually a susceptibility to develop a particular problem. Whether or not this predisposition is actually translated into clinical symp-toms depends to some extent on the experiences and support-ive networks a person has during his or her life. Before read-ing further try answering the questions in *Exercise 4.2* on page 64.

Common Sense and Personality

Here are some statements which reflect commonsense theories. Do you think they are true or false?

▶ ❛ *A youngster comes into the world with an inborn sense of good and evil.* ❜
▶ ❛ *A child who doesn't look you in the eyes is deceitful.* ❜
▶ ❛ *Red-haired children have more explosive tempers than blond ones.* ❜
▶ ❛ *Child prodigies tend to be physically weak and maladjusted.* ❜
▶ ❛ *Thin lips are a sign of cruelty in a child.* ❜
▶ ❛ *An expectant mother can influence the character of her unborn child by fixing her thoughts on particular subjects.* ❜
▶ ❛ *Mathematics helps a child to think logically.* ❜
▶ ❛ *Long, slender hands in a youngster indicate an artistic temperament.* ❜
▶ ❛ *Children with high foreheads are more intelligent than those with low foreheads.* ❜
▶ ❛ *Fat children are jollier than thin children.* ❜
▶ ❛ *Youngsters sometimes become feeble-minded from overstudying.* ❜
▶ ❛ *The marriage of cousins is practically certain to result in children of inferior intelligence.* ❜
▶ ❛ *Children have an instinctive fear of the dark.* ❜
▶ ❛ *Children have a greater capacity for learning than adults.* ❜

ANSWERS on page 74.

PERSONALITY TYPES

Extraversion–introversion

The psychologist Hans Eysenck, among others, has systematically studied personality traits like *extraversion–introversion*. He describes the typical extravert as a sociable person, who likes parties, needs to have people to talk to and does not like to be alone when reading or studying. Such persons tend to crave excitement, take chances, act impulsively, make decisions on the spur of the moment and jump in at the deep end. They are also carefree, easy-going, fond of practical jokes, like change, always have a ready answer, tend to be optimistic, laugh a lot and prefer to keep on the move. Extraverts are also inclined to be aggressive and lose their tempers rather swiftly. The typical introvert is a very different sort of person.

Introverts tend to be shy, quiet and retiring, introspective and more attracted to books than people. They are inclined to plan ahead, being cautious rather than impulsive, and try to avoid excitement, taking everyday life seriously and preferring a well-ordered style of life. Introverts keep emotions under tight control and are not aggressive or hot-tempered. This personality type is more reliable than the extravert, more pessimistic, and places a lot of emphasis on ethical values.

Of course these descriptions represent the extremes of a continuum. Many of us would come somewhere between these extremes – it's all a matter of degree.

Although it is commonly said that a person is a 'born' extravert or 'born' introvert, early family and other environmental experiences do also have their effect. Happy social experiences encourage the child to want to repeat them. By comparison, too many miserable social experiences tend to reinforce negative attitudes towards social experiences and towards other people. Children are particularly impressionable during their earliest formative years (the first six or seven) and can therefore be influenced in the direction of being sociable, unsociable or antisocial more easily in early childhood than later on. The first social experiences in the family and at home are significant in determining extraverted and introverted patterns of behaviour in adulthood. Undoubtedly environmental influences are important; but just how important are they?

Environmentalist theories

One of the results of the impact of thinkers like John B. Watson and B.F. Skinner was the almost exclusive emphasis placed on *environmental* influences in the development of behaviour. And, it follows from this that when things went wrong, mother (as the prominent feature in the child's early environment) tended, in the psychiatric literature, to receive all the blame. As Hilde Bruch, an eminent child psychiatrist put it:

Modern parent education is characterized by the experts pointing out in great detail all the mistakes parents have made and can possibly make in substituting 'scientific knowledge' for the tradition of the 'good old days'. An unrelieved picture of modern parental behaviour, a contrived image of artificial perfection and happiness, is held up before parents who try valiantly to reach the ever receding ideal of 'good parenthood', like dogs after a mechanical rabbit. . . .

For decades, psychiatric reports abounded in simplistic and often erroneous mother-scapegoating concepts such as 'maternal deprivation' and 'maternal overprotection'. Maternal attitudes were even blamed (incorrectly as we now know) for causing a serious developmental disorder of childhood called infantile autism. For a long time fathers escaped this sort of attention because, as we saw in Chapter 3, their role in infant care was minimal. The extreme environmentalist point of view was reflected in the philosophy of John B. Watson, a psychologist at Johns Hopkins University at the beginning of the twentieth century. He believed that precise, planned training of children's habits and ways of thinking could mould them in any desired shape:

Give me a dozen healthy infants, well-formed, and my own specified world to bring them up in, and I'll guarantee to take any one at random and train him to become any type of specialist I might select – doctor, lawyer, artist, merchant-chief, and yes, even beggarman, and thief, regardless of his talents, penchants, tendencies, abilities, vocations, and race of his ancestors.

Watson underrated the influence of the difference in *inborn* temperament of individual infants, and failed to take into account the power of proactive (as opposed to merely reactive) characteristics (the child's ability to think for him or herself, the coercive child's power to get his or her own way) to modify the environment itself. Children's individual capacities to process information and to superimpose meanings (i.e. their own interpretations) on events, as well as their differences in sensitivity to their environment, make it impossible to claim that two apparently similar environments will have identical effects on any two children (see the discussion of this point in Chapter 13). This makes nonsense of Watson's notion of a purely environmental 'programming' of a passive child.

TEMPERAMENT

The 'difficult' child

Temperament is a term applied to those aspects of personality pertaining to mood, activity, tempo and general level of energy. A group of New York psychiatrists, Stella Chess, Alexander Thomas and Herbert Birch, have demonstrated just how crucial these inherited or constitutional aspects of personality can be in the quality of the

relationships and interactions between parent and child. They followed the development of a large number of infants over several years,
and found that there were certain children who, very early in life,
stood out quite clearly as 'difficult children'. Of these, approximately
70 per cent later developed quite serious behaviour problems. In
Exercise 4.3 on page 68 you can see some of the ways in which babies
can be classified, according to temperament, very early in life; this
exercise enables you to explore the notion of 'difficult' more fully.

The 'easy' child

Another group of children participated in the study under discussion.
Their type of temperament was such that it usually made early
care remarkably easy. They frequently enhanced their mothers'
sense of well-being and of being 'good' and effective parents (see
Exercise 4.3).

EARLY EXPERIENCE

The impressionable age

It is commonly believed that the child's first five or so years of
life constitute a 'critical' or 'sensitive' period, when they show a
heightened susceptibility to the effects of their environment and are
therefore vulnerable to adverse experiences and learning situations.
The young, as Chapter 1 showed, have always been said to be
more easily influenced, more impressionable, than their elders. In
addition, these early effects are thought to be lasting. In the writings
of Plato, the Bible and the Jesuits in the past, and, more recently, the
psychoanalysts, there is a belief that 'character' is so set by about the
age of six or seven, that whatever happens to a child thereafter is but
a ripple on the surface.

What precisely are the facts, as opposed to the speculations, about
the later effects of early experience and learning? The psychologist,
Alan Clarke, who (as we saw in Chapter 3) has reviewed the
available evidence concerning early experience and its effects, comes
to the conclusion that, at present, valid scientific knowledge is still
sadly lacking. Nevertheless, he has been able to identify certain
consistencies in the research findings. He suggests that there is little
reason to suppose that infants learn and remember more easily than
adults. In fact, experiments suggest that infants and young children
are strikingly inferior to adults in many dimensions of learning. The
long-term effects of short, traumatic incidents seem to be negligible

Temperament: Jekyll or Hyde?

Research has shown that very early in life babies can be classified according to their 'temperament' – inborn or constitutional attributes of personality. They include characteristics such as:

Activity level: which can range from very fidgety and active to relatively still and passive.

Quality of mood: this may range from predominantly positive, happy, contented to mainly negative, fretful, miserable.

Approach versus withdrawal tendencies: the child, when exposed to new features of the environment, reacts *positively* or *negatively* to particular types of stimulation or sensory stimulation (e.g. touch or taste) or to new people.

Rhythmicity: habits of eating, sleeping, bowel movements, etc. relatively predictable rather than erratic or unpredictable.

Adaptability: child settles down relatively easily versus resistance to change when exposed to new routines or situations.

Threshold of responsiveness: child is hypersensitive to sounds, touch, etc. versus relatively insensitive.

Intensity of reaction: some babies may cry loudly and intensely for example; others react more moderately to stimuli.

Distractability: some children attend to things for considerable periods of time; others flit from one thing to another.

Persistence: some babies are very 'single-minded' and stick to 'goals' with great persistence.

One group of babies (about 10 per cent of those studied by Stella Chess and her colleagues (1968)) was described as 'difficult' (and unkindly, in some instances, as 'mother killers'); another group was characterized as 'easy' to rear (about 40 per cent). Think through and/or call on your knowledge of babies and parental tasks to describe what *combination* of temperamental attributes *and* what behavioural implications are likely to feature in:

(a)   easy babies,
(b)   difficult babies.

ANSWERS on page 74.

both in animals and in young human beings, and the specific effects of an infant's experiences before the age of seven months appear to be of very short duration. Only when early learning is, by repetition, continually reinforced, do long-term effects appear, and these may well be more the result of the later reinforcement than of the original learning, as such.

This must be reassuring to parents who worry a great deal about 'mistakes' they have made in dealing with their child, or about severe emotional upsets the child has suffered. The important thing is to deal sensitively and sensibly with trauma in order to prevent negative experiences being repeated to a point at which their transitory ill-effects become chronic and ingrained.

Clarke's review of the evidence leads him to be sceptical about the rigidity of the structuring of character which is thought to occur during infancy. The unchanging nature or fixity of the child's psychological attributes at a very tender age seems to have been exaggerated. Early learning experiences do not appear to set the child an inevitable 'tramline' route for his or her later development.

STYLES OF CHILD REARING

Despite extensive research, there is much doubt as to how different styles of child rearing might influence the development of the child's personality. Thus, we do not really know whether the psychological development of children is affected by feeding methods (breastfeeding versus bottlefeeding, or set-interval feeding versus on-demand feeding) or by early or late weaning, and so on. The available evidence suggests negligible effects for these early events.

Notwithstanding variations in family pattern and style of parenting, all societies seem to be broadly successful in the task of transforming helpless, self-centred infants into more or less self-supporting, responsible members of their particular form of community. Indeed, there is a basic 'preparedness' on the part of most infants to be trained – that is, an inbuilt bias towards all things social (see Chapter 10).

Later parent–child relationships

So what about later relationships and interactions between parents? Given the intimate, protracted and highly influential nature of parents' relationships with their children, it seems obvious that the quality of such relationships, the power and reach of early experiences must have a vital bearing on the development of the child's personality and general adaptation. The scientific inquiry into these matters is based upon this belief; sadly the quest has produced relatively meagre results.

Leaving aside the complexity of this kind of long-term research (which is self-evident), there are still particular doubts about many of the studies of human parenting. This is due largely to flawed research designs, biases in sampling, and a tendency for social class and ethnocentric values to determine the questions asked and the assumptions made in various investigations. Despite the many methodological hurdles researchers have at least reached a consensus about a predictable dimensional structure underlying parental attitudes and behaviour: two major dimensions with in-dependent (orthogonal) axes ascribed as warm–hostile and control–autonomy.

The dimensions in *Exercise 4.4* on page 71 have been combined with lists describing the sort of behaviour and problems produced by different combinations of parental attitude.

Another useful source of information about child care and devel-opment is the research carried out on prosocial (socially acceptable) behaviour in children. The major factors which foster prosocial personality attributes are:

- parental affection and nurturance;
- parental control (setting limits);
- consistency in child care and training;
- the use of reasoning in disciplinary encounters (so-called inductive methods);
- modelling; and
- giving children, and especially adolescents, responsibility.

The balancing of these components is perhaps best illustrated in the philosophy of what the American developmental psychologist Diana Baumrind calls the 'authoritative' mother. This kind of parent attempts to direct her child's activities in a rational manner determined by the issues which are pertinent to particular disciplinary situations. She encourages verbal give-and-take and shares the reasoning behind her policy with the child. She values both the child's self-expression and his or her so-called *instrumental attributes* (respect for authority, work and the like); she appreciates both independent self-will and disciplined conformity. So the authoritative mother exerts firm control at points where she and the child diverge in viewpoint, but does not suppress him or her with restrictions. She recognizes her own special rights as an adult, but also the child's individual interests and special ways.

Parental Behaviour and Child Outcomes

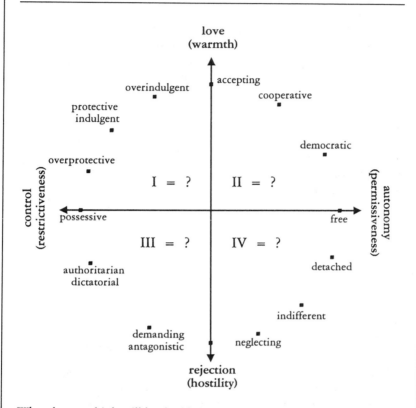

What do you think will be the likely outcomes for children's behaviour in the longer term when exposed to the following combinations of parental behaviour:

I   Warmth and restrictiveness (i.e. overindulgence, protective, overprotective) = ?

II Warmth and autonomy (i.e. accepting, cooperative, democratic) = ?

III Hostility and restrictiveness (i.e. possessive, authoritarian, demanding, dictatorial) = ?   .

IV Hostility and permissiveness (i.e. detached, indifferent, neglecting) = ?

ANSWERS on page 75.

Disruption of personality development

Substantial deviations from this 'ideal', as outlined by Diana Baumrind, are usually regarded as entailing risks to the child's healthy development. Examples of such deviations include at one 'extreme' authoritarian parenting (as opposed to authoritative parenting), and at the other, overly permissive or lax parenting. However, the most serious consequences for children result from punitive methods persistently used against a background of hostile and rejecting attitudes.

Where parenting breaks down altogether or is deficient in one way or another (see Chapter 11), society provides substitute care (adoption, foster care, residential care) or psychological help (child and family centres). Much of the help received by children in need is informal: the support provided by siblings, friends, kindly neighbours, teachers and voluntary community organizations. Fortunately, from the perspective of the survival of the species, most children are remarkably robust; the 'resilient' or 'stress-resistent' child is the subject of much contemporary research.

Recommended reading

Damon, W. (1983) *Social and Personality Development*. London: Norton. [A readable introduction.]

Hardyment, C. (1983) *Dream Babies: Child care from Locke and Spock*. London: Jonathan Cape. [Discusses the fads and fashions in child care.]

Herbert, M. (1989) *Discipline: A positive guide for parents*. Oxford: Basil Blackwell. [The positive why's and wherefore's of discipline.]

Howe, J.A.M. (1990) *Encouraging the Development of Exceptional Skills and Talents*. Leicester: BPS Books. [Challenges the assumption that we have no control over the growth of outstanding ability.]

Schaffer, H.R. (1990) *Making Decisions about Children: Psychological questions and answers*. Oxford: Basil Blackwell. [Invaluable guide to research required for decision making.]

Schaffer, H.R. & Collis, G.I.M. (1986) Parental responsiveness and child behaviour. In W. Sluckin and M. Herbert (Eds) *Parental Behaviour in Animals and Humans*. Oxford: Blackwell. [Discusses the important ingredients of parental behaviour.]

Yule, W. & Williams, R. (1990) Post traumatic stress reactions in children. *Journal of Traumatic Stress*, 3, 279–295. [Covers major and minor disasters and their effects.]

References

Baumrind, D. (1971) Current patterns of parental authority. *Developmental Psychology Monographs*, 4, (1), part 2, 1–103. [How parents differ in their nature and influence.]

Becker, W.C. (1964) Consequences of different kinds of parental discipline. In M.L. Hoffman and L.W. Hoffman (Eds) *Review of Child Development Research*. New York: Russell Sage Foundation. [Where does discipline lead?]

Belsky, J. & Nezworski, T. (1988) *Clinical Implications of Attachment*. Hillsdale, NJ: Erlbaum. [Attachment theory and its importance.]

Bornstein, M. & Sigman, M. (1986) Continuity in mental development. *Child Development*,

57, 251–274. [How stable is mental development?]

Bretherton, I. (1985) Attachment theory: Retrospect and prospect. In I. Bretherton and E. Waters (Eds) *Growing Points in Attachment Theory and Research*. Monographs for the Society for Research in Child Development, Vol. 50, No. 209. [The influence and nature of attachment theory.]

Brimm, O.F. & Kagan, J. (Eds) (1980) *Constancy and Change in Human Development*. Cambridge, Mass.: Harvard University Press. [What are the continuities and discontinuities of behaviour?]

Bruch, H. (1954) Parent education or the illusion of omnipotence. *American Journal of Orthopsychiatry*, 24, 723–5. [The 'burden' of parenthood.]

Clarke, A.D.B. (1968) Problems in assessing the later effects of early experience. In E. Miller (Ed.) *Foundations of Child Psychiatry*. Oxford: Pergamon Press. [The impressionable child.]

Erikson, E. (1965) *Childhood and Society*. Harmondsworth: Penguin. [Erikson's theory of development.]

Quinton, D. & Rutter, M. (1988) *Parental Breakdown: The making and breaking of intergenerational links*. Aldershot: Gower. [How one generation affects another.]

Rothbart, M.K. & Goldsmith, H.H. (1985) Three approaches to the study of infant temperament. *Developmental Review*, 5, 237–260. [Temperament: a vital aspect of personality – explained.]

Rutter, M.L. (1989) Pathways from childhood to adult life. *Journal of Child Psychology and Psychiatry*, 30, 23–52. [Cause and effect from childhood to adulthood.]

Seligman, M.E.P. (1975) *Helplessness: On depression, development and death*. San Francisco: Freeman. [Learned helplessness and its relationship to depression.]

Staub, E. (1975) *The Development of Prosocial Behavior in Children*. Morrison, NJ: General Learning Press. [How to enhance positive social behaviour.]

Thomas, A., Chess, S. & Birch, H.G. (1968) *Temperament and Behaviour Disorders in Children*. London: London University Press. [Discusses the work of Stella Chess and her colleagues on 'difficult' children.]

Watson, J.B. & Watson, R.R. (1928) *Psychological Care of the Infant and Child*. New York: Norton. [An early behaviourist view of childhood.]

————————————ANSWERS TO EXERCISE 4.1————————————

MAJOR HAZARDS TO ACHIEVEMENT

Birth to 1 year
Neglect, abuse, or deprivation of consistent and appropriate love in infancy; harsh or early weaning.

1–4 years
Conditions which interfere with the child's achieving a feeling of adequacy or the learning of skills such as talking.

4–5 years
Overly strict discipline, internalization of rigid ethical attitudes which interfere with the child's spontaneity and reality testing.

6–11 years
Excessive competition, personal limitations, or other conditions which lead to experiences of failure, resulting in feelings of inferiority and poor work habits.

12–15 years
Failure of society to provide clearly defined roles and standards; formation of cliques which provide clear but not always desirable roles and standards.

15 to adulthood
Cultural and personal factors which lead to psychological isolation or to formal rather than warm personal relations.

————————————ANSWERS TO EXERCISE 4.2————————————

By careful experiments, the truth or falsity of the statements has been ascertained – all of them are false. Yet 'common sense' might suggest the opposite.

————————————ANSWERS TO EXERCISE 4.3————————————

Easy children usually seem to be in a good mood, have regular sleep and bowel movements, adapt readily to new surroundings, and are not timid in new situations. They tend to be cheerful and are easy to care for and love. Not surprisingly, such a 'rewarding' infant makes parents feel effective and good. It is possible to really enjoy parenting.

Difficult children do not readily establish regular feeding or sleep patterns, react intensely to parental insistence and frustration, and withdraw passively from strange people or events. They require a long time to adjust to a novel situation or routine and hence are not very rewarding to rear. They can make a parent feel ineffectual and unskilled; indeed the often prolonged struggles and confrontations can lead to tension and resentment.

It is important to note that although these infants are at risk of going on to develop psychological problems, parents *can* (by sensitive, sensible but firm management) bring such youngsters up to be perfectly well-adjusted or normal.

———————————ANSWERS TO EXERCISE 4.4———————————

The following attributes have been found to be consequences of the parental attitudes:

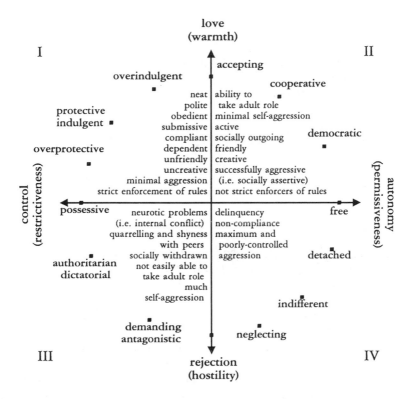

5. *Playing and Learning*

∇ *The development of children's play*
∇ *The purpose of play*
∇ *What do children learn through play?*
∇ *Learning social roles*
∇ *Learning at home, learning at school*
∇ *Children and television*

A three year old sings the words 'lee-la, lee-la' over and over again to herself, varying the pitch and timing; a group of nursery school children are engrossed in an elaborate make-believe game, dressed as doctors and nurses; two seven-year-old boys roll over one another in the school playground, laughing and tussling; an out-of-practice father takes his sons to the park to play cricket, trying to relive past glories on the field.

All of these would be widely accepted as examples of playful behaviour, and some are more organized than others. But what about a factory worker, who after a hard day at work, relaxes by attending an evening class on psychology? Or even the tutor of that class, who after teaching undergraduate students all week and adult education classes at night, relaxes by digging the garden? Which is play, or leisure, and which is work? The dividing line is by no means clear. Although the Victorians saw play very clearly as the *opposite* of work, our examples show that a given activity could function as either work *or* leisure, according to the circumstances in which it takes place.

Even if we stick to the examples of children's play in the opening paragraph, is it possible to come up with a precise definition? Is play behaviour spontaneous, or an end in itself? Is it behaviour which gives pleasure to the player? Does it lack structure and organization, and is it free from the demands of everyday life? All of these questions describe certain types of play, but we can think of exceptions to each possible definition. Some play *is* organized; some play *does* have a clear aim; some play *does* meet the demands of everyday life; and so on. The problem of definition stems from the fact that 'play' is a kind of umbrella term which embraces a wide range of different kinds of activity.

Explore first, play later

Corinne Hutt carried out a well-known study in 1966 which demonstrated the difference between *exploration* and play. She invited 30 three to five year olds to eight consecutive ten-minute play sessions, at roughly two-day intervals. In the first two 'familiarization' sessions the children played with five familiar toys: but in the next six 'experimental' sessions a 'supertoy' was introduced alongside the familiar toys. This was a red metal box on four brass legs with a lever on top, quite unlike anything they had seen before. Pulling the lever in different directions could result in the lever movements being recorded on four counters on the top of the 'supertoy'; it could also make a buzzer sound, and a bell ring (see *Figure 5.1*).

Hutt recorded the children's reactions to the supertoy over the

Children eagerly investigate the properties of things when they explore . . .

. . . and take off into the realm of the imagined when they start to play with what they have explored.

FIGURE 5.1: *Corinne Hutt's 'supertoy' experiment*

course of the six experimental sessions, varying the functions of the lever: in some sessions the bell and the buzzer were switched off and the counters were covered up, and in others some or all of them were working. Whilst a casual observer might loosely describe everything that the children did with the object as 'playing' with it, Hutt identified a distinctive pattern of reaction over the six sessions. In the early sessions, children *explored* the unfamiliar object: their behaviour was serious and focused, reflecting the implicit question 'What does this object do?'

In the later sessions this gave way to what Hutt identifies as true *play* behaviour. This was more varied and relaxed: some children sat on the supertoy, pretending it was a car, some used the lever as a microphone to sing into, and so on. Here the implicit question was 'What can *I* do with this object?' Hutt showed that the amount of exploration decreased over the six sessions, and that the amount of play correspondingly increased. She also found that the more complex the supertoy, in terms of the operation of the bell, buzzer and counters, the more exploration took place.

This is a good example of how psychologists can study the elusive phenomenon of play 'in the laboratory', that is, under fairly carefully controlled conditions. The complementary approach is to observe play in its natural setting – in the playground, or in the nursery school – and there are also studies which combine aspects of both of these two approaches. Using these methods, a picture has been built up of the distinctive character of children's play, and of how it changes with age.

THE DEVELOPMENT OF CHILDREN'S PLAY

Practice play. Jean Piaget, whose well-known theory of child development is described in Chapter 7, proposed that children's play progresses through three stages as they get older. The first of these is *practice play*: this largely occurs in the first two years of life, and involves the simple repetition of different actions for what Piaget calls 'functional pleasure'. Some practice play *does* take place after the first two years, for example, the vigorous mock fighting, chasing and wrestling which is termed *rough and tumble play*, and which usually occurs between friends. However, rough and tumble play cannot be categorized as practice play if it involves any symbols or rules, such as in the chasing game of tig.

Symbolic play. The use of different *symbols* is the major achievement of the preschool period (see Chapter 7), and one of the main expressions of this is in *symbolic play*: the world of pretence, make-believe and fantasy. Piaget pointed out that early pretend play often involves the identification of one object with another. He describes how his two-year-old daughter Jacqueline pretended that a pebble was a dog; that a biscuit was a lion; that a brush, held over her head, was an umbrella, and so on. A little later than this, by the age of about three years, children start to use parts of their own body to identify with other people or things. Piaget describes how:

at 2;7(4) [two years, seven months and four days old] having seen a little boy who said "I'm going home", she [Jacqueline] went in the same direction, said "I'm going home", and imitated his gait. The same day she was a lady whom we know. At 2;7(23) she was a cousin of her own age (several times during the day but without imitating either his way of talking or his gait). At 2;8(5) she crawled into my room on all fours, saying "miaow".

As the preschool period progresses, children construct increasingly elaborate sequences of *sociodramatic* play. These can be completely imaginary, not bound to the objects or people available, and they can involve several different players. They are frequently based on imitations of adult activities, such as teachers and pupils or doctors and patients, who carry out 'scripted' episodes such as going shopping, or having a meal. *Language* play is another prominent feature of preschool play: Peter and Iona Opie have compiled a

comprehensive and charming collection of the use of rhyme, nonsense, wit and repartee, 'tangle talk' and much more besides (see *Table 5.1*).

TABLE 5.1: *'Tangletalk'*

Two features which are apparent in Peter and Iona Opie's collection of the playground language of some 5,000 primary and secondary children in the British Isles are their historical continuity, and the wide range of regional variation on the same theme. What they call 'tangletalk' is a traditional form of language play which involves the deliberate juxtaposition of incongruities. According to the Opies, 'The best known of these travesties is also probably the oldest:

> *One fine day in the middle of the night,*
> *Two dead men got up to fight,*
> *Back to back they faced each other,*
> *Drew their swords and shot each other.*
> *A paralysed donkey passing by*
> *Kicked a blind man in the eye,*
> *Knocked him through a nine inch wall*
> *Into a dry ditch and drowned them all.*

. . . In William IV's time the verse children knew, according to an edition of *Ditties for the Nursery* printed about 1830, was:

> *Two dead horses ran a race,*
> *Two blind to see all fair,*
> *Two dead horses ran so fast,*
> *The blind began to stare.*

And nearly five centuries ago, about 1480, a professional minstrel noted down in his pocket book . . . the crude rhyme:

> *I saw iij hedles playen at a ball,*
> *an hanlas man served hem all,*
> *Whyll iij movthles men lay & low,*
> *iij legles a-way hem drow.'*

[From Opie and Opie, 1959.]

Games with rules. The increasing organization of make-believe play culminates in what Piaget called *games with rules*, at the age of around six or seven years. These might be games like football or netball, in which the rules are public: or they may be made-up games with rules which are spontaneously created. Piaget's celebrated study of the game of marbles showed that children between the ages of approximately five and ten saw rules as being determined by a higher authority than the players themselves, and as therefore being unchangeable: above this age they could understand that rules were created for the benefit of all, so that they could be changed by mutual agreement.

Do girls and boys play differently?

There is a good deal of research evidence which shows that girls and boys choose different toys, and play different games. At the preschool level, boys tend to prefer activities which require large-scale physical effort such as throwing and kicking balls, riding on trucks and cars, and rough and tumbling; girls prefer activities such as dressing up or doll play. Similar differences persist in school-age children: generally speaking, boys are more likely to be interested in outdoor play and in 'mechanical' or 'scientific' activities such as machines, construction sets or computers, whereas girls are more likely to prefer indoor, sedentary activities such as domestic play. It has been suggested that boys are more oriented towards *objects* and girls towards *people*.

Of course, there is a great deal of overlap. There are many activities which do not show any bias towards one sex or the other, such as drawing, painting, reading, or playing musical instruments. But the general trend is nevertheless apparent, and it is reinforced by the powerful stereotypes which are present in books, magazines, on television and radio, and even by the way in which toy shops are typically laid out. School-age children are increasingly likely to choose same-sex partners for play as they get older: observations of school playgrounds show quite distinct segregation between the sexes by the age of seven years or so.

Are boys more sporting and competitive than girls?

The play of boys and girls leads directly on to the important question of sex differences in sport. There is plenty of evidence that males participate in sport more than females at all ages, and it also seems that males *value* sport more highly than females. This is probably because certain important aspects of sports behaviour, particularly the desire to compete and to win at all costs, are incompatible with the feminine gender role. Whereas competitiveness, independence and self-assertion are encouraged in the upbringing of boys, these qualities are typically discouraged in many girls, and so they experience 'role conflict' in sports. One idea is that many women may display 'fear of success' in competitive situations, and maybe also in other areas of life: in sports, they may lack the 'killer instinct' that is characteristic of the champion.

George Sage and Sheryl Loudermilk gave a questionnaire to 268 female college athletes which investigated their perceptions of this

---

Sex-Stereotyping of Sports

Below is a list of 20 sporting and physical activities. Which ones do you consider to be more appropriate for females, and which for males? Ask a boy and a girl under the age of 11, and a male and female adult to complete the same task, and record their answers. How do these differ from your own, and from each other?

(1)	boxing	(11)	polo
(2)	weightlifting	(12)	showjumping
(3)	swimming	(13)	wrestling
(4)	netball	(14)	popmobility
(5)	cricket	(15)	gymnastics
(6)	running	(16)	potholing
(7)	lacrosse	(17)	rugby
(8)	rounders	(18)	yachting
(9)	soccer	(19)	yoga
(10)	baseball	(20)	mountaineering

Now turn to page 92 to compare your results with those of a recent study of sex-stereotyping in sports.

'role conflict'. About one quarter of them felt that it affected them greatly, but that this varied between different sports. Women in tennis, swimming and gymnastics experienced lower levels of conflict than those in softball, basketball and hockey. Along similar lines, Eleanor Metheny suggested that 'acceptable' sports for female participation are those which are aesthetically pleasing to watch, which are relatively low on body contact and physical strength, but which may nevertheless be competitive (tennis, fencing, golf, gymnastics and skiing). 'Unacceptable' sports, on the other hand, include wrestling, boxing, rugby, and other team sports. *Exercise 5.1* contains a list of 20 sports, and readers are invited to rate them as appropriate to males and females.

Another interesting idea is that people may have different goals, or motives, when they take part in sports. John Nicholls suggests that some people are *ego-involved*, focusing mainly on their own performance in competition with others ('success was when I won the game'), whereas others are more *task-involved*, focusing on the improvements within their own performances ('success was when I beat my personal best time'). Not surprisingly, the research so far suggests that males are more likely to be ego-involved in sports than females. In children, levels of ego-involvement may increase with age.

THE PURPOSE OF PLAY

Over the last century, many different theories have been put forward to explain the purpose of play. Herbert Spencer, for example, proposed in 1878 what has become known as the 'surplus energy' theory of play. His view was that animals lower down the evolutionary scale need to spend much more of their time on survival activities such as hunting and gathering than do those which are more highly evolved: humans and other 'higher' animals therefore have spare capacity, or 'surplus energy', which is expended in play. Almost the exact opposite of this view was advanced by George Patrick, who proposed in 1916 that play arises from a *deficit* of energy. In this view, play serves to replenish energy which has been expended in children's lives as they perform new or unfamiliar tasks: it 'recharges the batteries'.

Karl Groos published two books, *The Play of Animals* (1898) and *The Play of Man* (1901), in which he put forward what has become known as the 'pre-exercise' theory of play. He saw play as a kind of rehearsal for the skills which are required for survival in later life. Far from being merely the 'opposite' of work, play is seen to have a very distinct function in development. This basic idea has many contemporary supporters. The importance of play in children's development is a cornerstone of the educational philosophies of Friedrich Froebel, Maria Montessori and Susan Isaacs, for example, and this view has had a powerful impact on early childhood education.

Freud's view of play

Sigmund Freud saw play as a means by which children could *compensate* for the anxieties and frustrations that they encounter in everyday life. Their 'desire for mastery' for example, whereby they want to emulate their parents by going to bed late, being able to buy things, and generally being free from normal childhood restrictions, can be 'acted out' through play in a safe, stress-free environment. The idea of play as cathartic, as a vehicle for the release of tension, is the basis of play therapy. Children are encouraged to express their hidden impulses, which may be aggressive or sexual, in a harmless, therapeutic context. In an everyday sense too we may see children's worries and anxieties represented in their play. Anxiety about going to the doctor or taking medicine may be released in play with teddy who has to visit the doctor or be dosed with some imaginary mixture.

Piaget's account of play

Whilst Freud emphasized the *emotional* content of play, Piaget's account of play is clearly set within his general theory of the development of *thinking*. Piaget saw playful behaviour as that which shows a bias towards assimilation in the balance between assimilation and accommodation (see glossary and Chapter 7). When children *assimilate* new objects and experiences to their existing schemes of thought, they are effectively 'in control' of their immediate world. Reality is moulded to fit the child's own thinking, and that, for Piaget, is the essence of play. *Imitation*, on the other hand, occurs when the world is 'in control' of the child's thinking, when accommodation predominates over assimilation.

This account of play has not been without its critics. Brian Sutton-Smith, for example, has argued that Piaget's theory cannot explain the creative character of play: that it is only able to deal with behavioural 'copies' of the real world, and not with the invention of new actions. He also argued that although the theory is supposed to deal with developments in thinking, some of its details are in fact more concerned with emotional adjustments in play, just as in Freudian theory.

Almost certainly, play serves cognitive, social *and* emotional functions: differences amongst the theories arise because so many different kinds of behaviour are included. The contemporary world of preschool education has clearly got the message that 'children learn through play', but is it possible to be any more precise about exactly what it is that they learn from different kinds of play? Some experimental work has been carried out which has tried to unravel some of these strands.

WHAT DO CHILDREN LEARN THROUGH PLAY?

One approach to this question has been to give matched groups of children different play and non-play experiences, and to compare their performances on measures of cognitive or social ability before and after these experiences.

Play studies

In one study by Jeffrey Dansky and Irwin Silverman, for example, four-to-six-year-old children were divided into three groups. The 'play' group were allowed to play freely for ten minutes with a number of common objects: some paper towels and some wet plastic cups; a screwdriver with some screws mounted on a board; some paperclips and blank cards, and some matchboxes. Children in the 'imitation' group imitated an adult doing conventional things with these objects, for example, fastening cards together with the paperclip; those in the 'control' group simply coloured in some sketches with a box of crayons. When the children were later given the *Uses for Objects* test, a measure of creativity which involved thinking of numerous different uses for the same objects, the 'play' group came up with many more non-standard answers than either of the other two groups, whose performance was fairly similar.

This result seems to show that free play can promote creative thinking ability, at least as measured by the *Uses for Objects* test, and the same suggestion has been made by other researchers. Another study by Kathy Sylva, Jerome Bruner and Paul Genova showed that free play experience improved three to five year olds' problem-solving ability, measured by a task in which sticks were clamped together to produce an elongated tool which could then be used to open a box containing a prize. But if free play promotes creative thinking and problem solving, which are normally seen as quite distinct and independent abilities, are we in danger of accepting it uncritically as a kind of universal source of cognitive development?

Peter Smith has argued that this may indeed be the case. He carried out a thorough review of the research literature on play with Tony Simon, and concluded that some of the experiments may be methodologically unsound. In a number of them, the same experimenter administered the different experimental conditions and then carried out the supposedly independent tests of ability, so that the results may be biased. In others, the play and non-play conditions also differed in *other* important respects, such as the amount of contact with the experimenter, so that it is impossible to know whether it was the play experience *as such* that gave rise to the improvements in independent measures of ability.

Smith and Simon's review led them to conclude that there is little evidence that 'play' conditions are superior to other experimental conditions once these other factors are taken into account, but it may well be that the time span of these studies is far too short to expect any significant or long-lasting effects in any case. Certain play experiences undoubtedly give rise to certain types of learning, but we must be careful not to overgeneralize. Smith concludes that 'play is only one way to learn'.

LEARNING SOCIAL ROLES

The *social* function of play is clear in Piaget's description of 'games with rules' – the understanding that the public rules of the game extend beyond the interests of any single player is an important development in moral thinking. In his classic book *Mind, Self and Society* (1934) George Herbert Mead put forward a theory of how people develop their views of themselves, or *self-concepts*, as they grow up in society. One of his proposals was that play and games serve to develop that part of our self-concept which takes into account other people's views of us: he called this the 'generalized other'. As we grow older, we gain an increasingly complex picture of ourselves in relation to others.

Mead's book is an important landmark in *role theory*, which forms part of sociology as well as psychology. According to this, children's personalities develop by their imitating, or 'taking the roles of' a variety of *models*. In young children, it is easy to see that the first models come from their immediate family: by imitating the characteristics of father and mother, for example, boys and girls learn what constitutes typical 'masculine' and 'feminine' behaviour. As they get older, a wider range of people act as models: siblings, playmates, grandparents, neighbours, teachers at school, and many more.

Media influences

These are all models drawn from the immediate circle of personal acquaintances, but many influential models who are *not* known personally are drawn from the mass media. Girls and boys alike are served by a huge industry of comics, books, newspapers, fan magazines, films, videos, television and radio programmes which create heroes and idols out of pop stars, footballers and others. The all-pervasive influence of the mass media is apparent at a very early age, and this has stimulated a good deal of psychological research.

One of the main areas of investigation has been on sex-role stereotyping, especially in television advertisements and programmes. Surveys show that the stars of popular TV shows are much more likely to be male than female, and that this may be even more true of children's programmes than of adult ones. Recent television offerings include *Knight Rider*, *Dr Who*, *Star Trek*, *Happy Days*, and *Dastardly and Muttley*. Females are typically portrayed as weak, passive partners of powerful effective men, and the *range* of roles which they play is much less varied – they are usually typecast as lovers or mothers.

Adult roles

In adults, the process of *role taking* becomes very complex: each person can think of him or herself as being at the centre of an elaborate web of interlinking roles. For instance, a woman might perceive herself as mother, wife, employee, neighbour, motorist, trade union member, churchgoer, and so on at different times of the day: in any given situation a set of appropriate roles is 'called up'. These roles are *normative* (i.e. typical) descriptions of the behaviour expected of people in different social positions: and they can be 'taken on' on three different levels.

The most superficial of these is *role enactment*. A man who carries out a job he dislikes purely for the pay, or a stage actor in an unsympathetic part, is merely 'going through the motions': they have no personal investment in that behaviour. In contrast to this is the commitment to a certain role which is so strong that it becomes an essential part of the person's personality: a nurse, for example, may well act well 'beyond the call of duty' in displaying caring behaviour when he is not at work. In this case we would say that he has *internalized*, or *identified with* the behaviour and attitudes associated with that role and he acts them out unconsciously.

In between these two is *role taking*. At this level, certain parts of the role are internalized and others are not. A schoolteacher, for example, may have completely internalized the educational ideals concerning the welfare of pupils: faced with discipline problems, however, they may be forced to resort to punishments of which they do not approve. A good deal of our everyday behaviour probably operates on this level: we act out some parts of the prescribed role, but not others. We may also experience *role conflict* in some situations, as in the case of female athletes which was described earlier.

Children can learn by observing other people

One distinctive explanation of the processes of imitation and identification is that of *social learning theory*. The central idea behind this is that children learn by being *reinforced* for displaying different kinds of behaviour. For example, parents might 'reward' masculine behaviour in boys by encouraging them to play with transport toys, or in 'play fighting' with them, and they might correspondingly 'punish' feminine behaviour by expressing disapproval, for example, of doll play. ('Action Man', essentially a doll for boys, is an interesting intermediate case!) There is a good deal of research which confirms that parents do indeed behave in this way.

Social learning theory proposes that children can learn by *observing* the behaviour of models as well as by direct reinforcement. A well-known demonstration of this was carried out by Albert Bandura and his colleagues in 1961. Seventy-two nursery school children watched two adult models: one played quietly with a set of toys, ignoring a large inflated 'bobo doll' which was in the same room as the toys; the other reacted violently towards the doll, throwing it in the air, hitting it with a mallet, and shouting 'kick him' and 'hit it in the nose'. When the children were allowed to play with the doll later, those who had observed the violent model imitated the aggressive behaviour. Not only did they do the same violent things as the model, but they also invented new types of aggression towards the doll, such as pretending to shoot it with a toy gun that was also in the room (see *Figure 5.2*).

Interestingly, the boys in this experiment were more likely to imitate *physical* violence than the girls, although there was no sex difference for *verbal* aggression. In subsequent experiments, Bandura found that boys were more likely to imitate male models and girls to imitate female models even when the opposite-sex model was made 'more powerful', in reinforcement terms, by

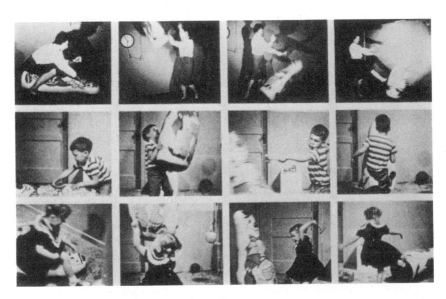

FIGURE 5.2: *Learning aggression by observation*

by dispensing rewards. In other words, children do not simply imitate and identify with those models which provide the most reinforcement: the process is also influenced by cultural stereotypes. We must take account of the cultural, or social setting in which learning takes place: and the most important of these settings are the home and the school.

LEARNING AT HOME, LEARNING AT SCHOOL

Recent studies of children's conversations show quite clearly that they 'present themselves' very differently at home and at school. A six year old may appear tongue-tied and monosyllabic when asked questions about number work by the teacher, for example. If the topic of discussion is pocket money, however, and if the setting of the conversation is the kitchen at home rather than the classroom, the same child may display a sophisticated grasp of arithmetical reasoning. We must be very careful to distinguish between whether children *cannot* use language appropriately in certain situations, or whether they simply *do* not. The absence of successful performance does not necessarily imply a lack of competence.

One of the best-known sources of evidence for this point of view comes from a study by Barbara Tizard and Martin Hughes, in which they tape-recorded four year olds in conversation with their mothers at home, and with their teachers at school. At home, children talked freely about a wide range of topics; they were likely to initiate activities, to hold sustained conversations about them, and to ask spontaneous questions. This richness and variety of language was much less likely to occur in classroom talk with the teacher. David Wood has suggested that *natural* learning takes place in the home: this is spontaneous, it is embedded in real-life activities, and in particular, the child is actively in control. In *contrived* learning in the classroom, on the other hand, this control is firmly in the hands of the teacher.

Classroom observation studies in the UK show that teaching in the modern primary classroom is still very didactic, with a strong emphasis on giving information and routine instructions. The picture of the classroom which emerges from this research is one in which bargaining takes place between teacher and pupil, such that each can negotiate conditions which satisfy their respective needs. The teacher wants co-operation, attention, discipline and good work from the pupils, who in turn seek some degree of success, or at least the avoidance of failure on the task which is set. The course of learning is shaped by these explicit and implicit 'ground rules'.

CHILDREN AND TELEVISION

Apart from the home and the school, the other major influence on children's learning in the real world is the mass media. Children learn from books, newspapers, magazines, and from the radio; and perhaps the single most powerful influence is that of television. Television is now present in most homes in Western society, and recent surveys suggest that most children typically spend between two and four hours viewing per day. With the rapid developments which have occurred in personal computing and video technology in recent years, many children are part of a TV culture which includes video and computer games as well as TV programmes.

Opinions differ as to whether the powerful influence of TV is a good or a bad one. We mentioned earlier that television programmes and advertisements are an important source of stereotypes, particularly in the area of sex roles, and their reinforcement is clearly detrimental to the case for equality between the sexes. Let us consider two further areas of debate: the use of TV in education, and children's learning of aggression.

Does TV encourage learning?

Television (and computers) are a common feature of most of today's school classrooms, and broadcasting organizations like the BBC have pioneered TV as a medium for learning. The BBC programme *Playschool*, and its successors, explicitly encourage their preschool viewers to participate actively in learning, rather than watching passively: the presenter may ask questions directly of the viewer, and may suggest ideas for different activities and games.

Perhaps the best known and most explicit attempt to use TV as an educational medium was in the programme *Sesame Street*, in North America. This programme uses puppets, animation and sound effects to attract the attention of its viewers. It follows the principle that new information is best learnt when it is explicitly related to something that the child already knows, and it also employs repetition as a means of encouraging active learning by the viewers. The programme has been found to be successful in teaching specific knowledge, such as of the alphabet, and of numbers, as well as in conveying TV literacy skills, such as the comprehension of the meaning of a close-up. There is also some evidence that disadvantaged preschoolers may learn more effectively from *Sesame Street*, which takes place in a familiar and comfortable medium, than from other forms of schooling from which they may feel alienated.

Does TV encourage violence?

Clearly TV can be beneficial, but the opposite side of the coin may be in the learning of violence. Debate has raged for some time about whether viewing violent TV programmes encourages violent behaviour in young, impressionable viewers. If Bandura's 'Bobo doll' experiment is anything to go by, we would predict that children would indeed learn aggressive behaviour from violent TV models by the process of observational learning, and public concern is frequently expressed about the number of violent episodes which are shown on television. Some programmes which are specifically made for children feature a good deal of violence (for example *The A Team*, *Knight Rider*), and many children watch adult adventure programmes or films in which violence is a prominent feature (*James Bond*, *Miami Vice*, *Indiana Jones*).

If anything, research on this emotional issue suggests that TV violence is more likely to encourage aggressive behaviour than inhibit it: but the evidence for this tentative conclusion is by no means clear. The effects depend upon the way in which violence is portrayed – as realism, fantasy, or entertainment. For example, few would argue that the extreme violence portrayed in the ever-popular children's cartoon *Tom and Jerry* is likely to be harmful. The effects have also been found to vary according to the context of viewing (alone, with peers, or with parents), and on the previous levels of aggression of the viewer. Whilst television may serve to provide aggressive models, factors like parental discord at home are probably much more likely to provoke violent crime than fictitious violence.

Such questions will increase in importance as technology advances. As communications become ever more sophisticated, as our 'global village' becomes effectively smaller, and as the amount of information in our everyday lives increases, television and the media will assume an increasingly important part in play, leisure and learning.

Recommended reading

Greenfield, P.M. (1984) *Mind and Media*. London: Fontana. [Children's use of computers, TV, and video games.]

Hargreaves, D.J. & Colley, A.M. (1986) (Eds) *The Psychology of Sex Roles*. Milton Keynes: Open University Press. [A comprehensive review of the psychological literature on childhood, adolescence and adulthood.]

Smith, P.K. (1984) (Ed.) *Play in Animals and Humans*. Oxford: Basil Blackwell. [Advanced collection of papers on animal play, children's play, and games.]

References

Bandura, A., Ross, D. & Ross. A. (1961) Transmission of aggression through imitation of aggressive models. *Journal of Abnormal and Social Psychology*, 63, 575–582. [The classic 'Bobo doll' study.]

Colley, A., Nash, J., O'Donnell, L. & Restorick, L. (1987) Attitudes to the female sex role and sex-typing of physical activities. *International Journal of Sports Psychology*, 18, 19–29. [See Exercise 5.1.]

Dansky, J.L. & Silverman, I.W. (1973) Effects of play on associative fluency in pre-school children. *Developmental Psychology*, 9, 38–43. [Free play promotes creative thinking.]

Groos, K. (1898) *The Play of Animals*. New York: Appleton. [An early theory of play.]

Groos, K. (1901) *The Play of Man*. London: Heinemann. [See above.]

Hutt, C. (1966) Exploration and play in children. *Symposium of the Zoological Society of London*, 18, 61–87. [The 'supertoy' study.]

Mead, G.H. (1934) *Mind, Self, and Society*. Chicago: University of Chicago Press. [Mead's theory of the development of the self.]

Metheny, E. (1965) *Connotations of Movement in Sport and Dance*. Dubuque: William C. Brown. [Sex-stereotyping of sports activities.]

Nicholls, J. (1984) Achievement motivation: Conceptions of ability, subjective exerience, task choice, and performance. *Psychological Review*, 91, 328–346. [Differing motivations for sports participation.]

Opie, I. & Opie, P. (1959) *The Lore and Language of Schoolchildren*. Oxford: Clarendon Press. [A rich and fascinating collection of material from all over the British Isles.]

Patrick, G.T.W. (1916) *The Psychology of Relaxation*. Boston: Houghton Mifflin. [An early theory of play.]

Piaget, J. (1951) *Play, Dreams and Imitation in Childhood*. London: Routledge & Kegan Paul. [Piaget's theory of play.]

Sage, G.H. & Loudermilk, S. (1979) The female athlete and role conflict. *Research Quarterly*, 50, 88–96. [Questionnaire study of role conflict.]

Simon, T. & Smith, P.K. (1985) Play and problem solving: A paradigm questioned. *Merrill-Palmer Quarterly*, 31, 265–277. [Some research on the effects of play may be methodologically unsound.]

Spencer, H. (1878) *The Principles of Psychology*. New York: Appleton. [The 'surplus energy' theory of play.]

Sutton-Smith, B. (1966) Piaget on play: A critique. *Psychological Review*, 73, 104–110. [See also Piaget's reply, and Sutton-Smith's rejoinder, in the same issue.]

Sylva, K., Bruner, J.S. & Genova, P. (1976) The role of play in the problem-solving of children 3–5 years old. In J.S. Bruner, A. Jolly & K. Sylva (Eds) *Play*. Harmondsworth: Penguin. [The effects of free play on a stick-clamping puzzle.]

Tizard, B. & Hughes, M. (1984) *Young Children Learning*. London: Fontana. ['Natural' and 'contrived' learning at home and at school.]

Wood, D. (1988) *How Children Think and Learn*. Oxford: Basil Blackwell. [Wide-ranging survey of current issues in developmental psychology and education.]

──────────── SCORING FOR EXERCISES 5.1 ────────────

As a comparison you may like to know that items 1, 2, 5, 9, 10, 11, 13, 16, 17 and 20 were described as 'suitable for males only' and items 4, 7, 8, 14 and 19 as 'suitable for females only' by at least 22 per cent and 15 per cent respectively of a sample of 168 male and 123 female 16–18 year olds from a sixth-form college in Leicester (Colley *et al.*, 1987). Items 3, 6, 12, 15 and 18 are included as neutral 'filler' items.

6. *Developing Language*

Perhaps our most remarkable achievement as children is our development and mastery of language. Although most of the time we use language easily and automatically, human language is a very complex system of communication.

CHARACTERISTICS OF LANGUAGE

People can, and do, communicate by using gestures, postures and facial expression, and when we talk to each other some meaning is conveyed by the pace, tone, pitch and volume of our speech. But we communicate with each other principally by using words and sentences which convey meaning, and our use of words and sentences is highly creative even in the most ordinary conversations. Language is organized at two levels: the level of sounds, which are meaningless in themselves, and the level of meaning – words, parts of words and combinations of words. There are reckoned to be about 50 or fewer separate speech sounds, but we can combine speech sounds to form large numbers of words, and combine words to form even larger numbers of sentences, including sentences which we have never heard before. This characteristic of language is called *productivity*, or *creativity*, and it means that there is no limit to the number of possible sentences in any language. More complicated still, although some words in our language – like 'crash' or 'gurgle' – sound rather like their meanings, the vast majority of them are arbitrary. The word 'dog', for example, doesn't sound or look more like a dog than it sounds like a cat, or a canary, or an easy chair; and 'cat' or 'cot' are very similar words in structure, but quite different in meaning. If I produced a sound halfway between 'cat' or 'cot', you would understand it as meaning either cat, cot, or perhaps 'cut'; you would not give it a meaning which is somehow halfway between a cat and a cot. The very specific meanings of different speech sounds and combinations are referred to as *discreteness*.

Is there an innate potential for language?

These and other characteristics of language make it so sophisticated that it seems quite a puzzle that any but the most intelligent of us manage to master the system. Yet virtually all humans acquire language, and young children normally use it fluently and creatively from a very early age. Some psychologists and linguists (for example, Noam Chomsky and Eric Lenneberg) have argued that this presents too great a task to be learned 'from scratch', and that since all humans readily acquire language there must be some innate potential, or *language acquisition device* (LAD), which predisposes infants to extract linguistic information and form grammatical hypotheses from the language to which they are exposed. They also argued that the LAD is species-specific – that is, exclusive to humans, since while all humans acquire language, often in spite of imperfect exposure to it, no non-human appears capable of acquiring it.

In many respects human language does seem to be unique and species-specific. Charles Hockett identified a number of language features which, he argued, non-verbal communications systems in other animals do not share, though further evidence shows that some of them do have 'human' features such as discreteness, the use of symbols and the ability to communicate about things remote in time and space. Attempts to teach animals (for example, chimpanzees) human language or something like it have had only very limited success. The use of signs to communicate can be sophisticated and creative, but any evidence that animals can combine symbols into grammatical 'sentences' is very doubtful. It seems that this crucial aspect of language, at least, may well be a quality not found in communication systems of other animals.

THE COURSE OF LANGUAGE DEVELOPMENT

In describing how children learn their first language, three points must be made at the outset. First, it is abundantly clear that language, virtually from its beginning, is lawfully patterned. Children don't just learn words and sentences; they learn rules, and the job of the psychologist is essentially to discover the rules which most economically and adequately describe their language behaviour without either underestimating or overestimating their capacity.

The second important point is that at all stages of language development, understanding exceeds, and precedes, production. Children can understand certain words and respond appropriately to them before they use them spontaneously in speech; this is true also for grammatical features of many kinds, and it is also true for phonological development (the development of speech sounds). Children can appreciate phonological distinctions before putting those distinctions into practice: for example, they may say 'tum' instead of 'come' and may also use 'tum' as a short form of 'tummy', but 'tum' and 'come' will be differently responded to in adult speech. There are in fact exceptions to this general rule, in which production exceeds performance, particularly in the use of words and phrases taken from songs and nursery rhymes. These cases, though, are overwhelmingly outnumbered by evidence in the opposite direction. Studies of the spontaneous speech of young children are often in danger of underestimating their capacity, though occasionally of overestimating it; they need to be supplemented by other evidence such as imitation, speech in answer to questions and 'prompts'.

Third, it should be stressed that language development does not happen in a vacuum; it depends on, and largely parallels, cognitive and social development. For example, certain cognitive structures, notably *representation* and *object permanence*, are generally held to be prerequisite for naming behaviour and therefore language; and much current research stresses that the proper unit of study in language development is not so much the child as the child and the caregiver together. As we shall see, 'what the child says' can't very meaningfully be studied without consideration of 'what the caregiver says' as well.

The beginnings of language

Babies vocalize from birth, though we do not normally describe their early crying as language. The first evidence for language is usually taken, by parents and professionals alike, to be the production of a child's first recognizable word (although what's a recognizable word to one adult may not be one to another). 'Normal' children may produce their first word at any age between seven months and two years or even later; but even before the first word is produced a great deal of development will have occurred which is relevant to language. The child will have established a high degree of communicative skill, with the use of gesture and facial expression, and will be having 'conversations' with caregivers. These early conversations consist of talking on the adult's part, and vocalizations, movements, smiles and 'funny faces' from the child; they are regulated, as adult conversations are, by variations in pitch and intensity and by the establishment and variation of eye contact between the speakers to indicate *turn taking*. More specifically, over the months before language proper begins the child's vocalizations develop phonologically in ways which have considerable implications for speech.

Babbling and phonological development

Babies cry more or less as soon as they are born, but although some mothers and other caregivers reckon that they can identify different kinds of crying in their children it is not generally until a child is a month or two old that clearly varied vocalization can be heard. At this age children begin to produce identifiable vowel sounds, particularly 'i' and 'oo' sounds. (This has suggested the general description of this language stage as *cooing*.) Somewhat later, at perhaps four to six months of age, there is an often dramatic increase in the frequency and variety of vocalizations which is generally described as *babbling*. Consonant sounds as well as vowel sounds begin to occur, particularly 'back' consonants (in which the airflow from the larynx is interrupted at the back, rather than the front, of the oral cavity), such as *k* and *g*, and a little later the 'labial' consonants such as *b* and *m*. The child also begins to produce combinations of consonant and vowel sounds, such as *ka* and *ga*, and after a while these syllables are repeated in combinations like *kagagaga*. Also during the babbling stage the child's speech becomes enormously varied in stress, pitch, intonation and rhythm. The babbling stage lasts until the first few words are produced. At this point, the frequency and variety of babbling decline fairly sharply, and phonological development becomes much more gradual, although it does continue beyond infancy well into childhood.

Babbling is such a spectacular phenomenon that it's tempting to regard it as significant for language development. It has been suggested that babbling is a phonological preparation for speech. According to this argument, early on in babbling a wide variety of sounds occur, including sounds from many languages and perhaps some sounds used in none; but during the course of the babbling stage the sounds which are used in the child's local language are in some way 'reinforced' and become more frequently babbled, while sounds which are not so used tend to drop out – a process which can be described as *acculturation*. In this way babbling, and the acculturation which occurs in it, equip infants with the sounds which they will need to use when language begins.

In fact the relationship between babbling and early speech is not as straightforward as this: for example, sounds which a child acquires early in babbling and uses frequently may not be so readily used when words appear. The consonants *k* and *g* appear early in a child's repertoire and are fairly frequently used in babbling, but in early speech they are almost always replaced by so-called 'front' consonants such as *t* and *d*: a child says 'tum and det it' rather than 'come and get it'. There are a number of possible reasons for sound substitutions of this kind, which are very consistent in young children's speech and are also mirrored, as we shall see later, by adults' talk to children, but they do indicate a certain discontinuity between babbling and speech. However, we should be cautious about accepting too easily that one is an obvious preparation for the other.

Early words

The age at which children produce their first word varies greatly; it depends upon the child's sex and social class, upon whether he or she is a twin or an only child, upon whether the home is monolingual or bilingual. The first words produced are usually nouns, at least partly because these are frequently used in caregivers' speech at this stage, and also adjectives. Verbs tend to come later, and words of other types hardly at all until sentences are produced (and not very early even then).

It has been suggested that at this earliest language stage a child is simply *labelling* – learning to attach names to things and people; but one-word speech is more complicated than that. One-word utterances may have several functions: some may be simply labelling, but others refer to absent objects and appear to be orders for the caregiver to provide them; some are self-imperatives apparently announcing the child's intention to do or get something, and some express emotion. So single-word statements may be more semantically complex than we at first give them credit for; and some psychologists have suggested that they are also more grammatically complex. According to this view, a single-word statement is a *holophrase* – a sentence, with an underlying grammar, which however is only one word long. Its length is not limited by an absence of grammar, but by the child's limited vocabulary, memory and attention span and perhaps by a failure to recognize the need to verbalize all parts of a sentence. After all, if you mean to tell your mother that you want some milk, why bother to name yourself when you are obviously the speaker and saying 'milk' will do the job? But this interpretation of single-word statements has been challenged by other researchers, who claim that at the one-word stage children's cognitive development is not far enough advanced for them to possess grammar; clear evidence of grammatical behaviour can only appear when sentences are more than one word long.

Words and sentences: inventing and following rules

A sentence can be defined as the occurrence of more than one word in a single utterance, joined together in a pattern. It is not always easy to know when a young child has produced a sentence. For one thing, an utterance which is more than one word long for an adult may not be more than one word long for a child. The daughter of one of the authors, when she was less than two years old and at her one-word stage in development, often produced an expression best written as 'ereyare' when handing something to another person. While this could have been interpreted as the three-word and quite complex sentence – 'here you are' – it would have been quite inappropriate to do so. Second, it is not always clear what constitutes a single utterance rather than two utterances in succession: the usual interpretation is in terms of context, intonation and respiration, but these criteria are not foolproof. Third, 'pattern' needs to be defined: generally this is in terms of linear order. If a child often says 'Mummy coat' and never says 'coat Mummy', this is evidence that he or she possesses a *rule* governing the order in which different words (or types of word) should be combined in a sentence.

What do early sentences look like? First, and not surprisingly, they are very short, mostly only two words long with a few longer utterances and probably quite a few one-word utterances as well, so that the *mean length of utterance*, or MLU, is less than two. Second, they consist of *content* words – nouns, verbs and adjectives for the most part – and very few so-called 'function words': these are words such as *to*, *for*, *and*, *but*, *the* and *a*, which essentially bind content words together in a sentence without substantially adding meaning of their own. Also missing are auxiliary bits of verbs, such as *is*, *am*, and *will*, and inflections – endings such as -ing, -s (for a plural word or for the present tense) and -d (for the past tense of a verb). The result is speech which has been described as 'telegraphic': sentences like 'Adam coat', 'big car', 'doggie bite'. Telegraphic speech occurs both spontaneously and in imitation: children frequently imitate adults' speech, and when they do they preserve the word order of the original but shorten the utterance by dropping its function words and keeping in the content words (probably largely because those are the words most heavily stressed by the adult 'model').

Finally, it is strikingly clear that early sentences are lawful. Children show considerable consistency in the ordering of words within a sentence. Finding the appropriate rules to describe children's early grammar is not an easy task, and in a sense every child has his or her own grammar, obeying rules which are not necessarily quite the same as those of another child or of the adults around. Sometimes the rules have been strictly defined with respect to 'privileges of occurrence' – that is, the sentence position which a given word is seen to occupy, and the other words with which it occurs, in a systematic way, in the available sample of a child's utterances. This can be an extremely rigorous definition, producing rules which are very reliable and not affected by preconceptions of what a sentence ought to be from an adult standpoint. But it is not very sensitive to distinctions in meaning, and distinctions in grammar, which can be seen from the context of utterances. For example, 'Mummy sock' is likely to mean one thing when Mummy puts her own sock on in front of her child, and another when the child's own sock is being put on by her Mummy. (This real-life example of the same phrase being used by a little girl twice on the same day, but in different contexts, was reported by Lois Bloom). The same phrase in different contexts has not only two meanings but also two underlying grammatical structures. Lois Bloom, Roger Brown and others have suggested that it is important to define the structure of a child's speech with respect to the semantic (or meaning-related) functions of the words in it: agent, action, object, location and so on. By such criteria, too, early speech is lawfully patterned, and order rules are observed in the expression of semantic categories.

Inflections

Although young children follow rules in speaking, the rules they follow are not adult rules. One obvious difference, already mentioned, is that they do not use *inflections*, that is, word endings which convey extra meanings. Where an adult would say 'Daddy goes . . .' a young child says 'Daddy go', and 'Mummy's sock' is 'Mummy sock'. Some inflections come into a child's repertoire earlier than others. Plural endings (saying, for example 'socks' rather than 'sock' when there are two of them) begin to be used quite early, while past tense endings ('washed' instead of 'wash' when the washing has already been done) appear later, and usually at a time when the MLU is longer than two; saying 'goes' instead of 'go' may come later still. One explanation for the difference in timing is the frequency with which the inflections are used in caregivers' speech; plurals are used more often than past tenses, so the child's exposure to plural forms is greater. This is a good explanation of some differences, but not of others, such as the late appearance of 'goes' for 'go'. Other factors are likely to be the complexity of the meaning conveyed by the inflection, and the amount of change to the original word which is required; this is more noticeable in languages which are more heavily inflected than English, such as German and Russian.

When children do use inflections, it is clear that they are again following rules rather than producing, say, plural words or past-tense verbs learnt piecemeal. Oddly enough, some of the best evidence for this comes from children's mistakes. The English language is full of exceptions and irregularities: we say 'grew' instead of 'growed', 'dug' instead of 'digged', 'feet' instead of 'foots', 'mice' instead of 'mouses'. But young children, by the time they are three to four years old, regularly produce sentences such as 'I digged in the garden', 'The sheeps runned away', 'Look at the mouses'. At the same age they can apply plural and past tense endings appropriate to nonsense words, as Jean Berko and Roger Brown, amongst others, showed. Children might be shown a picture of a nonsense animal and told 'This is a wug. Now, [adding a second picture] this is another one. There are two. . . .' and children as young as four years old have no difficulty in finishing the sentence with 'wugs'. They can also tell you that a man who 'wugs' today (and every day) 'wugged' yesterday. Incidentally, they also tell you with confidence that a man who 'glings' today 'glinged' yesterday, although adults in the same situation are apt to suggest that he 'glang', 'glung' or even 'glought'!

Complex sentences

Adults speaking to each other use not only simple sentences of the kind used by youngish children, but also sentences which are in some way *transformed*, for example into a negative form – 'I don't want any supper' – or an interrogative form – 'Who took my pen? Was it you?' – or a passive form – 'The match was stopped by the referee'. These transformations are complex and may involve several rules for supplying the elements within the sentence. Children may take some time to produce sentences of this kind, and they seem to master and apply the different rules one by one. Early negatives and questions, for example, may be like 'No want some supper' and 'Why he's got my car?' because transportation, or reordering, rules are not yet learned. Indeed, adult forms in many cases cannot emerge until a child has learned quite complex verb forms employing auxiliaries such as 'is' (followed by a verb ending in -ing), 'can', 'may', 'will' and so on.

Adults can also use *embedded* sentences, in which one sentence is included within another: 'Here's the book I was reading yesterday'; 'I don't want you to do that'; 'The girl I wanted to marry turned me down'. They produce, and understand, sentences in which the semantic relations among the words don't closely mirror the surface structure of the sentence: for example, in the sentence 'John is easy to please' who is doing the pleasing and who is being pleased? Is your answer the same if the sentence is 'John is eager to please'? Adults observe a number of rules of which most of them have never heard in so many words, such as the *minimal distance principle* (MDP) and its exceptions: if John persuaded Bill to leave, who left, John or Bill? If John promised Bill to attend the funeral, which of them attended? (Ask your friends and see if you all agree on the answers. If you do, you may be surprised to learn that you have all learned the MDP, which is that when a sentence contains a 'complement clause' with an infinitive verb and no subject, the implied subject of that verb is the noun, or noun phrase, immediately before it. You have also all learned that certain verbs, such as 'promise', consistently violate the MDP).

Children take time to acquire these features of adult speech, and a number of studies have shown imperfections in their understanding. Carol Chomsky, for example, showed children aged five to ten years old a blindfolded doll and asked them 'Is the doll hard to see or easy to see?'. Younger children were apt to answer with confidence that the doll was hard to see, because it was blindfolded; in other words, they interpreted that sentence as though the doll was expected to do the seeing. The 'adult' interpretation, that the doll is to be seen rather than to see, only appeared reliably in children of seven or eight. Similarly, Richard Cromer showed children a toy duck and a toy wolf and told them 'the wolf is happy to bite'; or 'the duck is fun to bite'; or, an ambiguous sentence from the adult's point of view, 'The wolf is nasty to bite'. In each case he then asked the children which animal was biting, the wolf or the duck. Children less than about five and a half years old invariably said that the animal named in the sentence was doing the biting. In the second sentence quoted, for example, they assumed that the duck was biting (and having fun doing it), whereas adults assume from the sentence that the duck is being bitten. Only at about seven years old do the children agree with adults.

It is misleading, then, to think of language development as something which is more or less over by the time a child is about four or five. Important language learning continues throughout much of childhood. Nevertheless, the ready and lawful mastery of language shown by very young children remains an amazing achievement. How is such achievement possible?

HOW DO CHILDREN LEARN LANGUAGE?

Psychologists and linguists have sometimes argued that there must be an innate component to language, because the language system is too complex, exposure to it from caregivers and others too imperfect and confusing, and the speed with which it is mastered too impressive,

"Not ŏ, dummy, ōō."

Drawing by Modell: © 1983 The New Yorker Magazine, Inc.

for it to be learnt from scratch. However, whether or not human babies have a biologically given predisposition to help them to acquire language, it is clear that they have a lot to learn.

Obviously, they learn the particular language to which they are exposed, and human languages are so different from one another in vocabulary and structure that the individual characteristics of any one language could not possibly be in-built. Also, although language learning seems an immense task, it may not be quite as immense as the argument above suggests. Young children almost invariably receive an 'easy introduction' to language from their caregivers, and the natural interactions between children and caregivers provide plenty of opportunity for teaching and learning.

Baby talk

When adults talk to young children, their speech is different from that used with other adults; they use what is known as an *adult–child register*, or, more colloquially, baby talk or 'motherese'. Most studies of baby talk have been based on observation of caregivers, particularly mothers, talking to their children in their own homes; but baby talk features are also used by teachers in day nurseries and playgroups, by other adults, even those unused to babies and young children, and by older children talking to younger ones. The characteristics of 'baby talk' have been studied for several different languages, and while naturally details do vary for different languages they tend to show common features.

What are the essentials of baby talk? There are probably well over 100 separate features; some of the most notable are listed in *Table 6.1.*

TABLE 6.1: *Some Characteristics of baby talk*

UTTERANCES are:

- *shorter* (in MLU or mean preverb length)
- *simpler* (fewer clauses)
- *better formed* (fewer disfluencies, errors, interruptions)
- *more limited in vocabulary*
- *more repetitive*

SPEECH is:

- *slower*
- *more articulated* (longer pauses at end of clause; more stress on separate syllables of long words and phrases)
- *higher and more varied in pitch* (so-called 'nursery tone')

PHONOLOGY is often modified by:

- *substitution of 'front' for 'back' consonants* (e.g. 'tum' for 'come')
- *consonant cluster reduction* (e.g. 't' instead of 'st')
- *deletion or weakening of final syllable* (e.g. 'tummy' instead of 'stomach')

VOCABULARY and SYNTAX are often modified by:

- *replacement of pronouns* (by proper names or kin terms – 'Mummy' instead of 'me', 'Katie' instead of 'you')
- *pet names and affixes* ('dolly', 'Johnny', 'Katykins')
- *'let's . . .' and 'shall we . . . ?'* (instead of orders)

Catherine Snow and Charles Ferguson argued that there are essentially three components: 'simplifying', 'clarifying' and 'expressive'. Speech is simplified, in that sentences are shorter and simpler in structure and vocabulary; it is clearer, in that it is slower and more clearly articulated; and its expressiveness is shown by such features as the use of pet names and euphemisms. Some parents resolve that they will not use baby talk to their children, but it is almost certain that while they avoid a few characteristics (for example, pet names and consonant substitution) they retain many others, such as the simplicity of sentence structure and vocabulary and the slowness and clarity of delivery. As we have already mentioned, baby talk is similar in some ways to the speech of young children, both in its simplicity and, for example, in the use of 'consonant substitution': adults talking to little children are apt to say 'tum on' rather than 'come on', just as the children themselves do. You may like to observe some features of babytalk for yourself by trying out *Exercise 6.1* on page 107.

It is sometimes reported that parents of very young (for example three-to-four-month-old) babies don't use baby talk to them; baby talk is used when a mother or other adult feels, for one reason or another, that some communication is possible. Once baby talk is introduced, it does not stand still. We have talked so far of an adult–child register, but in fact there are rather different registers for children of different ages. As children develop, and as they show more signs of comprehension and more elaborate language production, caregivers' speech becomes more complex. Several investigators have found that the speech of mothers is finely tuned to that of their children, slightly more advanced in its complexity, and increasing in complexity as the child's production grows. In other words, the developing child is presented, in the mother's speech, with a well-designed set of language lessons. However, we still do not know exactly what baby talk accomplishes, and how. It is clear that what Catherine Snow termed 'conversation with an interested adult' is important for children's language development in general terms, but not so clear whether they actually learn specific features of language from exposure to the mother's conversation. More evidence concerning the specific results of 'teaching' comes from the study of other caregiver–child interactions, involving training and imitation.

Imitation

Children frequently *imitate* the utterances of their caregivers; by one estimate, about ten per cent of children's speech at two to three years of age consists of repetition of what an adult (or sometimes an older child) has just said. At first sight the tendency to imitate seems likely to aid language learning, but its role is not straightforward. For one thing, there is plenty of evidence that children are very resistant to imitating forms that don't fit their current rules. When Jean Berko, for example, showed four-year-old children pictures of geese, saying 'Here is a goose, and here are two geese; now there are three. . .', the children replied 'gooses'. Also, as we have already seen, children imitate 'with reduction', so that their imitative speech is remarkably like their non-imitative speech in length and complexity rather than more advanced. If imitations are not 'progressive' – that is, more linguistically advanced than non-imitative speech – there is not much of a case for regarding them as a learning device.

In fact there is some evidence that imitations can be progressive, in vocabulary and also in grammatical structure though not in length, and particularly if the criteria for what is an imitation are not too strict. For example, is a child's statement an imitation if it occurs ten minutes after the 'model', and how exact a repetition of the model does it have to be? On the other hand, there is not much evidence that imitation helps a child to understand a given phrase or a grammatical structure. It is more likely that imitation is a way of learning to produce words and structures which the child already understands but hasn't yet produced in spontaneous speech.

How do we teach children language?

It is obvious that in some sense or other parents, and other caregivers, 'teach' their children language. But most observers (including parents themselves) have found that explicit teaching, for example correcting the child's ungrammatical sentences, is not a very successful technique. For one thing, parents don't often do it; they may correct pronunciation, the use of 'naughty' words, and, sometimes, the use of regularized irregular forms such as 'digged' and 'goed', but they don't normally bother to correct syntax and are more likely to approve or disapprove the truth of their children's utterances than their grammaticalness. For another thing, when parents do try explicitly to correct children's speech the children are usually very resistant to being corrected, and there is some evidence that children whose speech is often corrected may develop language more slowly, rather than faster, than others.

It is much more likely that parents train their children in less direct and less formal ways, through natural, everyday communicative exchanges. For example, mothers frequently imitate their children's utterances (rather more often, in fact, than children imitate theirs!); when they imitate, they expand the child's utterance, filling in function words and elaborating its grammatical and semantic content. They also use 'new' sentences to comment on the child's speech, or on the situation, or on the nonverbal behaviour of the child or themselves, and in this way they 'model' grammatical and semantic forms for the child to observe.

The effects of 'modelling' may be quite specific, as some controlled studies have shown. If children receive specific exposure, in adults' speech, to particular constructions (for example, complex forms of verbs or questions) they may show faster linguistic development than other children with respect to those constructions, but not in other respects. It's not clear, though, whether these specific effects are long-lasting, or whether in the end the general effects of 'conversation with an interested adult' are more important.

In any case, in everyday conversations between children and caregivers, modelling, imitation (on both sides), corrections and comments generally exist side by side, so that it's perhaps an artificial exercise to try to separate out their effects. Linguistic interactions are also cognitive interactions, in which children learn about the world, about concepts of time and space and causality, and they are social interactions in which children explore their relationships with others. Language does not develop in isolation. It develops within the context of cognitive and social development and is best studied within that context, where it has a central and crucial part to play.

Recommended reading

Brown, R. (1973) *A First Language: The early stages*. Cambridge, Mass.: Harvard University Press. [A classic, and very entertaining, account of early language development.]

Dale, P.S. (1976) *Language Development*, 2nd edn. New York: Holt, Rinehart & Winston. [A full and detailed, but very readable, introduction to all principal areas.]

Ellis, A. & Beattie, G. (1986)*The Psychology of Language and Communication*. London: Lawrence Erlbaum Associates. [Chapter 15 deals with several aspects of development, in more detail than other readings, but more selectively: other chapters provide useful information on other aspects of the psychology of language.]

Naremore, R.C. & Hopper. R. (1990) *Children Learning Language*. New York: Harper & Row. [A good, up-to-date, fairly introductory discussion.]

Yule, G. (1985) *The Study of Language*. Cambridge: Cambridge University Press. [Chapters 4 and 15 give brief but very informative accounts of 'language in animals' and language development: other chapters give useful background information.]

Talking to Children

Ask a number of friends, acquaintances or relatives to help you with a study of children's stories. Take one person at a time into a quiet room with a tape recorder, turn on the tape and give your helper a picture – it could be from a children's book or from a magazine. Ask the helper to make up and tell a story suitable for a nursery group of three-year-old children. You can discuss the story together, but the helper must eventually tell it, in his or her own words and without interruption, for the hypothetical children. When the story has been told, chat to your helper for a few minutes, encouraging him or her to talk to you as much as possible, before switching the tape off.

Compare the speech of your helpers (a) when they are supposedly talking to young children and (b) when they are talking to you. If you can extract from your recording a passage in which your helper is telling you something, at some length and without interruption, this will give you the best basis for comparison. Some useful measures to choose from are:

▶ **Mean length of utterance.** An utterance is usually a sentence, but can also be an incomplete sentence or phrase if it is clearly marked off from the speech around it by pauses and intonation (use your judgement as consistently as possible).

▶ **Sentence complexity.** An easy way to measure this is by counting, and averaging, either the number of verbs or the number of 'compound verbs' (such as 'will go', 'have done', 'were saying') per utterance.

▶ **Mean preverb length.** This means the average number of words preceding the main verb in an utterance or clause, and is really another measure of complexity.

▶ **Incidence of third-person pronouns.** Count the number of occurrences of 'she', 'he', 'it', 'they', 'her', 'him', 'them', 'hers', 'his', 'its', 'theirs' and express it as a proportion of the total number of words.

▶ **Rate of speech.** Record the number of seconds taken to produce an uninterrupted passage of, say, 50 words under each condition; take more than one sample of each if you can.

Other possible measures are suggested in *Table 6.1* on page 103, which describes some differences which you might expect to find, in your samples, between adult-to-adult and adult-to-child speech.

More questions which you might explore:

• If some of your helpers are more experienced with children than others (for example, if some of them are parents while others are not) does this seem to make a difference?

• How does a story told into a tape recorder for absent children compare with one told directly to a young child?

• What happens to helpers' speech if you ask them to tell a story for ten year olds, or for elderly people at a day centre? Do they speak as they would to adults, or do they use baby talk, or is their speech different from both?

References

Berko, J. (1958) The child's learning of English morphology. *Word*, *14*, 150–177. [A classic experiment on children's possession of grammatical rules.]

Bloom, L. (1970) *Language Development: Form and function in emerging grammars.* Cambridge, Mass.: MIT Press. [An account of language development which emphasizes the semantic characteristics of children's early speech.]

Bloom, L. (1973) *One World at a Time: The use of single word utterances before syntax.* The Hague: Mouton. [A critical assessment of the 'holophrastic speech' hypothesis.]

Brown, R. (1973) *A First Language: The early stages.* Cambridge, Mass: Harvard University Press. [A classic account of early language development.]

Chomsky, C. (1969) *The Acquisition of Syntax in Children from 5 to 10.* Cambridge, Mass.: MIT Press. [As its title indicates, a study of language development in older children.]

Cromer, R. (1970) Children are nice to understand: Surface structure clues for the discovery of deep structure. *British Journal of Psychology*, *61*, 397–408.

Demetras, M.J., Post, K.N. and Snow, C.E. (1986) Feedback to first language learners: The role of repetitions and clarifications. *Journal of Child Language*, *13*, 275–292. [An examination of negative as well as positive feedback.]

Hockett, C. (1960) The origin of speech. *Scientific American*, *203*, 89–96. [An analysis of language features and their 'human exclusiveness'.]

Lenneberg, E.H. (1967) *Biological Foundations of Language.* New York: Wiley. [Although now out of date, an excellent exposition of the biological argument that language is species-specific to man.]

Linden, E. (1976) *Apes, Men and Language.* Harmondsworth: Penguin. [A readable discussion of the evidence that non-humans may acquire 'language', though a little too much on the side of the 'linguistic apes'.]

Lyons, J. (1970) *Chomsky.* London: Fontana. [An account and assessment of Noam Chomsky's views on language and psycholinguistics.]

Moerk, E. (1972) Principles of interaction in language learning. *Merrill-Palmer Quarterly*, *18*, 229–257. [A discussion of the potential language-learning devices in everyday interactions between caregivers and children.]

Nelson, K.E. (1977) Facilitating children's syntax acquisition. *Developmental Psychology*, *13*, 101–107. [The effects of specific 'modelling' on children's language development.]

Penner, S.G. (1987) Parental responses to grammatical and ungrammatical child utterances. *Child Development*, *58*, 376–384. [A study which finds that parents are more likely to expand ungrammatical utterances.]

Snow, C. & Ferguson, C.A. (Eds) (1977) *Talking to Children: Language input and acquisition.* Cambridge: Cambridge University Press. [A fascinating collection of papers on baby talk and its implications at different ages and for different cultures.]

Terrace, H.S. (1985) In the beginning was the 'name'. *American Psychology*, *40*, 1011–1028. [A sympathetic review of the evidence for naming behaviour, if not for grammar, in chimpanzees and other apes.]

Wanner, E. and Gleitman, L.R. (Eds) (1990) *Language Acquisition: The state of the art.* Cambridge: Cambridge University Press. [A collection of essays, detailed and fairly technical.]

Wells, G. (1985) *Language Development in the Preschool Years.* London: Cambridge University Press. [Report of a large-scale longitudinal study; detailed accounts of methodology and of emerging grammatical structures in children aged 1–5 years.]

Whitehurst, G.J. & Vasta, R. (1975) Is language acquired through imitation? *Journal of Psycholinguistic Research*, *4*, 37–59. [An examination of the role of imitation in language learning.]

7. *Children's Thinking*

▽ *Jean Piaget and his theory*
▽ *How do babies perceive the world?*
▽ *The symbolic world of the preschooler*
▽ *Logical thinking at school*

The following dialogue took place between one of the authors and his son, aged three years and nine months. The 'props' were a large plastic bowl full of water, a wooden toy boat, and various other household objects.

Dad: 'What's happened to the boat now we've put it in the water?'
Jonathan: *'It's splashed'*
D: 'Yes – and what's it doing on top of the water?'
J: *'Floating'*
D: 'And why is it floating?'
J: *'Because the water is too little. . .shall I see if this crayon works?'*
D: 'What's happened to the crayon?'
J: *'It's floated!'* [laughs]
D: 'No it hasn't – what's happened to it? Why do you think the boat floats but the crayon goes to the bottom? Think carefully. . .'
J: *'Because. . .I don't know why'*
D: 'Let's try this stone: has it floated?'
J: *'No'*
D: 'Why has the stone gone to the bottom?'
J: *'Because it doesn't float'*
D: 'Why does the boat float?'
J: *'Because it's big. . .shall I see if this [button] does?'*
D: 'Has that floated?'
J: *'No, it's sinked on the stone poor button'*
D: 'Why do you think the button's not floating?'
J: *'Because it's a stone in'*

This brief conversation illustrates several features of Jonathan's think-ing, and indeed of his whole approach to the problem. He clearly does not understand the physics of flotation, which he disarmingly admits at one point, though he advances two explanations of his own, based on the size of the objects in the water and the presence of other objects already there. He also shows a lively interest in trying out new things to float, and an anthropomorphic concern for the 'poor button' which had the misfortune to sink to the bottom of the bowl. You can try this out for yourself in *Exercise 7.1* on page 124.

What makes children's thinking different from that of adults, and how does it change with age?

JEAN PIAGET AND HIS THEORY

By far the best-known attempt to explain these questions is the monumental theory of Jean Piaget (1896–1980), who was born, and worked, in Switzerland. In order to understand how Piaget's theory about children's thought developed we need to know something of his background. The young Piaget was something of a child prodigy: he published his first paper (a description of an albino sparrow he had observed in the park) at the age of ten. This began a lifetime of scholarship in which he wrote over 50 books, and hundreds of articles.

Biology, philosophy, and genetic epistemology

Piaget's theory is rooted in biology, the discipline in which he carried out his undergraduate and postgraduate studies. However, he had always been interested in that branch of philosophy called *epistemology*, the study of knowledge, and his life's work can be seen as an attempt to explain epistemological problems from a biological perspective. Piaget discovered that this endeavour led him into the study of children's thinking: and his own research into what he called 'genetic epistemology', the study of the origins of knowledge, became the single most powerful influence on developmental psychology. The theory has also had a profound influence upon education-al practice, although Piaget himself never claimed to be an educational expert.

Piaget's approach

Piaget adopted a method of studying children's thinking which he called the 'clinical interview', and the 'flotation' dialogue above is a fairly typical example. He was less interested in the number of correct answers that children give to a set of questions (for example in intelligence tests) than in the *reasons* behind those answers, whether right or wrong. This had its advantages as well as its disadvantages. Piaget's methods led him to discover a wealth of important phenomena about child development, but they could in no sense be described as rigorous or scientific: it has been left to the numerous critics of the theory to carry out more scientific investigations.

Piaget's theory rests on several important concepts whose biological origins are obvious. He saw *adaptation* as a fundamental feature of development: all organisms, including humans, adapt to their environment. Adaptation itself consists of two interrelated processes, *assimilation* and *accommodation*. When you eat an apple, we could say that it is assimilated into your body, and at the same time your body accommodates to the apple in the sense that a number of physiological changes take place. This metaphor is not intended to be flippant, for Piaget himself used the term 'aliment' – food – to describe the new objects and experiences which are assimilated to the thinking of the developing child.

Piaget suggested that thinking is built up from *schemes*, or *schemata*, which are the sets of related *operations* which children perform upon the world. A scheme, in a young infant, might be the set of actions concerned with sucking. In 'assimilating new objects to his or her sucking scheme', the infant might suck dummies, fingers, or toys – and then maybe a piece of soap, which results in the scheme's accommodation to the fact that some classes of objects are less suckable than others! This example helps to explain Piaget's powerful idea that the development of thinking is an *active* process. Children have an internal drive to explore the world actively rather than being acted upon by it, and this concept has provided a strong foundation for the promotion of child-centred learning, in the world of education.

A well-known feature of Piaget's theory is the proposal that thinking proceeds through a series of four broad developmental stages, which are described in more detail later in this chapter. The *sensori-motor stage*, which lasts from birth to about two years, gives way to the *pre-operational stage*, between the ages of two and seven years. The *concrete operational stage* lasts from the ages of seven to eleven years, and is finally succeeded by the *formal operational stage*. Piaget's stage theory has inspired others to propose similar theories in specific areas such as moral thinking and aesthetic appreciation, and it has had a profound influence upon curriculum development in mathematics and science.

Although the final stage is intended to deal with developments in adolescent and adult thought, such as hypothesis testing and formal logic, most Piagetian research has been concerned with developments in childhood. In the rest of this chapter we will concentrate on the first three stages.

HOW DO BABIES PERCEIVE THE WORLD?

Piaget's approach to infant perception was rather different from that outlined in Chapter 2 because, in his view, babies' actions reveal how they make sense of their world. Piaget's sensori-motor stage is divided into six substages. In the first of these, *use of reflexes* (0–1 months), simple physical actions like sucking are exercised, with only the very beginnings of adaptation to the world. Although babies may prefer sucking nipples to fingers when hungry, for example, there is no real accommodation to different classes of 'things to be sucked'. In the next substage, *primary circular reactions* (1–4 months) this accommodation does begin. For example, the baby may suck his or her hand if it accidentally touches his or her mouth: and having discovered this experience, the baby may repeat it (in 'circular' fashion) because it is pleasant.

Primary circular reactions, like thumb sucking, centre on part of the baby's body; in *secondary circular reactions* (4–8 months), in the third substage, the reaction is between the baby's actions and objects in the outside world. Here is an example from one of Piaget's observations of his own son Laurent:

At 0;3 (29) [three months and 29 days old] Laurent grasps a paper-knife which he sees for the first time; he looks at it a moment and then swings it while holding it in his right hand. During these movements the object happens to rub against the wicker basket of the bassinet: Laurent then waves his arm vigorously and obviously tries to reproduce the sound he has heard, but without understanding the necessity of the contact between the paper-knife and the wicker and, consequently, without achieving this, contact otherwise than by chance.

At 0;4 (3) same reactions, but Laurent looks at the object at the time when it happens to rub against the wicker of the bassinet. The same still occurs at 0;4 (5) but there is a slight progress towards sys-tematisation.

Finally at 0;4 (6) the movement becomes intentional: as soon as the child has the object in his hand he rubs it with regularity against the wicker of the bassinet. He does the same, subsequently, with his dolls and rattle.

Here we see the beginnings of *intentionality*; Laurent deliberately and systematically creates a simple effect upon the world around him. At this early stage, Piaget suggests that thought is action. What babies do to the objects and toys around them *is* what they think about them. It follows that when objects are not physically present, they cease to exist as far as the baby is concerned: – this idea has been captured in the saying 'out of sight is out of mind', and we will return to it shortly.

The fourth stage, *co-ordination of secondary schemes* (8–11 months) sees the beginning of the separation of objects and actions. If the baby can see her or his doll behind a cardboard box, for example, the baby can set aside the box to retrieve the doll: and this involves the co-ordination of two separate schemes. However, if the baby sees the doll hidden under cloth A, and then watches an adult move it from under cloth A to under cloth B, she or he will search for it under the first cloth, A. Piaget explains that this is because the doll still forms part of the sequence of actions which identified it with cloth A.

In the fifth substage, *tertiary circular reactions*, (12–18 months), babies start to experiment with their actions. One of the authors vividly remembers how his son used to drop his cup of orange juice from his high chair on to the kitchen floor. When this produced an interesting parental reaction, he tried dropping it from a different height. Further explorations of the scheme included throwing it at the wall, throwing it up in the air, and so on; all of this experimentation took place with a great deal of enjoyment and fun (in spite of the state of the kitchen carpet!). By experimenting with schemes, babies are able to discover new means of solving problems. In the earlier example, the baby might have discovered that a rattle could have been used to set aside the box which was in the way of the doll.

By the sixth and final substage, *invention of new means by mental combinations* (18 months +), babies can solve such problems by *mental* means: they can anticipate the likely effects of pushing the box with a rattle without having to observe it directly. This marks an extremely important development – the emergence of *symbolism*. By the end of the sensori-motor stage, infants are able to make mental predictions about the likely effects of their actions without actually having to carry out those actions.

Is 'out of sight, out of mind'?

The later substages of the sensori-motor period incorporate an important Piagetian discovery which has been challenged by a number of infancy researchers. The idea that 'out of sight is out of mind' implies that objects have no permanence – they effectively cease to exist when they are not directly visible. According to Piaget, full *object permanence* is only acquired by the final substage. In our substage 4 example of the baby searching for the doll under cloth A after observing an adult move it to cloth B, we might say that objects possess 'semi-permanence'. Such an infant could retrieve the doll if part of it was hidden under the cloth and part was visible, but nevertheless makes the 'stage 4 search error' (see *Figure 7.1*).

In the fifth substage, infants overcome this error: when they see the doll moved from cloth A to cloth B, they search correctly under cloth B. But if the doll is first hidden under A and then moved to cloth B *without the child seeing this move* (for example if the two cloths are partially overlapped at the point of switching over) they will still search under the wrong cloth A. In this case, to use Piaget's terminology, they cannot cope with 'invisible displacements'. It is only by the end of the sensori-motor stage that this problem can be solved, which indicates that the infant has an internal concept of the doll even when it cannot be seen.

Was Piaget right?

Some researchers have claimed that infants do in fact possess object permanence at earlier ages than Piaget's theory predicts, and have devised alternative ways of testing it. For example, Tom Bower carried out an impressive series of experiments at Edinburgh University. In one of these, conducted with infants under the age of eight months, a screen was passed in front of an object that the infants were watching, and their interest in the object was measured by monitoring their heart rate. In half the experimental trials the object was still present after the screen passed by, but in the other half it had disappeared. If these babies do not possess object permanence, argued Bower, they should not be surprised when the object has disappeared. In fact, the heart rate measures suggested that they were more surprised when it did not reappear than when it did.

In another experiment, the screen stayed still and the object moved behind it. In some trials the object stopped behind the screen, and in others it emerged from the other side. Bower found that infants even as young as eight weeks turned their eyes to anticipate the reappearance of the object from the other side of the screen. Both of these results cast some doubt on the simple notion that 'out of sight is out of mind', and Bower advances a more complex explanation.

His view is that infants of this age do not realize that place and movement are linked; that they think that the same object, when moved from place to place, effectively becomes a series of different objects. This is supported by the results of a study in which multiple

(a)

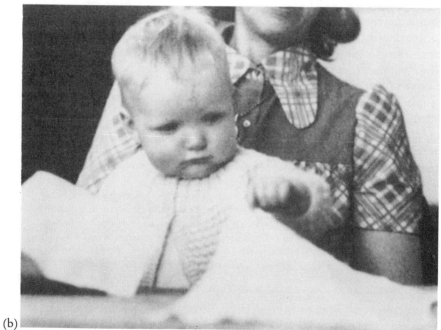

(b)

FIGURE 7.1:   *The stage 4 search error*

images of babies' own mothers were shown to them by means of mirrors. Below the age of five months, babies were quite happy to view three images of their mothers, and interacted with each one in turn. Above this age, however, the babies were distressed by the multiple images: Bower suggests that they realized that they only have one mother, and that she can no longer be identified by a place or a movement.

It seems that Piaget may well have underestimated the perceptual capabilities of the infant, and that some sensori-motor developments take place at an earlier age than he suggested. However, there can be no doubt that the acquisition of object permanence is an extremely important milestone in children's early development. It heralds the end of the sensori-motor stage in that children are finally liberated from physical actions which take place in the immediate present.

THE SYMBOLIC WORLD OF THE PRESCHOOLER

The ability to form and use symbols is the key feature of the pre-operational stage. Symbols (or 'internal mental representations') are organized into different *symbol systems*, which are developed in every aspect of life. Language is one of the most obvious and immediately useful symbol systems, but similar developments are occurring in the areas of number, drawing, music, dance, modelling, and so on. Piaget put forward his own account of what he called the *symbolic function*, which is displayed in four different areas of activity.

The first of these, *deferred imitation*, is illustrated by Piaget's observations of his daughter Jacqueline:

At 1;4 (3) [one year, four months and three days old] Jacqueline had a visit from a little boy of 1;6, whom she used to see from time to time, and who, in the course of the afternoon got into a terrible temper. He screamed as he tried to get out of a play-pen and pushed it backwards, stamping his feet. Jacqueline stood watching him in amazement, never having witnessed such a scene before. The next day, she herself screamed in her play-pen and tried to move it, stamping her foot lightly several times in succession. The imitation of the whole scene was most striking. Had it been immediate, it would naturally not have involved representation, but coming as it did after an interval of more than twelve hours, it must have involved some representative or pre-representative element.

Here the action sequence was repeated some time after it had originally occurred: and in *verbal evocation*, the second area, the repetition is carried out with words:

At 1;7 (28) Jacqueline told her mother about a grasshopper she had just seen in the garden: "Hopper, hopper jump boy", meaning that the grasshopper jumped as a boy had made her jump. A boy cousin had in fact made her jump two days earlier. At 1;11 (28), after she had been on a visit she said to me "Robert cry, duck swim in lake, gone away".

Make-believe play and drawings

Symbolic play and *drawings*, the third and fourth areas, have both been the subject of a great deal of theory and research in developmental psychology. In many ways, symbolic or make-believe play captures the essence of the preschool period. We have all seen children pretending to be parents, teachers, nurses, or astronauts, and they are presumably acting out roles which they see around them in the adult world. The functions of play, and its role in children's learning, are discussed in more detail in Chapter 5.

Children's drawings are of immense interest to the psychologist because they bring together two quite different 'poles' of children's thinking. On the one hand, they are obviously expressive: children can give full rein to their feelings and imagination in drawing, without the constraints of reality. At the same time, many children's drawings *are* attempts to represent the world around them. Piaget explains this combination by describing drawings as 'graphic images', which are midway in between play on the one hand, and mental images on the other. They are discussed at more length in Chapter 9.

Pre-conceptual and intuitive thought

Piaget divided the pre-operational stage into two substages, which he called the *pre-conceptual* stage (2–4 years) and the *intuitive* stage (4–7 years). In the former, children's concepts are not fully formed. One of the authors' children, for example, used the term 'co-co' to refer to all drinks for a period of some weeks: differentiation between cocoa, orange juice, water, milk, and so on emerged only gradually. Children do not yet possess the class concepts which are used to organize the thinking of adults: similarly, they are unable to perceive the individual identities of the objects within a given class. Piaget quotes the example of Jacqueline who, on seeing a number of different slugs whilst walking along a road, thought that they were all the same slug!

As children progress beyond the pre-conceptual stage their ability to classify, order and quantify things gradually develops, but they are still unaware of the principles which underlie these abilities, and so their thinking is still described as *intuitive*. It is only in the next stage of concrete operations that these principles become more explicit, so that children can explain their logical reasoning in a satisfactory way.

Piaget's account of the transition from the pre-operational to the concrete operational stage, which takes place around the age of seven, has stimulated an immense amount of research. Developmental psychologists have devoted a great deal of effort in attempts to show that children can display concrete operational reasoning well before this age, and the debate still goes on. We will follow up two lines of this debate after looking at some of the more prominent features of the concrete operational stage.

LOGICAL THINKING AT SCHOOL

Exercise 7.2 on page 125 illustrates one of Piaget's most famous demonstrations of concrete operational thinking. Children are first shown two rows of counters, A and B, and asked 'Are there more black counters, more white counters, or the same number of each?' Children of all ages should correctly answer that there are the same number of each, and this serves as a check on their answers in the rest of the demonstration. The experimenter next spreads out the white counters in row B, transforming it into row B1, and repeats the question. According to Piaget, pre-operational children are now very likely to answer that there are more counters in row B1 than in row A: if asked why, they are likely to reply along the lines of 'because it's longer'. When the experimenter finally reshuffles row B1 so as to return it to its original form, children assert once again that there are the same number of black and white counters.

The answer to the second question is clearly wrong, and Piaget suggests that it occurs because children of this age do not possess *number invariance*, the ability to realize that number stays constant regardless of other properties of the array, such as length, or the distance between each counter. Children only acquire this concept in concrete operations and Piaget goes on to explain that the acquisition of this understanding of number involves a synthesis of two other operations: *class inclusion*, and *seriation*.

Putting objects into classes and into orders

Class inclusion is the ability to understand how a set of objects can be grouped into categories, and to appreciate the relationship between these categories and the whole set of objects. For example, a five year old is quite likely to be able to sort out the horses from the cows in a set of farmyard animals, but Piaget claims that children cannot understand the relationship between horses, cows and the superordinate class 'animals' until concrete operational thinking has been achieved.

Seriation is the ability to order objects in a logical series. If the ten sticks shown in *Figure 7.2* are jumbled up and children are asked to match them to the ordered set of dolls, for example, Piaget suggests that pre-operational children will fail. They may be able to sort out small groups of two or three sticks in the correct order, but they will not be able to integrate these small groups into an organized series. The ability to do so involves another very important Piagetian principle, the *transitive inference*. If a child realizes that stick A is longer than stick B, and that stick B is longer than stick C, the ability to work out that A is longer than C *without directly comparing them* involves a transitive inference. Piaget's claim that children are only able to make such inferences when they have acquired concrete operations has generated a great deal of research which has tried to disprove it.

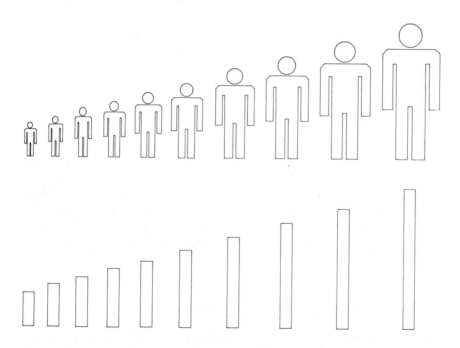

FIGURE 7.2:   *Piaget's seriation problem*

Number invariance, class inclusion and seriation are just three examples of the application of Piaget's theory of concrete operations to different areas of primary school mathematics and science. Other well-known examples include Piaget's famous *conservation* tasks. Conservation of volume, for example, involves understanding that a given volume of liquid remains constant even though its shape may be changed by pouring it into another vessel. This idea has also been applied to physical properties including length, time, mass, as well as number. The general principle which underlies all of the conservation experiments is that of *decentration*: the ability to recognize that two dimensions of a display can vary simultaneously, and that these dimensions may interact to determine a third, higher-order property of the display. The same principle has been extended into the social world, as we shall see next.

Are young children egocentric?

Another important feature of Piaget's account of the pre-operational stage is the idea that young children cannot decentre from their own point of view: that they are *egocentric*. Four-year-old Rebecca fully understands that she has a little sister called Amy, for example, but she cannot grasp the idea that she is herself a sister to Amy. One of Piaget's most famous experiments, which he devised as a demonstration of egocentric thought, is the 'three mountains' task.

The three mountains task

This consists of a display of three model cardboard mountains, arranged on a table such that the view of them is different from each side of the table. Children were shown pictures of these different views, and asked to predict the viewpoint of a doll which was placed at a particular side of the table. Piaget found that pre-operational children usually made a choice that was based on their own perspective rather than that of the doll: it was only by the age of nine or so that they could accurately predict the doll's point of view (see *Figure 7.3*).

Once again, a number of subsequent studies have challenged this finding. Maureen Cox, for example, has shown that a number of different factors affect pre-operational children's tendency to respond egocentrically. She also found that they are better able to predict the view of another *person* than that of a doll, which indicates that the social aspects of the test situation may be important. She also found that children as young as five years old could be trained to improve their performance on the task, and that this improvement persisted over time, although it did not generalize to other tasks.

Helen Borke argued that although predicting views of Alpine mountain scenes may have produced reliable findings from Piaget's child participants in Switzerland, the task may seem strange and remote to the American children who are involved in many published experiments. She repeated Piaget's original experiment, but included three additional settings of the task which were likely to be much more familiar. In one of these, for example, Piaget's doll was replaced by Grover, a well-known character from the popular American children's television series *Sesame Street*. The task was to predict Grover's views of a model fire engine which was mounted on a revolving turntable. Borke found that three and four year olds showed much less evidence of egocentric thought when the task was familiar to them, and when they rotated the display themselves rather than responding by selecting photographs. In other words, children seem to be much less egocentric when the task 'makes sense' to them: and this argument has been followed in conservation research, as we shall see next.

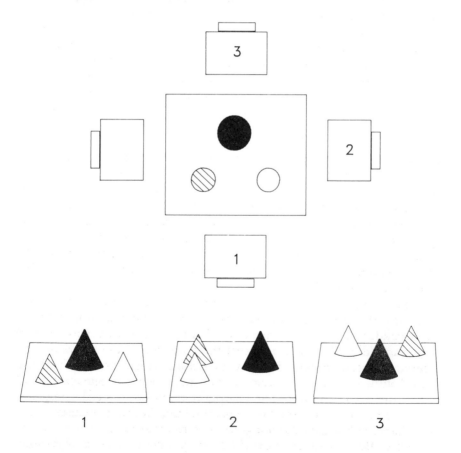

FIGURE 7.3: *Piaget's 'three mountains' task*

'Cognitive sense' or 'human sense'?

Consider the child's point of view in the number invariance task, which we described earlier (see *Exercise 7.2*). The experimenter sets out the counters as rows A and B; transforms B to B1; then asks whether there are still the same number in each row. Any test-wise five year old is likely to argue 'the experimenter wants me to say that B1 is longer now, otherwise the question wouldn't have been asked'. In other words, the wrong answer may emerge not from the absence of number invariance, but from the perception that 'B1 is longer' is the answer that the experimenter wanted.

In *Children's Minds*, which has become a classic book, Margaret Donaldson has explored the implications of this phenomenon at some length. She contends that a direct response to the literal wording of the questions in Piagetian tasks represents only one of several possible channels of communication between the experimenter and the child. In reality, children respond to many other channels: they attempt to perceive the motives and intentions of the experimenter by picking up non-verbal clues, by attending to the *form* of language that is used, by working out the role of the experimenter in relation to the school staff, and so on. Donaldson suggests that they construct 'human sense' explanations of the task situation. Incorrect answers may therefore reflect a much more complex response than the simple absence of concrete operational thinking.

This point was elegantly demonstrated in a famous experiment by Donaldson and her research student, James McGarrigle. They found that only about 30 per cent of the five to six year olds they tested gave the correct answer to standard Piagetian tests of number and length conservation, in which the displays were *intentionally* transformed by the experimenter. However, when the transformations of the displays were made to appear *accidental* by the ingenious introduction of a 'naughty teddy bear', who 'spoilt the game', the children's success rate approximately doubled.

A number of subsequent researchers have repeated this study, and some have introduced additional variations on the procedure so as to alter children's perceptions of the purpose of the experimenter. There can be no doubt that these variations exert a significant influence on children's performance, though researchers differ as to the precise implications of the findings for Piaget's theory of concrete operations. Nevertheless, it is clear that the cognitive and the social aspects of child development are inextricably linked, and that these experiments enable us to examine the interaction. The emergence of the field of 'social cognition', which goes well beyond the bounds of Piagetian research, is another reflection of this.

PIAGET'S THEORY
AND THE STUDY OF CHILDREN'S THINKING

We have seen that although research has shown Piaget's theory to be inaccurate in a number of important respects, it continues to dominate the explanation of children's thinking. Above all, Piaget's talent for spotting the key phenomena of cognitive development has shaped the course of research. We have concentrated on *children's* thinking in this chapter, and there is a good deal which has not been covered. Piaget proposed a fourth stage of *formal operations* which begins at around the age of 11, in which the ability to propose hypotheses and deduce consequences is developed in the absence of concrete experience. His work on the development of moral thinking beyond childhood formed the basis for Lawrence Kohlberg's influential stage theory of moral development, which is discussed in more detail in Chapter 10.

Apart from the lack of rigour in Piaget's methodology, there are three main criticisms of his theory. The first concerns the four developmental stages: although this concept has had a significant impact on the design of the primary school curriculum, it seems quite likely that the four stages are not as coherent as the theory implies, and that some of the abilities which characterize each stage may appear earlier than Piaget proposed. The second concerns the idea of adaptation as the basis of developmental change. Although the general idea of children being internally motivated to learn *actively* has been an important part of the promotion of 'child-centred' teaching methods, there is a current move towards the view that teachers should be seen as directors of learning rather than merely as facilitators. The third concerns the idea that development gradually proceeds towards higher forms of *logical* thinking. The focus on scientific, problem-solving activity may not be appropriate for those types of thinking which predominate in the arts, as we shall see in Chapter 9.

Some so-called 'neo-Piagetian' theorists, such as Robbie Case and Kurt Fischer, have tried to get round some of these problems by combining parts of Piaget's theory with concepts from information-processing theory. They have retained the idea of developmental stages but have allowed for a great deal more flexibility within each stage than in Piaget's version, suggesting that children can show the characteristics of any stage at any age. This seems a promising development, and may well solve some of the more pressing problems. In the meantime, the fact that researchers continue to challenge and reformulate Piaget's theory, rather than to ignore it, speaks for itself.

Children's Causal Thinking

Fill a large plastic bowl with water, and assemble some everyday objects which will float, such as a cork, a toy boat, or a small piece of paper, as well as some which will not, such as a coin, a stone, or a nail. Ask a three year old to predict whether these different objects will float, and then tape-record your conversation as you test your predictions.

The dialogue between Jonathan and his father at the opening of this chapter gives some examples of how your questioning might probe the child's understanding of *causality*: of how one event can give rise to another in the physical world. Play back your recording, and look for the following features:

▶ 'Magical' thinking: does the child show evidence of associating his or her own actions (e.g. dropping the objects into the water) with the tendency to float?

▶ 'Phenomenalist' thinking: does the child show evidence of believing that the mere association of two events makes them causally related (e.g. 'the coin sinks because it is brown')?

▶ Anthropomorphism: does the child attribute human motives to the inanimate objects (e.g. 'the stone sinks because it is tired')?

Repeat the exercise with a five year old: how do the responses differ?

Conservation of Number

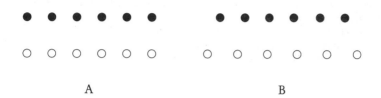

A   B

(1)   Set out one row of six black counters and one row of six white counters, as shown in A above, and ask the child 'Are there more black counters, more white counters, or the same number of each?' Record the child's answer by writing it down, or by tape recording it.

(2)   Spread out the white counters so that the display appears as in B, and repeat the question.

(3)   Replace the white counters in their original positions, so that the display appears as in A once more, and repeat the question.

Try this exercise with a five year old, a seven year old and a nine year old.

Do your results support Piaget's theory of number invariance?

Recommended reading

Boden, M. (1979) *Piaget*. Glasgow: Fontana. [A concise and sophisticated account.]

Donaldson, M., Grieve, R. & Pratt, C. (Eds) (1983) *Early Childhood Development and Education*. Oxford: Basil Blackwell. [A collection of readings of research, many of which deal with Piagetian topics.]

Ginsberg, H. & Opper, S. (1979) *Piaget's Theory of Intellectual Development: An introduction*. Englewood Cliffs, NJ: Prentice-Hall. [A popular textbook which includes applications to education.]

Piaget, J. & Inhelder, B. (1969) *The Psychology of the Child*. London: Routledge & Kegan Paul. [The authors' own attempt to present a brief, clear account of the whole scope of their work.]

References

Borke, H. (1975) Piaget's mountains revisited: Changes in the egocentric landscape. *Developmental Psychology*, *11*, 240–243. [Children display less 'egocentricity' on tasks which are familiar to them.]

Bower, T.G.R. (1982) *Development in Infancy*, 2nd edn. San Francisco: WH Freeman. [Includes Bower's own research on object permanence.]

Case, R. (1985) *Intellectual Development: Birth to adulthood*. Orlando, Florida: Academic Press. [A theory which combines Piagetian concepts with those from information processing approaches.]

Cox, M. (1986) *The Child's Point of View*. Brighton: Harvester. [Extensive review of the research literature on egocentricity, including details of Cox's own research.]

Donaldson, M. (1978) *Children's Minds*. London: Fontana [Donaldson's classic study of the effects of social influences on children's thinking.]

Fischer, K.W. (1980) A theory of cognitive development: The control and construction of hierarchies of skills. *Psychological Review*, *78*, 477–531. [Fischer's 'skill learning' theory.]

McGarrigle, J. & Donaldson, M. (1975) Conservation accidents. *Cognition*, *3*, 304–310. [The original 'naughty teddy bear' study.]

Piaget, J. (1951) *Play, Dreams and Imitation in Childhood*. London: Routledge & Kegan Paul. [Piaget's theory of play.]

8. *Intelligence and Experience*

What is intelligence? This is probably one of the most difficult and important questions in the whole of psychology. In a famous study in the *Journal of Educational Psychology* in 1921, 14 experts were asked to explain their understanding of the nature of intelligence – and they came up with 14 different views. These included:

❝ *the power of good responses from the point of view of truth or fact* **❞** *(Edward Thorndike)*

❝ *the ability to carry on abstract thinking* **❞** (Lewis Terman)

❝ *the capacity to acquire capacity* **❞** (Herbert Woodrow)

. . .and there were many more.

The reason for this apparent disagreement is that it is probably unrealistic to try to define intelligence in the abstract – to think of it as a kind of general property which people have to varying degrees, and which is then 'applied' to different activities. In everyday life, people are more intelligent in certain activities than in others. Those who are good with numbers and computers may be relatively poor at writing and spelling; others who are good at writing may be hopelessly impractical in carrying out jobs around the home, and so on.

In other words, we probably need to define a number of different 'intelligences' in these different areas of activity, rather than to think in terms of a single, unitary capacity. Unfortunately, the idea of the *intelligence quotient*, or IQ, still has a great deal of currency in the public mind as well as in psychology. The IQ is a single number, on a scale with an average of 100, which is supposed to summarize one's intellectual powers independently of the situation in which they are employed.

INTELLIGENCE AND THE IQ

One probable reason for the ascendancy of the IQ is that the early psychologists were eager to establish the scientific validity of the discipline. They wanted to follow the example of the natural sciences in quantifying and predicting human behaviour, and the establishment of scales of measurement seemed an important step. The subsequent study of intelligence has been dominated by the *psychometric* approach, which relies on tests and measurements. A large amount of research effort has been devoted to the development of a range of different IQ tests, and to their use as predictors of success or failure in different areas of life.

Many psychologists have lamented the fact that the psychometric approach has been so influential in the study of intelligence, and one of the main reasons has been their uncertainty as to the *validity* of IQ tests. The validity of a test is the extent to which it measures the property which it is supposed to measure – and this is usually assessed by comparing scores on the tests with some external *criterion* measure of that property. IQ tests have usually been validated by reference to measures of educational attainment, such as exam successes and grades – but then exam success itself involves the ability to perform well in activities like completing IQ tests! In other words, the definition of intelligence in terms of the abilities that are needed for scholastic success is a circular definition as well as a narrow one.

A number of current developments in thinking about intelligence are showing a movement away from the definition of intelligence solely in terms of IQ tests. For theorists like Howard Gardner and Robert Sternberg, for example, 'academic intelligence' is only one part of a much broader spectrum of abilities, as we shall see later. There have also been developments *within* the field of intelligence testing in recent years: creative, or divergent abilities are now commonly assessed alongside problem-solving, or convergent abilities, for example (see Chapter 9), and some of Piaget's experimental tasks have been adapted into psychometric tests (see Chapter 7).

TESTS OF INTELLIGENCE

One of the earliest and best-known tests was originally devised by Alfred Binet and Theodore Simon in 1905. This was designed to enable the French government to identify children who were failing to make progress within the school system. The tests involved comprehension and reasoning, word definition, and work with numbers. From this starting point, Binet and Simon went on to develop more general assessments of general intelligence, which they defined as 'judgement', and they formulated this in terms of the idea of *mental age*.

What is mental age?

Mental age was defined in terms of the child's ability to pass increasingly difficult sets of test items in relation to the typical performance of children of different ages; and IQ was later defined in terms of the ratio of mental age (MA) to chronological age (CA) (IQ = MA ÷ CA × 100). Thus if a four year old could not only pass the 'four years' test items but also the 'four and a half years' and 'five years' items, for example, he or she would be said to possess a mental age of five, and an IQ of $5 \div 4 \times 100 = 125$. This scaling by reference to *age norms*, and the adoption of an average or mean score of 100, has become a standard feature of many subsequent tests, but of course it only applies to children and adolescents. The concept of mental age is not applied to adults. Binet and Simon's tests were adapted by Lewis Terman at Stanford University, and have undergone several revisions over the course of the century. The Stanford-Binet test, as it is now known, is still widely used today.

Intelligence tests

The Stanford-Binet test, which is administered to children individually, is now just one of a vast number of IQ tests which are available. Amongst the other better-known individual tests are the *Wechsler Intelligence Scale for Children* (WISC), which is accompanied by the *Wechsler Adult Intelligence Scale* (WAIS), and the *British Ability Scales*, which were first published in 1979. Amongst the better-known *group* tests of intelligence in the UK are the *Moray House* and *NFER* tests, *Raven's Progressive Matrices*, and Alice Heim's *AH4*, *AH5* and *AH6* tests. In North America, the *Lorge-Thorndike* tests, the *Scholastic Aptitude Test* (SAT), and the *School and College Ability Tests* (SCAT) are widely used.

It is important to remember that these tests are intended to be measures of *ability* rather than of *attainment*; they are supposed to measure people's natural capabilities regardless of their learning or experience. Although they clearly differ from attainment tests such as school examinations, in practice the distinction is often blurred. Performance on IQ tests is inevitably influenced by learning and experience to a certain degree, and all the testers can do is to try and keep these outside influences to a minimum.

VARIATIONS IN INTELLIGENCE AND ATTAINMENT

In the UK, the psychometric view of intelligence has had a powerful influence on educational practice. Cyril Burt, one of the most influential figures in British educational psychology, firmly believed that intelligence was a fixed innate capacity which was only influenced to a small degree by education or training, and which could be measured objectively by IQ tests. As a result of this kind of thinking, it was widely believed that children should be separated into different groups with different educational needs, ranging from 'mental defective' (IQ below 70) through to 'scholarship pupils' (IQ above 130).

Selection and streaming

One of the clearest applications of this view was in the categorization of UK children at the age of 11 by the '11 plus' examination, which included tests of English, mathematics and intelligence. Those with the highest scores were selected as being suited to an academic education in the 'grammar schools'. Those with lower scores were allocated either to 'technical schools' or to what eventually became known as 'secondary modern schools'. Even within the schools, the children were streamed into ability groups: the higher or alpha streams as they were often called concentrated on academic courses, and the lower ones (beta, gamma, and so on) on more practical and technical subjects.

Educators gradually came to realize that selection could have extremely detrimental effects, particularly on high ability pupils from underprivileged backgrounds who were prevented from fulfilling their true potential. This eventually led to the abolition of the '11 plus' in most regions. The psychometric view of intelligence and ability has nevertheless had a powerful influence on educational thinking and the debate about equal opportunities, educational assessment and standards of attainment continues.

Educational attainment

The differences which occur between individual children on measures of intelligence and educational attainment are strongly related to the children's social background and ethnic origin. Studies in Great Britain and the USA have consistently found that children from lower social class groups achieve lower scores than those from middle-class backgrounds, and that children from ethnic minorities typically show lower levels of educational attainment than their white counterparts.

For example, the National Child Development Study in the UK followed up all children born in one week in 1958 throughout their school careers. Detailed information was collected about their educational progress, home background and psychological development at the ages of 7, 11 and 16 years. The data revealed a very close relationship between social class and educational attainment. On tests of arithmetic and reading, for example, the proportion of children with poor test scores was much higher in children from manual working-class homes than in those from non-manual, middle-class homes.

This kind of finding has frequently been explained in terms of the idea of educational disadvantage, or 'cultural deprivation'. Children from lower-class homes are more likely to live in families with a large number of children, and with a single parent, to have a low family income, and to live in poor housing. All these factors combine to restrict the cognitive and linguistic stimulation which children receive in the home and this, along with the lack of parental encouragement, gives rise to underachievement at schools, and poor performance in tests.

Along with this explanation came the view that 'cultural deprivation' could be remedied: that remedial education programmes could be provided which could compensate for the effects of a disadvantaged background. Now if this is the case, it implies that the IQ is 'malleable' – that although environmental circumstances may prevent a child from fulfilling its full potential, appropriate intervention ought to be able to reverse the effect. This is quite the opposite of Cyril Burt's view that IQ is relatively impervious to training or experience. The outcomes of the *compensatory education programmes* which were mounted in the USA ought to provide crucial tests of these conflicting points of view.

COMPENSATORY EDUCATION

Perhaps the best-known compensatory education programme was Project Head Start, which began in 1965. The idea was to give preschoolers from disadvantaged homes a 'head start' by providing them with educational experiences which were likely to be absent from their homes. In particular, attempts were made to remedy their cognitive and linguistic deficiencies. A variety of local Head Start programmes were instituted across the USA, and these varied quite widely in their content and duration, and in the age, socioeconomic and ethnic composition of the children.

Evaluating 'headstart' programmes

National evaluations of the effects of the project in 1969 and 1985 produced disappointing results. Although there was an average gain of 9–10 IQ points immediately after the training programmes had taken place, this gain had typically disappeared by the first year of schooling. Some psychologists, notably Arthur Jensen of the University of California, chose to interpret this as evidence that intelligence was not malleable; that the low ability of the children in the programme could not be compensated for by environmental enrichment. Others argued that the gains were only short term because the Head Start programmes did not provide enough enrichment; that they should have been more intensive, have started when the children were younger, and have involved parents as well as children.

The Milwaukee project

Another study which appeared to overcome these problems by providing a much more intensive intervention programme was the Milwaukee project, which was carried out by Rick Heber and his colleagues at the University of Wisconsin. Forty low social class black mothers with IQs below 75 and their newborn infants were assigned either to an 'experimental' or to a 'control' group.

Those in the experimental group received parental education as well as a children's programme. The mothers were given job placement training as well as parenting workshops to improve their child-rearing and home-keeping skills. The children received an intensive daycare programme, five days a week, which began when they were only three months old. This emphasized language, reading, mathematics and problem-solving skills, as well as social and emotional support. The children and their families were encouraged to form warm relationships with the teachers, and home visits were arranged.

The control group received no intervention, but were assessed on different measures of IQ, learning, language, problem solving, and personality and social development at the same intervals as the experimental group. The results showed that the IQ scores of the two groups were roughly equivalent for the first 18 months or so, but that they then began to diverge. By the age of five and a half years, the children in the experimental group had a mean IQ of 124, whereas those in the control group averaged 94 – a difference of some 30 points. This difference decreased somewhat as the two groups entered regular schooling, but it remained at around 20 points throughout the school years.

Miracle or mystery?

This appears to be a dramatic demonstration of the power of intensive early intervention, and it contradicts the disappointing Head Start results. Unfortunately, some doubt surrounds the Milwaukee project since its results have seldom been published in refereed journals. Charles Locurto refers to the project as the 'mystery in Milwaukee' for this reason: he also calls it the 'miracle in Milwaukee', since its dramatic results have not been replicated in any comparable studies. The Abecedarian project at the University of North Carolina, for example, failed to replicate the Milwaukee project even though its intervention programme was roughly equivalent in duration and intensity.

A radical interpretation of these generally disappointing findings is that the 'deficit' or 'cultural deprivation' model on which the intervention programmes are based might be inappropriate. An alternative view, the 'difference' model, is that because schools and educational institutions tend to be permeated with white, middle-class values and attitudes, children from different backgrounds may simply fail to adapt to this. The black working-class children in these studies may not be 'deprived' in relation to their white middle-class counterparts; they may simply be 'different', and it may be at best patronizing, and at worst racist, to assume the former. If this is true, there is no reason why compensatory programmes *should* produce any increase in IQ scores.

INSTITUTIONS AND ADOPTION

More convincing evidence for the benefits of environmental enrichment comes from studies of adoption. Children who are brought up in large, impersonal institutions such as orphanages are typically adopted by parents who are generally from the higher socioeconomic status groups. Their superior housing and income means that they can provide a much richer cognitive and social environment than is possible in an institution.

One well-known long-term study was carried out by Harold Skeels. In the 1930s, Skeels had noticed that two orphanage babies who were regarded as 'mentally retarded' had shown considerable improvements, both cognitively and socially, when they had been transferred into a women's ward in an institution for the mentally retarded. The two babies had been affectionately 'mothered' by staff and patients, and they received a great deal more attention and stimulation than they would have done in the orphanage.

Marie Skodak and Harold Skeels then carried out a more systematic study of two groups of children. One group of 13 infants was transferred to a ward for 'mentally retarded' older children at an average age of 19 months, and a 'comparison group' of 12 children remained in the orphanage. After about one and a half years, the average IQ of the transferred group had increased from 64 to 92, whereas that of the comparison group had actually decreased from 87 to 61. In a follow-up some two and a half years later, Skeels found that 11 of the transferred children had been adopted by families, and their IQ levels now averaged 101. The unfortunate children in the comparison group who remained in the orphanage had a mean IQ of 66 at this point, and were therefore classified as 'retarded'.

A follow-up study Some 20 years later, when the 'children' were 25–35 years old, Skeels carried out another follow-up. Of the 12 members of the comparison (orphanage) group one had died in adolescence, four were still under state care, and the rest were either in unskilled occupations, or unemployed. In contrast, all of the transferred group were self-supporting. They had a much higher level of educational and occupational achievement, and income; in fact, Skeels considered the progress of the 11 adopted members of the group to be 'equivalent to what might be expected of children living with natural parents in homes of comparable sociocultural levels'.

Skeels' study is a powerful demonstration that the effects of a deprived early environment can be reversed, and other studies of adoption have come to similar, if not quite so dramatic, conclusions. Charles Locurto's review of the major studies suggests that the IQs of adopted children, assessed at the age of seven to ten years, average 106; that the average for adoptive parents is 116; and that the average for the biological children of those parents is 114. If we take 100 as the presumed average for the biological mothers of the adopted children, this means that adoption produced an average gain of 6–7 IQ points. This evidence for the malleability of IQ is much more convincing than that from the compensatory education programmes.

LANGUAGE AND SOCIAL CLASS

One recurring theme in studies of the effects of disadvantage is that the quality of children's language is probably a crucial factor; that the linguistic stimulation which children receive in the home is a vital foundation for other aspects of cognitive and social development, and that it may be lacking in some institutions and in lower social class groups.

Language codes

Basil Bernstein developed a well-known theory which attempted to explain the relationship between language and social class. He proposed that structures such as social class groupings give rise to particular social situations and relationships, and that these in turn produce distinctive speech systems or 'language codes'. The head waitress's patter whilst she is serving you at the table may be very different from the speech style she adopts just a few minutes later when she is in the kitchen giving orders to the chef. Another similar example comes from John Cleese's memorable character Basil Fawlty, from the well-known TV series *Fawlty Towers*, who also hilariously illustrates these different language codes. Different social situations elicit different sentence structures and word selections, and these selections define the nature of the relationship between the speakers.

Bernstein proposed that two distinct 'language codes' were typically adopted by speakers from middle and working-class backgrounds. Consider the following two stories, which were collected from five year olds as part of Bernstein's research work, and which describe a series of four pictures which tell a story. In the first picture some boys are seen playing football; in the second the ball goes through the window of a house; in the third a man is seen making a threatening gesture; and in the fourth the children are seen moving away. The first story is told by a middle-class child:

" *Three boys are playing football and one boy kicks the ball and it goes through the window   the ball breaks the window   and the boys are looking at it and a man comes out and shouts at them   because they've broken the window   so they run away   and then that lady looks out of her window   and she tells the boys off.* **"**

The second is by a working-class child:

❝ *They're playing football   and he kicks it and it goes through there   it breaks the window and they're looking at it   and he comes out   and shouts at them   because they've broken it   so they run away   and then she looks out and tells them off.* **❞**

It is easy to see that the first story is much more informative: we can gain a fairly good idea of the content of the pictures without seeing them because the story has *explicit* meaning: it is free of the context in which it was originally produced. This is not true of the second, however, in which the meaning is implicit: it makes little sense in the absence of the pictures themselves.

The 'elaborated' and the 'restricted' code

Bernstein described the first as an example of an *elaborated* language code, and the second as illustrating a *restricted* code. In comparison to the elaborated code, speech in the restricted code tends to have shorter sentences; to be grammatically more simple; to contain more unfinished sentences; to contain fewer adjectives and adverbs; and to use repeated conjunctions (the second story is strung together by a series of 'ands'). It is also much more likely to contain redundant phrases like 'you know', 'and that', or 'know what I mean?'.

Bernstein proposed that despite a common potential to use either code, middle-class speakers were much more likely to use the elaborated code. Most working-class children could only use the restricted code, and this led to a lower level of conceptualization and learning. Furthermore, this difference had effects on other aspects of psychological development. In matters of discipline and moral judgement, for example, elaborated code users are more likely to use reasoning than coercion. Whereas a middle-class mother might explain to her child why it is wrong to take another child's toy, for example, and to ask the child to return the toy herself, the working-class mother would be more likely to say that the toy should be returned 'because I say so'. Reasoning emphasizes moral thinking · which centres on the self – taking responsibility for one's own actions – whereas coercion is based on the demands of an external authority figure.

Bernstein's original theory received a good deal of criticism, and his later writings have modified it in certain respects. It has been suggested that the distinction between 'working-class' and 'middle-class' groups is oversimplified, and that it is dangerous to assume lower levels of *competence* from a restricted code speech *performance*. Perhaps the most serious criticism has been that the view of working-class speech and culture as in some way 'restricted' is at best patronizing, and at worst quite wrong. Working-class speakers may well use elaborated codes when discussing topics which are of particular interest to them, but these topics are not usually those which are valued in the predominantly middle-class education system. In other words, more attention should be paid to the *context* in which speech occurs.

Deficient or just different?

This returns us to the conflict between 'deficit' and 'difference' theories of disadvantage, which we discussed earlier. Working-class speakers may simply be different from middle-class speakers rather than in any way inferior. This point was made very graphically by William Labov, in his studies of the speech of underprivileged black children from the ghetto area of Harlem, New York.

Labov compared the structure of Black English vernacular (BEV), the language of the ghetto, with standard English (some examples are shown in *Table 8.1*). His analyses show that the vernacular form, with its double negatives and non-standard constructions ('he don't know nothin', 'don't nobody know that') is just as expressive, economical and organized as standard English when considered in terms of its own ground rules. Children who would appear uncooperative, monosyllabic and tongue-tied when questioned in the regular school environment became fluent, expressive and indeed witty when talking to a non-threatening interviewer, in an informal setting, about topics which particularly interested them. In this sphere at least, the 'difference' model seems to be much more appropriate than one of 'cultural deficit'.

'HOTHOUSE' CHILDREN

Until now we have discussed attempts to use environmental stimulation to improve the lot of children who, for different reasons, are well below the norm. But suppose one gives equivalent stimulation to children who start from that norm, or indeed from above it; can this produce exceptional levels of achievement? There is a great deal of interest in the notion of 'hothousing' children, which came to public notice as a result of the book *Hothouse People* by Jane Walmsley and Jonathan Margolis. Youngsters whose parents had given them intensive education in basic skills at an early age were shown to display precocious abilities that would normally be quite exceptional, and the impression was created that any child could acquire these talents, given similar experiences.

TABLE 8.1: *Labov's studies of Black English Vernacular*

William Labov found that black children from the urban ghettos of the United States typically appeared monosyllabic and tongue-tied in standard interview or test situations. When the setting was informal and the interviewer non-threatening, however, their language was anything but 'restricted' or 'deprived'. Here is a brief excerpt from an interview between 15-year-old Larry, one of the loudest and roughest members of a New York gang called the Jets, and the interviewer John Lewis:

JL: *... but, just say that there is a God, what color is he? White or black?*

Larry: *Well, if it is a God ... I wouldn' know what color. I couldn' say – couldn' nobody say what color he is or really would be.*

JL: *But now, jus' suppose there was a God –*

Larry: *Unless'n they say ...*

JL: *No, I was jus' sayin' jus' suppose there is a God, would he be white or black?*

Larry: *... He'd be white, man.*

JL: *Why?*

Larry: *Why? I'll tell you why. 'Cause the average whitey out here got everything, you dig? And the nigger ain't got shit, y'know? Y'unnerstan? So – um – in order for that to happen, you know it ain't no black God that's doin' that bullshit.*

Although Larry's responses are non-standard and unconventional, there can be little doubt that his is a clear, complex and indeed witty response to a difficult and abstract question. Labov claims that utterances in BEV should be evaluated in terms of their own internal rules rather than in terms of those of standard English, and his work has been devoted to the identification of those rules.

Can any child become a genius?

There are two distinct views that could be taken about these achievements, which represent both sides of the perennial *nature–nurture* debate. The first, represented by the more exaggerated of the 'hothouse' claims, is that IQ and other abilities are malleable to such an extent, especially at very early ages, that prodigious achievement can be cultivated – that any child can learn to become a genius! The second view is that genius is somehow inherent – that people are 'born with it', and that training can therefore only help up to a certain point.

    Which of these two views is correct? The answer is that both are – but only up to a point. Research evidence leaves little doubt that those babies whose parents invest considerable amounts of time, patience and care to the early acquisition of their basic skills will show accelerated development, and that the benefits can be long-lasting; but this is far from saying that all children can become exceptionally talented.

Michael Howe has pointed out that the second viewpoint is much more common – that it is widely believed that exceptional achievers are somehow *inherently* gifted. But this view is not wholly true either, and Howe suggests that there are several common misconceptions about such people. It is often thought that their creative activity takes place without conscious effort; that they can take short cuts, bypassing the learning of difficult skills; and that their genius is all the more apparent because they usually come from unexceptional, ordinary home backgrounds. None of these turn out to be true! Howe provides plenty of evidence that masterpieces are *not* created without conscious effort and hard work; that eminent creators always master their craft through extensive training before going on to innovate; and that they typically come from a home background which provides enriched opportunities for early development.

To summarize, exceptional achievement in a given field of endeavour requires inherent talents as well as a stimulating environment. Unfortunately, 'hothouse babies' cannot all be geniuses. The effects of intensive early education can nevertheless be very impressive, and Howe concludes that: 'the babies of parents who make conscientious efforts to promote the early acquisition of basic skills will show accelerated development. Moreover, providing that the parental support and encouragement is not abruptly terminated after early childhood, the effects of accelerated development will be cumulative and long-lasting'.

ALTERNATIVES TO THE IQ

As we have seen throughout this chapter, a tremendous burden of evidence has been placed on the IQ – it is used as the single most important index of the effects of many different kinds of experiences on human development. Yet virtually all psychologists would agree that IQ scores possess many limitations, and should only be used with caution, and in conjunction with other information about the testees.

One of the most serious objections is that the IQ is based entirely on academic abilities – and that these are only part of the full spectrum of abilities which constitute intelligence as a whole. In his book *Frames of Mind*, Howard Gardner has put forward what he calls a theory of 'multiple intelligences'. According to this, there are seven basic 'intelligences': musical, bodily-kinaesthetic, logical-mathematical, linguistic, spatial, interpersonal, and intrapersonal. An intelligence, according to this view, is a set of abilities which enable a person to solve problems, fashion products, or create problems within real or genuine cultural settings.

Assessment in context

The implication of this view is that the assessment of these intelligences must be carried out 'in context', that it should take place as a natural part of the child's learning environment, rather than as an external imposition. Assessments can then be carried out which are more directly tailored to the child's particular strengths and weaknesses, which is clearly not possible with standardized testing. Gardner is developing these techniques in *Project Spectrum*, which covers the preschool curriculum, and in *Arts Propel*, which deals with arts assessment at secondary level, and a similar approach is being followed in the DELTA project at the University of Leicester.

The same line of argument is taken even further by Robert Sternberg: rather than stopping at seven 'intelligences', he effectively argues for as many as are necessary to describe the full range of intelligent activities. Sternberg's book *Practical Intelligence* is based on the idea that 'intelligent behaviour' is displayed in everyday life – at home and at work – and not just in academic testing situations. His book draws on studies of the practical thinking which is carried out by milk processing workers, bartenders, waitresses, sales engineers, managers, and business executives, amongst others, and these are carried out using naturalistic methods as well as conventional psychometric techniques.

As these developments continue, the IQ will increasingly be seen as a useful but fairly limited part of a much broader range of human abilities. Our opening question 'what is intelligence?' will never be answered, though we may get further with 'what are intelligences?'. There will be many different answers to the second question, and they will come from well beyond the bounds of psychometrics.

Recommended reading

Anastasi, A. (1990) *Psychological Testing*, 6th edn. New York: Macmillan. [A standard and widely-used guide to the field.]

Kail, R. & Pellegrino, J.W. (1985) *Human Intelligence: Perspectives and prospects*. New York: Freeman. [Includes Piagetian and information-processing approaches as well as psychometric ones.]

Sternberg, R. (1985) *Beyond IQ: A triarchic theory of human intelligence*. Cambridge:

Raven's Progressive Matrices

This well-known nonverbal intelligence test was originally produced in 1936, and has been revised several times since then. Test participants (who may be of any age above six years or so) are shown patterns 'with bits taken out', and are asked to identify which of a set of alternatives is the missing bit. Can you solve the two items below? Also try them out with one or two children.

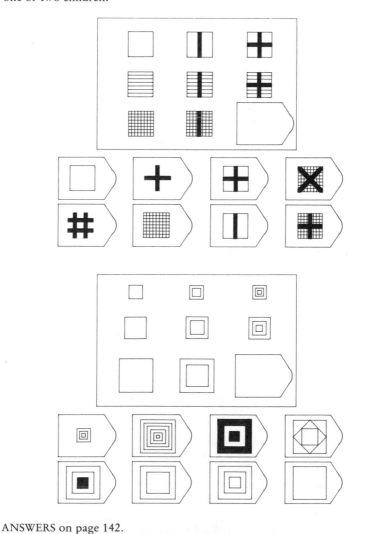

ANSWERS on page 142.

Cambridge University Press. [Sternberg's information-processing theory of intelligence.]

Sternberg, R. & Davidson, J. (1986) (Eds) *Conceptions of Giftedness*. Cambridge: Cambridge University Press. [A collection of papers which looks at different aspects of giftedness in education, in psychology, and in fields of endeavour including mathematics and music.]

References

Bernstein, B. (1971, 1973, 1975) *Class, Codes and Control*, Vols. 1, 2 and 3. London: Routledge & Kegan Paul. [Bernstein's original theory of language codes.]

Binet, A. & Simon, T. (1905) New methods for diagnosis of the intellectual level of subnormals. *L'Année Psychologique*, *14*, 1–90. [One of the earliest tests of intelligence.]

Gardner, H. (1983) *Frames of Mind*. London: Paladin. [Gardner's theory of multiple intelligences.]

Head Start Bureau (1985) *Final Report: The impact of Head Start on children, families and communities*. Washington, DC: US Government Printing Office. [Head Start programmes.]

Heber, R., Garber, H., Harrington, S., Hoffman, C. & Falender, C. (1972) *Rehabilitation of Families at Risk for Mental Retardation: Progress Report, December 1972*. University of Wisconsin: Rehabilitation Research and Training Center in Mental Retardation. [Report on the Milwaukee Project.]

Howe, M.J.A. (1988) "Hot house" children.*The Psychologist*, *1*, 356–358. [A clear-headed look at some of the claims which have been made.]

Jensen, A.R. (1969) How much can we boost IQ and scholastic achievement? *Harvard Educational Review*, *39*, 449–483. [The article which sparked off heated controversy on race and intelligence.]

Labov, W. (1969) The logic of non-standard English. Reprinted in abridged form in P.H. Mussen, J.J. Conger & J. Kagan (Eds) (1975) *Basic and Contemporary Issues in Developmental Psychology*. New York: Harper & Row. [Describes Labov's analyses of Black English Vernacular.]

Locurto, C. (1988) On the malleability of IQ. *The Psychologist*, *1*, 431–435. [Review of environmental influences on IQ.]

Ramey, C.T. & Campbell, F.A. (1984) Preventive education for high-risk children: Cognitive consequences of the Carolina Abecedarian project. *American Journal of Mental Deficiency*, *88*, 515–523. [A failure to replicate the Milwaukee project.]

Skeels, H. (1966) Adult status of children with contrasting early life experiences: A follow-up study. *Monographs of the Society for Research in Child Development*, *31*, No. 3. [Skeels' final follow-up of his original sample.]

Skodac, M. & Skeels, H. (1949) A final follow-up study of one hundred adopted children. *Journal of Genetic Psychology*, *75*, 85–125.

Sternberg, R. & Wagner, R.K. (1986) (Eds) *Practical Intelligence*. Cambridge: Cambridge University Press. [Studies of intelligence as manifested in everyday life.]

Thorndike, E.L. *et al.* (1921) Intelligence and its measurement. *Journal of Educational Psychology*, *12*, 123f. [A report of the famous 1921 symposium on defining intelligence.]

Walmsley J. & Margolis, J. (1987) *Hot House People: Can we create super human beings?* London: Pan Books. [An optimistic look at the future possibilities of 'hot housing'.]

Wedge, P. & Essen, J. (1982) *Children in Adversity*. London: Pan. [The consequences of living in deprived conditions].

───────────── ANSWERS TO EXERCISE 8.1 ─────────────

The correct answers are 8 and 7.

9. Creativity and Artistic Development

▽ *Developing creativity in children and adults*
▽ *Developing aesthetic appreciation*
▽ *Children's drawing*
▽ *Drawings of music*
▽ *Children's singing*
▽ *Children as storytellers*

From the earliest years we see children creating their own drawings and paintings, acting out their own episodes in make-believe play, inventing their own songs and dance routines, and modelling in clay and playdough. All children take part in the arts – indeed the open-ended, expressive character of many arts activities, with no obvious right or wrong solutions to a problem, make them uniquely available to children of all ages.

Surprisingly perhaps, children's development in the arts has been sadly neglected in comparison to what we might call their scientific development. This neglect has occurred both in psychology and in educational practice. The study of children's thinking, perhaps as a result of the strong influence of Piaget's theory, has been dominated by investigations of their capacity to solve problems, and to display logical reasoning. In today's hard-pressed schools, the arts are frequently regarded as 'frills' which are the first to suffer whenever financial cuts are to be made; mathematics, science, and reading are generally seen as the core of the curriculum.

Changing attitudes to the arts?

In developmental psychology there is an upsurge of interest and research in what we might call *artistic development*. Howard Gardner, one of the most prominent psychologists working in this field, has proposed that children develop three 'systems' in relation to the arts, and this turns out to be a useful way of thinking about the whole topic.

- The *making* system deals with production: children invent their own art works, and they may also perform these works.
- The *perceiving* system deals with children's distinctions and discriminations between different art works: they gradually learn to take on the role of the critic.
- The *feeling* system is concerned with the emotional side of the response to art: children gradually develop the response of the audience member.

These three systems do not exist in isolation from one another: rather, they become increasingly interlinked as children grow older.

DEVELOPING CREATIVITY IN CHILDREN

One way of trying to assess children's creativity has been by means of so-called 'creativity tests', or tests of *ideational fluency*. One well-known example is the *Uses for Objects* test, in which children are asked to think of as many unusual uses as they can for everyday objects, such as a brick or a cardboard box (see *Table 9.1*). Another is the *Circles* test, in which they are asked to fill sheets of empty circles with as many different kinds of drawing as they can think of. The responses to these open-ended test items are scored for fluency (how many different ideas are thought of), for flexibility (how many different *types* of idea are thought of), for originality (how unusual or infrequent the ideas are), and for elaboration (how much detail appears in the responses).

Ups and downs in creative thinking

Paul Torrance gave his own well-known *Minnesota Tests of Creative Thinking* to large numbers of preschool and school-age children, as well as to groups of adults. As expected, there was an overall increase in scores from the youngest to the oldest groups: but this *age curve* included some interesting and unexpected ups and downs. Torrance found that a steady increase between the ages of 5 and 8 years was followed by a sudden dip at the age of 9 years. This has been confirmed by other researchers, and has become popularly known as the 'fourth grade slump'. Torrance found that scores then recovered at the ages of 10 and 11 years, dipped once again at the age of 12, and then carried on rising steadily throughout adolescence.

Why should there be 'dips' in creative thinking scores at the ages of 9 and 12 years? Torrance's explanation is that these are important

TABLE 9.1:   *The 'Uses for Objects' test*

Below are two everyday objects. Think of as many uses as you can for each, and write them in the answer space.

(1)   A brick

Build a building, Make a bicycle ramp, Hold a shelf up, throw it through a window, Hold something with wheels so it doesn't roll off, Make a sculpture with it, use it as a wedge, Use it to hold something down, use it to stand on and make you taller, use it to crush something and use it to hold something up.

(2)   A cardboard box

use it to hold something, use it to make a sculpture, use it to hide in, make it into something, use it to make a den with, use it to put something on, use it to hold something up, use it to carry shopping in and use it as a table.

transition points in the American education system. The age of 9 marks the change from primary to intermediate grades, and the age of 12 from elementary to high school. These transitional periods are times of stress, because children are forced to abandon their old routines and attitudes, and to adapt to new competitive pressures. The result is a temporary decline in creativity scores, which may also be accompanied by a lowering of motivation to succeed in school activities as a whole.

An acid test of this explanaton would be to see whether or not the same 'dips' occurred in children in an education system with different school transition points. One of the authors did in fact find some evidence of something like a 'fourth grade slump' in a comparable study of 199 British schoolchildren, even though the pressure of competition and assessment was much less marked in the UK than in North America in 1982, when the study was carried out. We need further evidence before we can draw any conclusions about the generality of these age changes.

DEVELOPING CREATIVITY IN ADULTS

If we carry on the age curve for creative productivity into adulthood, there is general agreement that it carries on rising up to the age of 40 or so, then begins to decline, and that this decline accelerates rapidly in old age. Most of the evidence for this pattern comes from two historical studies of well-known creators, in different fields of endeavour, over the course of their life span.

Measuring outstanding creativity

Harvey Lehman's study assessed the number of outstanding pieces of work produced by eminent individuals in science, philosophy, music, art and literature over successive five-year intervals. He found that they were generally most productive in their twenties and thirties, with a decline after that age. Wayne Dennis' study found a similar pattern, with a slightly later general 'peak' of achievement. He also found that the shape of the age curve varied from discipline to discipline. Creative individuals in the arts (composers, poets, and architects), and those in the sciences (biologists, chemists and mathematicians), were at their peak in their forties; those in the fields of history and philosophy did not decline in productivity even in their fifties and sixties.

It seems quite likely that these differences arise from the kinds of creative ability which are demanded in each field. Success in mathematics, music as well as in the game of chess can be achieved by the mastery of a relatively abstract, impersonal set of rules, and this can be achieved at an early age. This probably explains why child prodigies tend to be found in these fields, and not in others. Success in history or philosophy requires a lifetime of experience in human affairs, and prodigies do not occur in these disciplines.

But let us not be too gloomy about the prospects of our continuing to be creative and productive in old age. The decline in the later part of the curve is based on people's creative *output* rather than necessarily on their *ability*. The fact that people generally tend to produce less creative work in their later years does not necessarily mean that their ability to do so is impaired.

The decline may occur for many other reasons, such as physical frailties, or a decline in the motivation to maintain a high work output. There are numerous examples of great creators who carried on working well into old age, such as Elizabeth Lutyens, Pablo Picasso, and Iris Murdoch, as well as of 'late starters' who did not begin their creative careers until relatively late in life. The composers Alexander Borodin, Modeste Mussorgsky, and Emmanuel Chabrier had careers in chemistry, in the army, and in the civil service before devoting themselves to music! Amongst creative women, such as the writer Elizabeth Gaskell, domestic concerns and having a family often preceded the start of their artistic careers.

DEVELOPING AESTHETIC APPRECIATION

Howard Gardner and colleagues carried out a study in which 121 4–16 year olds were shown a picture, read a poem, or played some music, and then interviewed about different aspects of their responses. They were quizzed about the means of production of the work, about its style, about its formal properties, and so on. Analysis of the interview transcriptions revealed that there were three broad types of response, which increased in sophistication as the children got older.

The youngest children gave *immature* responses: between the ages of approximately four and seven, their main concern was with the concrete details of how the piece of work was produced, and with the techniques involved. The older children in the group (14–16 years old), in contrast, gave *mature* responses: these showed an understanding of the problems involved in producing art works, of the differences between different art forms, and of the concept of artistic style. In between these two were *transitional* responses, roughly between the ages of eight and 12 years, which contained some of the features of both mature and immature responses. One

FIGURE 9.1a

FIGURE 9.1b

of the most striking was an emphasis on *realism*: children at this age were particularly concerned about whether or not a piece of art was representative of real life.

This general pattern of development crops up frequently in the growing body of research on sensitivity to style in visual art, music and literature which has been carried out by the Project Zero research group at Harvard University, under the co-direction of Howard Gardner. Younger children tend to concentrate on the degree of realism in the subject matter of art works, and a true appreciation of their stylistic properties only emerges in adolescence.

CHILDREN'S DRAWING

Many psychologists have studied children's drawing over the course of this century, including Rhoda Kellogg, Helga Eng, and Florence Goodenough, and one of the main concerns of these early researchers was to describe how drawings change consistently with age – with establishing *norms* of development. Various accounts of the development of drawing were proposed, and these can be summarized in terms of four broad stages.

Scribbling

The first of these is the *scribbling* stage, which is self-explanatory: in the early years, children gain immense pleasure simply from making marks on the paper. These scribbles are initially disorganized and uncontrolled, and they gradually get more and more organized. This can be seen in the change between the scribbles shown in *Figure 9.1a* and *9.1b*. Children only gradually start to name their scribbles as being drawings of recognizable objects or people during this stage – and it is quite possible that the scribble will change its name several times as it progresses!

Intellectual realism

Preschematic drawings develop next, between the ages of four and seven years or so, and their main feature is what has been called 'intellectual realism'. What this rather cumbersome term means is that children draw 'what they know rather than what they see'. A man's arms may be drawn through his shirt sleeves because the child *knows* they are there rather than because they can necessarily be seen – this is called a 'transparency'. Norman Freeman and Rosemary Janikoun produced a neat experimental demonstration of this effect

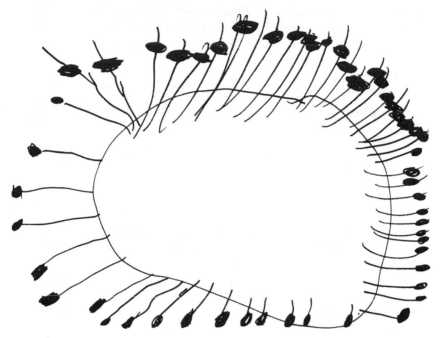

FIGURE 9.2a

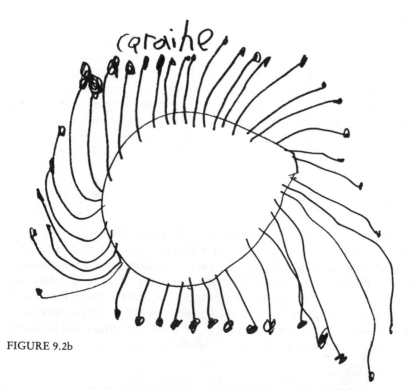

FIGURE 9.2b

when they asked children of different ages to draw exactly what they saw of a mug whose handle was facing away, so that it wasn't actually visible. Younger children tended to draw in the handle even though they couldn't see it, and this tendency declined with age.

Another feature of intellectual realism is 'turning over', which is illustrated in *Figure 9.2*: children of different ages were asked to draw a pond with trees around it. *Figure 9.2a* shows a typically 'turned over' drawing: the trees are splayed out at right angles to the pond all the way round. *Figure 9.2b* is a fascinating intermediate case which shows some realization that trees don't grow downwards – those on the left and right edges of the pond start to branch out horizontally, following the 'perpendicular' rule, but are then 'bent' upwards vertically. In *Figure 9.2c* the child organizes the drawing by creating a baseline which enables all the trees to 'grow upwards'. The drawing is still not fully realistic, however, since the pond is drawn as a circle 'from above' whereas the trees are drawn from a horizontal perspective.

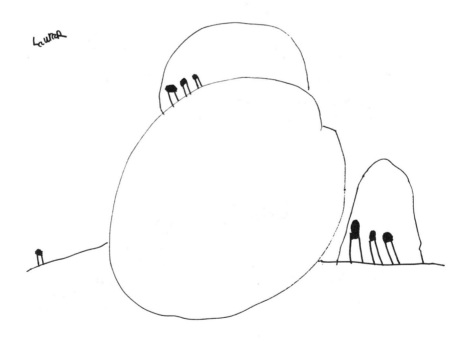

FIGURE 9.2c

Schematic drawings

Figure 9.2c takes us into the next stage, exemplifying what might be called *schematic* drawings. These are spatially organized according to baselines, skylines, or other reference markings, but they are still not visually realistic. In *Figure 9.2c* this is because the drawing incorporates two incompatible perspectives. In *Figure 9.3*, which illustrates what might be called the 'air gap effect', it is because of the problems created by splitting up the drawing into sky, ground, and air. If you ask children to look out of the window and show them that the sky 'comes down to the ground', they will readily

FIGURE 9.3: *Child's drawing showing the 'air gap effect'*

agree – yet they consistently produce 'air gap' drawings up to the age of ten or so. They seem to devise their own rules, or production strategies, in order to deal with the planning problems involved in producing a given drawing.

In *Figure 9.3* there is a fascinating glimpse of one particular strategy that the child has adopted. Many children draw stereotyped houses with a window in each corner, a door in the middle, a chimney on top – and these often have a path leading down the garden. In this case, the child has somehow contrived to put the bottom of the path, rather than of the house, on to the baseline – with unexpected Jacob's ladder-type results!

Visual realism

The fourth and final stage is the production of drawings which display *visual realism*. Children can by this stage draw objects as they actually look from any angle, and can start to tackle the problems of representing three-dimensional objects on a two-dimensional surface in a realistic manner. We should bear clearly in mind that realistic representation drawing is by no means the only 'end state' of drawing, of course: many abstract and expressionist artists use quite different criteria.

DRAWINGS OF MUSIC

Children create music, perform music, and perceive music: but how do they *represent* music? One fascinating line of research has investigated how young children, who may have no knowledge of musical notation, actually go about writing down short rhythms or familiar songs. This work is important because it brings together the study of children's thinking within two art forms simultaneously, and is able to cast light on both.

Representing rhythm

Some pioneering research was carried out by Jeanne Bamberger, working in conjunction with Harvard Project Zero. Bamberger carried out a series of studies which enabled her to work out a typology, or classification, of the strategies used by children of different ages in their drawings of rhythmic sequences. Bamberger asked groups of participants ranging from four year olds to adults to clap different rhythms (some of which they had invented themselves) until she was confident that each listener had a reasonable grasp of them. They were then asked to 'put down on paper whatever you think will help you to remember the rhythm tomorrow or help someone else to play it who isn't here today'.

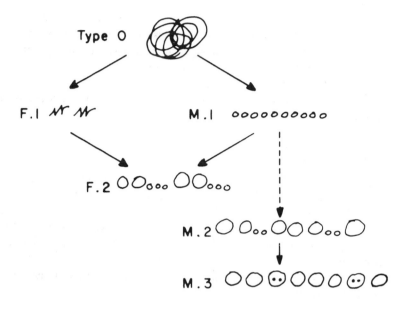

CLASS PIECE:

SOUNDS LIKE:

Three, four shut the door; five, six pick up sticks

FIGURE 9.4: *Bamberger's classification of children's drawings of rhythmic patterns*

These drawings formed the basis of Bamberger's typology, in which the main distinction is between *figural* and *metric* drawing strategies. Figural strategies are concerned with the overall shape, or figure, of the sequence, with its broad outline rather than its details. Metric strategies, on the other hand, are concerned with the details – with the metrics of what goes on within the broad outline shapes. Bamberger also proposed that there are three broad developmental levels (1, 2 and 3) on which figural and metric strategies can exist, so that there ought to be six basic types of drawing altogether, which she called F1, F2, F3, M1, M2, and M3.

In practice, it turned out that the youngest children produced drawings which could not properly be described as any of these types, and these were labelled type O. Also, the designation F3 did not turn out to be useful. *Figure 9.4* shows a typical example of each of the categories that finally were used. These are all drawings of a sequence called the 'class piece'. The conventional notation of this is also shown in the figure; it is something like the second and third lines of the nursery rhyme 'One, two, buckle my shoe'.

Rhythmic scribbles

Type O is an example of what Bamberger refers to as *rhythmic scribbles*: the child 'plays' the rhythm with the pencil on the paper, but the drawing itself gives no clue that there were a distinct number of separate claps. In type F1, however, the correct number is represented, by the up and down stokes of the two zig-zags, and the resulting drawing is figural because it clearly shows that the sequence had two distinct halves. As yet, however, there is no indication of the timing of the claps. The same is true in the M1 example: here we can see that the child has made what Bamberger calls a 'count-up' of the correct number of claps, but there is still no information about the timing, nor about the two-part 'shape' of the sequence.

The arrows on the figure show that F1 and M1 drawings gradually merge, with age, into F2 drawings. Here we can see that the child has indicated the relative timings of the claps by drawing large and small circles for slow and fast events respectively, and that the two-part shape of the sequence is shown. The drawing is still not accurate, however, because claps 5 and 10 appear as small circles when they should have been large ones. Bamberger's explanation of this is that the child perceives claps 5 and 10 as the 'end points' of groups 3–4–5 and 8–9–10 respectively. Because he or she thinks of them as integral parts of these groups, they are mistakenly drawn in the same way.

This error is overcome in type M2 drawings, where claps 5 and 10 are correctly shown as large circles: M2 is more advanced than F2. Finally, in M3 drawings, the underlying beat is shown by means of the large circles, and each clap is drawn in relation to this 'reference metric'. Bamberger found that most of the six to seven year olds in her studies produced either F1, M1, or F2 drawings, and that her 11 to 12 year olds tended to produce either F2 or M2 drawings. Hardly any of the children produced M3 drawings, and this is also likely to be true of adults without any musical training. You can investigate this yourself in *Exercise 9.1* on page 164.

Bamberger's typology is best regarded as a starting point for further research – there will be many exceptions to it, and situations in which it does not apply. But we have looked at it in some detail because it may have educational implications which go well beyond the drawing of rhythms. She draws the distinction between *formal* and *intuitive* understandings of music. Formal understanding is what many of us have gained through our musical education – we have learnt about time and key signatures, about note lengths and rests, and about expressive markings – there is a strong emphasis on formal musical notation. Intuitive musical understanding, on the other hand, is the unschooled 'natural' response which cannot be formally taught, and which is likely to be primarily aural rather than written.

Bamberger suggests that metric drawings, which approximate to the conventional way in which music is written on staves, reflect the child's formal musical understanding. Many music teachers would probably consider that they convey a higher level of musical under-standing than do figural drawings, which are more personal, subjective and indeed intuitive. She feels that this is very unfortunate because figural notations can actually convey some aspects of a piece, such as its phrasing and 'feel', in a way that metric ones cannot.

Does music education stifle musical creativity?

Bamberger argues further that the insistence on formal skills and understanding in traditional music education actually stifles musical feeling and creativity. As the children in her studies became more and more expert at reading and writing staff notation, so they apparently became less able to feel the 'musical sense' of the rhythms – she calls this the 'wipe-out' effect. In other words, some forms of traditional music education may actually be 'wiping out' pupils' natural feeling for music.

In the UK at least, this picture is changing rapidly. The recommen-dations for music in the National Curriculum now acknowledge that different skills, and thus assessment criteria, are required in different forms of music. Metric-type notation is indeed indispensable in Western 'classical' music, but it is much less important for the teaching and assessment of jazz and rock music, for example, where performance, improvization and aural skills may be more important than being able to write a piece down. There is now official support for the inclusion of 'intuitive' alongside 'formal' musical activity: creative music making may already be overcoming the 'wipe-out' effect in some school classrooms.

CHILDREN'S SINGING

Children's singing has received more attention than any other aspect of musical development. As with drawings, early researchers concentrated on describing the early course of song – Helmut Moog, Heinz Werner, and the researchers at the Pillsbury Foundation School, California, carried out some well-known studies. More recently, psychologists have tried to identify the thought processes which underlie the development of singing. Two of the best known of these are Jay Dowling, of the University of Texas, and Lyle Davidson, of Harvard Project Zero. From their detailed and comprehensive tape recordings of the spontaneous singing of a relatively small number of children, carried out in natural surroundings, a developmental pattern is beginning to emerge.

Up to the age of approximately two years, babies spend a good deal of time babbling. Helmut Moog has suggested that 'non-musical babbling' appears first: this emerges as a response to people and things around them, and is probably the precursor of speech, as we saw in Chapter 6. 'Musical babbling', on the other hand, is usually a specific response to music heard by the infant. Early 'babbling songs' consist of a few sounds, perhaps vowels or syllables, which are repeated at varying pitches. Although they initially have no clear organization with respect to pitch or rhythm, these features do gradually emerge. *Figures 9.5* to *9.7* show some spontaneous songs produced by

FIGURE 9.5: *'Babbling song' by a 12 month old*

one of the authors' children, which were tape-recorded at three different ages.

Figure 9.5 shows a 'babbling song' which was recorded at the age of 12 months. It contains some characteristic glissandi (sliding between pitches), as well as the beginnings of some musical organization in the form of a repeated four-note figure.

This organization gradually increases: the songs of the two year old consist of short phrases, perhaps of two or three notes, which are repeated over and over again. The repetitions may vary in pitch, but the *contours* of the notes within each phrase remain fairly constant. From these simple repeated phrases, more complex contours gradually emerge. These may be three, four or five-note phrases which are incorporated into a complete song, and which are once again likely to be varied in pitch. *Figure 9.6* shows another spontaneous song by the same child now aged 42 months: it shows the repetition of a distinct descending contour, as well as some early signs of harmonic organization.

By the age of three or so, children have learnt quite a few 'standard' songs from the world around them: nursery rhymes, lullabies, and maybe elements of pop songs from the radio or TV. One of the most interesting developments is the way in which these become enmeshed with children's own spontaneous songs: the resulting mixtures have been called 'pot-pourri' songs by Helmut Moog. *Figure 9.7* shows a short song produced by the same child at the age of 36 months, and it is notable in three ways. It clearly draws on the tune of 'Old Macdonald had a farm': its second half ('E–I–E–I–O') is pitched a tone lower than its first: and the made-up words may or may not provide convincing support for Freud's notion of the 'anal stage' at this age!

Lyle Davidson would describe this as an 'outline song'. The singer is

FIGURE 9.6:   *Spontaneous song by a 42 month old*

I   wan da on - ly   poo poo poo   pee   pee   hee!

FIGURE 9.7:   *Spontaneous song by a 36 month old*

clearly working towards a general 'song outline', or 'frame', but as yet the details are not 'filled in'. This gradually takes place after the age of three or so, when the pitch of notes, and the intervals between them, become much more accurate. By the age of five, children possess a wide repertoire of standard songs, and they improve their ability to reproduce new songs accurately. Davidson's research shows that they do so first by grasping the overall 'shape' of the song, and its words; then by extracting its surface rhythm; then by matching the pitch contours of each phrase, and finally by organizing all of these phrases or contours into a stable key. You can investigate these features yourself in *Exercise 9.2* on page 165.

There are obvious parallels between this shift from the 'outline' properties of songs to their accurate, detailed reproduction, and the development from 'preschematic' to 'visually realistic' drawings, which we described earlier.

CHILDREN AS STORYTELLERS

Children start to 'tell stories' very early on. Chapter 5 discussed the importance of make-believe play and fantasy in the early years: children carry out 'scripted' activities such as going shopping, having a meal, or going to bed. Peter Smith has suggested that these early activities are the precursors of imaginative story-telling or writing. They involve the creation of a *narrative*, and also an awareness of *social roles*, in the form of the inter-relationships between the characters in the story.

As early as two years or so, children are aware of the idea of 'writing' – or at least of making marks on paper – and they may try to imitate words on a page. Although the marks which appear on the paper may look like early scribbles, they are intended to create meaning in the form of a 'text', and this meaning can sometimes be deciphered in terms of the different types of mark which are made.

Children are clearly experimenting with different *symbol systems*: through play sequences, drawings, and early 'writing', as well as in talk and in song, they actively try to express their thoughts and feelings.

As writing gradually develops, children's use of narrative becomes more apparent and predictable: they use conventions to organize their stories. Stories emerge from a relatively unrelated string of events, to become coherent, organized wholes. Helen Cowie has suggested that children between the ages of two and five produce 'frame stories', with a clear beginning and end, about 'stock characters who experience unbalancing and unresolved adventures'. (Once again, there are obvious parallels between 'frame stories', 'outline songs', and 'preschematic drawings'.)

As children get older, their narratives have much clearer beginnings, middles and ends. This development can be seen very clearly in two stories produced by one of the authors' children. The first was written at the age of six:

❝ *Once apon a time there was a diver. And he lived near the sea. And once somebody siad to him are you a fisherman he siad it sounds a bit fishy to me. Then he went diving and he ran out of oxygen and a shark came he had to swim very quickly for sharks can swim very fast he managed to escap. then he saw a ship. And siad to the driver may I sleep on your boat yes said the driver and the diver did.* ❞

Four years later, the same child wrote a story called *The Exploding Dustbin*:

❝ *Once upon a time in the land of Dustbinia there was a dustbin called Edd. Edd was doing the normal thing; standing in the corner when he realised that he had an amazing talent. He could explode! He was the worlds first exploding dustbin! He had to tell someone. He went to his friend's house. Fred was really amazed at Edd's talent.*
"You must use your talent on NEW FACES 90!"
Edd had always wanted to be a Television star, so he did as he was told. He filled in the entry form very rapidly. He did well and got to the Finals. Then problems started: Nina Myscow was the judge! Edd was the last act and she had given everyone 3/10. Luckily by the time it was Edd's act she wasn't seeing so good and gave him 10 out of 10! Edd was the best of all the competitors. When he got home he was a local hero and was not condemned to standing in the corner anymore! He was now known as the biggest BIN IN SHOW BUSINESS. ❞

Although both stories begin with the conventional 'Once upon a time', several differences are immediately apparent. The first story, in spite of its rich detail and its joke, is essentially a string of events joined together by conjunctions. *The Exploding Dustbin*, on the other hand, has a clear setting, beginning, development and ending, as well as a few more jokes. It displays some effective writing techniques (such as the use of exclamation marks and capitals for emphasis), it conveys an understanding of the inter-relationships between the characters, and it also borrows from a talent show, with one of its well-known characters from the mass media.

Children's creative writing gives us access to the way in which children view the world, to the issues they perceive as important, and the problems which concern them. The same applies in different ways to drawings and to music, as well as to other areas of artistic activity which we have not had the space to discuss in this chapter, including drama, sculpture, and dance. Although children's art is one of the most difficult areas for developmental psychologists to study, it is by the same token one of the most potentially rewarding.

Recommended reading

Hargreaves, D.J. (1986) *The Developmental Psychology of Music*. Cambridge: Cambridge University Press. [A comprehensive account of the psychological basis of musical development in children and adults.]

Hargreaves, D.J. (1989) (Ed.) *Children and the Arts*. Milton Keynes: Open University Press. [A collection of research readings which cover most of the major art forms.]

Winner, E. (1982) *Invented Worlds: The psychology of the arts*. Cambridge, Mass.: Harvard University Press. [Comprehensive and wide-ranging yet very readable textbook.]

References

Bamberger, J. (1982) Revisiting children's drawings of simple rhythms: A function for reflection-in-action. In S. Strauss and R. Stavy (Eds) *U-shaped Behavioural Growth*. New York: Academic Press. [Summary of Bamberger's own research.]

Cowie, H. (1989) Children as writers. In D.J. Hargreaves (Ed.) *Children and the Arts*. Milton Keynes: Open University Press. [Review of research on children's writing.]

Davidson, L. (1985) Tonal structures of children's early songs. *Music Perception*, 2, 361–374. [Describes the underlying cognitive basis of early songs.]

Davidson, L., McKernon, P. & Gardner, H. (1981) The acquisition of song: A developmental approach. In J.A. Mason *et al.* (Eds) *Documentary Report of the Ann Arbor Symposium on the Applications of Psychology to the Teaching and Learning of Music*. Reston, VA: MENC. [Detailed studies of children's singing by members of the Harvard Project Zero group.]

Dennis, W. (1966) Creative productivity between the ages of 20 and 80 years. *Journal of Gerontology*, 21, 1–8. [Dennis' studies of the ages of peak productivity in different fields.]

Dowling, W.J. (1982) Development of musical schemata in children's spontaneous singing. In W.R. Crozier & A.J. Chapman (Eds) *Cognitive Processes in the Perception of Art*. Amsterdam: Elsevier. [Detailed analyses of children's songs.]

Eng, H. (1931) *The Psychology of Children's Drawings*. London: Routledge & Kegan Paul. [Early developmental descriptions.]

Freeman, N.H. & Janikoun, R. (1972) Intellectual realism in children's drawings of a familiar object with distinctive features. *Child Development*, 43, 1116–1121. [Do children draw what they know about, or what they see of an object?]

Gardner, H. (1973) *The Arts and Human Development*. New York: Wiley. [Includes Gardner's original theory of artistic development.]

Gardner, H., Winner, E. & Kircher, M. (1975) Children's conceptions of the arts. *Journal of Aesthetic Education*, 9, 60–77. [Study of children's reactions to a picture, a poem, or some music.]

Hargreaves, D.J. (1982) The development of ideational fluency: Some normative data. *British Journal of Educational Psychology*, 52, 109–112. [Children's performance on divergent thinking tests at different ages.]

Kellogg, R. (1969) *Analysing Children's Art*. Palo Alto., Calif.: National Press. [Developmental descriptions of drawings.]

Lehman, H.C. (1953) *Age and Achievement*. Princeton, NJ: Princeton University Press. [Creative productivity in different fields at different age levels.]

Moog, H. (1976) *The Musical Experience of the Pre-school Child*. London: Schott. [Large-scale study of some 500 children.]

Smith, P.K. (1984) The relevance of fantasy play for development in young children. In H. Cowie (Ed) *The Development of Children's Imaginative Writing*. London: Croom Helm. [Shows how early play is the precursor of drawing and writing.]

Torrance, E.P. (1962) *Guiding Creative Talent*. Englewood Cliffs, NJ: Prentice-Hall. [Describes the author's own tests of divergent thinking, as well as his research on the effects of age on performance on the tests.]

Drawings of Rhythms

Look carefully at *Figure 9.4* on page 155 and work out how to clap Bamberger's 'class piece', which appears at the bottom of it (ask a musician if you have any difficulties!). Now clap this rhythm to a seven year old, provide a pencil and paper, and ask the child 'to put down on paper whatever you think would help you to remember the rhythm tomorrow, or help someone else to play it who isn't here today'.

(1) Can you categorize the drawing as one of Bamberger's six types, i.e. F1, F2, F3, M1, M2, or M3?

(2) How would you categorize the four drawings below?

ta ta te te ta   ta ta te te ta

O O ♭♭O o o ♭♭o

♩♩ ♫♫   ♩♩ ♫♫

ı ııı ı   ıııı ı

(3) Repeat the exercise with a five year old and a nine year old. How do their drawings differ? You may also like to invent your own rhythm, or to use another familiar one, and repeat the exercise.

Children's Singing

Ask a child between the ages of two and five years to sing 'your favourite song' into a tape recorder. If you are able to do this successfully, ask also for renditions of well-known nursery rhymes such as 'Baa baa black sheep', 'Goosey goosey gander', 'Old MacDonald had a farm', or any other tunes with which the child is familiar. (If you are unsuccessful, ask another child, or try to record some spontaneous singing in a playgroup or nursery school.) Transcribe the songs, seeking a musician's help if necessary.

(1) Do the songs of the younger children (up to the age of three or so) show any evidence of the following features:

    (i)   *Repetitions* of vowels or syllables?
    (ii)   *Glissandi*, i.e. sliding pitches?
    (iii) *Rhythmic organization*, i.e. regularities in timing?
    (iv) Repeated *contours*, i.e. melodic shapes?

(2) Do the recordings of the older children (three to five year olds) show any evidence of:

    (i)   Whole songs being sung in tune?
    (ii)   'Pot pourri' songs, i.e. combinations between their own spontaneous inventions, and familiar songs from the outside world?

10. *Moral and Social Development*

▽   *The nature of moral awareness*
▽   *Learning the moral code*
▽   *Jean Piaget*
▽   *Lawrence Kohlberg*
▽   *Adolescent morality*

Two things fill the mind with ever-increasing wonder and awe, the more often and the more intensely the mind of thought is drawn to them: the starry heavens above me and the moral law within me.

(Immanuel Kant)

The moral law within: the voice of conscience

Moral development refers to the processes by which children adopt principles that lead them to judge certain behaviours as 'right' and others as 'wrong' and to govern their own actions in terms of these principles. If people are to live together in society – if social life is to be possible – they must share certain conceptions of what is right and what is wrong.

Parents cannot always be on the spot to check their children's actions. Eventually their voices and other voices (for example, teachers', religious leaders' and friends' who exemplify or enunciate moral and social values) are taken inside the psyche of the child so that the child has the choice of heeding his or her own voice from within – the voice of conscience. Many theorists draw a distinction between social values (norms or conventions) and moral rules. The former may vary from culture to culture and from society to society; they are also subject, as the years pass by, to radical changes. Moral rules, they suggest, are timeless, universal and foundational, in the sense that they are concerned with basics such as the maintenance of mutual help, trust and justice in human relationships. (This is an issue you might like to think about or debate, as it is contentious.) Moral behaviour consists of all the various things people do in connection with moral rules – rules that are positive (for example about altruism and generosity) as well as negative (for example prohibitions of lying or disloyalty).

According to psychologist Derek Wright, moral rules not only serve as guides to future actions but also provide the basis for judging the acceptability of things we have done in the past. Morality is not a game or activity among others, marked off from them by the nature of its rules. If we find the rules of a particular activity uncongenial or impossible to keep, we can, at least in principle, contract out and play a different game. However uncongenial and difficult moral rules may be to keep, we cannot contract out. Unless these exist in some measure it becomes virtually impossible to continue any social activity.

When children, over many years of development, have internalized the rules and values, they are usually able to restrain themselves from doing wrong even when no one else will ever know about the misdemeanour. If they give way to temptation they are likely to feel guilty afterwards. Not only can they be relied upon to keep the rules without constant supervision, but they will, in turn, teach the rules to their offspring. At the same time they will endeavour to ensure that there are sanctions for people who break the rules. It goes without saying that people's consciences are not equally strong. Going back to those early commands and prohibitions which are the foundation stones of conscience, it is apparent that some toddlers obey them more readily and consistently than others. And some parents convey them more effectively and constructively than others.

Social learning theorists suggest that children learn their parents' moral code and a willingness to act in accordance with the rules. It could be said that the first and most important step in the socialization of children occurs when a *willingness* to do as they are told develops. This is where strong bonds of affection and respect between children and parent/s become so important. Their identification with their parents, fuelled by a desire to please them, puts them on the same side as their mentors. Such bonds facilitate the adoption of the parent's point of view and value system; which, in turn, allows them to evaluate their own actions.

Ideally, parents will encourage a reasonable and rational conformity of the kind that enables the child to learn the patterns of prosocial (as opposed to antisocial) behaviour which guarantee social acceptance. It is important to be aware that persistent nonconformity is as prejudicial to good adjustment as is the slavish conformity that denies the person a mind of his or her own. The child who refuses to conform to the accepted standards of the group is likely to become a social outcast. This is serious for social development because such a child is deprived of the satisfactions of belonging to a group, and of the learning experiences which come from a sense of belonging and the feelings that go with comradeship.

A sometimes precarious balance is required by society – a balance which is often difficult to perceive, and difficult for the child to achieve. It is difficult enough for adults. In a series of social psychology experiments by Solomon Asch and others, evidence was found that adults conform to a judgement that they knew was contrary to fact, contrary to what they perceived, or both. Children also bend to these group pressures or feel anxious when they try to resist them.

THE NATURE OF MORAL AWARENESS

As many as four facets make up moral awareness and behaviour:

- *Resistance to temptation:* the 'braking' or inhibitory mechanism that works against misdemeanours even when the individual is not being observed.

- *Guilt,* or the acute emotional discomfort which we have all experienced both as child and adult that follows transgression and may lead to confession, reparation, or self-blame.

- *Altruism,* representing various prosocial acts that are often described as unselfishness such as: kindness, helpfulness, generosity, sympathy, empathy and service to others.

- *Moral belief and insight,* covering all aspects of what people think and say about morality, including their willingness to blame others who do wrong.

Each of these components is complex, and related one to the other in a complex manner.

The principle of reciprocity

The growing child's increasingly sophisticated cognitive processes – their developing ability to think and reason – contribute significantly to these moral and more general control mechanisms. As children grow older they are better able to conceptualize right and wrong; they gradually learn sets of rules taught them by parents and teachers. (Before you proceed further you might like to think about your own ideas on rules: see *Exercise 10.1* on page 180.)

These developments are facilitated first by interaction with authority figures who behave rationally, and who explain the reasons for their requirements, and second by the individual's own experiences of taking on the role of authority. Thus by exposure to others in authority and by the child's own experience of carrying out an authoritative role he or she acquires a better understanding of morality.

For Jean Piaget morality involves a powerful cognitive element. Moral behaviour depends on the consistent action of the mind, the cognitive framework supplied by recognition of the principle of reciprocity: the need to give and take in human interaction. As he put it, 'Morality is the logic of action, as logic is the morality of thought'. He believed that the concept of 'good' comes not from a sense of obligation based on learned obedience, but from the need for reciprocal affection – in other words the need to both give and receive love.

LEARNING THE MORAL CODE

Other psychologists less concerned with philosophical issues take the accepted moral code of society as the starting point for their research. They have studied children in situations where the types of response they can make are either desirable or undesirable, and where children learn to make one response rather than the other. It is not meaningful in this context to distinguish between social conformity and morality. Because behaviour is heavily influenced by previous learning experiences in similar situations, the idea of the individual's control over his or her behaviour assumes a different meaning. Self-control is consequent, to a significant extent, on the internalization of learned rules, rather than on an untrammelled and active freedom to choose between alternative actions in situations that present moral dilemmas (see example of Heinz's dilemma on page 181).

It is an assumption now prevalent among social scientists that the individual does not go through life viewing society's central norms as externally and coercively imposed pressures to which he or she must submit. Though the norms are initially alien, they are eventually adopted by the child, largely through the efforts of his or her early socializers – the parents – and they come to serve as internalized guides so that the individual follows them even when external authority is not present to enforce them. Control by others is replaced by self-control.

The development of conscience

Studies of moral development suggest that all disciplinary encounters that contribute to social and moral awareness and behaviour have a great deal in common, regardless of the specific technique used. The techniques have three components, any one of which may predominate:

- ### Assertion of power

Probably the most consistent finding is the inverse relationship between the assertion of power (authoritarian, harsh, domineering attitudes) and various measures or indices of moral behaviour. This finding applies to both sexes and the entire range of childhood. Severe punishment (for example harsh physical punishment) serves merely to alienate the child from the person who is using it to instil 'moral' lessons. Rather than identifying with the adult and internalizing the lesson (i.e. that the adult disapproves of the child's actions), all that is achieved is that the child will endeavour not be caught out next time.

- ### Withdrawal of love and approval

Anxiety about threatened withdrawal of parental love or approval is significant in child-rearing, but it is not the major contributing factor to the child's internalization of parental values. However, there is evidence that the threat of withdrawing approval (for example, 'Mummy doesn't love you when you do that!') may contribute to the inhibition of anger. It produces anxiety which leads to the renunciation of hostile impulses. While it may contribute to making the child more susceptible to adult influence, thereby giving the impression to parents of the desired outcome, this does not necessarily have a bearing on moral development (i.e. internal moral judgement). Thus the child may suppress his or her impulse to lash out at another child who receives the biggest slice of cake but not feel that it is wrong to use aggression to express a sense of grievance.

- ### Induction

This is the type of discipline which is most conducive to moral development; it involves pointing out the effects of the child's behaviour, giving reasons and explanations. A child might be shown the bruise that results from kicking his sister and reminded of how it hurt when he bruised himself in a recent fall. By this means the child learns to understand why he or she should or should not act in particular ways.

A learning theory perspective

Learning theorists base their investigations of conscience development upon the assumption that there is nothing about moral learning to distinguish it qualitatively from other forms of learning. Principles which derive from the study of classical conditioning on the one hand, and instrumental conditioning on the other, are used to explain the way children learn to resist temptation. Learning theorists consider that behaviours indicative of guilt such as confession, self-criticism and apology, are learned responses which have been found to be instrumental in reducing the anxiety that follows some transgression of the rules. Derek Wright makes the important point that learning theory (as opposed to the broader perspective adopted by social learning theorists) does not account sufficiently for the fact that punishment and reward are mediated by *human agents* (for example, parents, teachers) and are not simply the impersonal consequences of behaviour. The individual's relationship to this agent is a crucial factor in moral development. For instance, the words of a mother whose child wishes to emulate and please her will carry much more force than those of a person for whom the child feels nothing or (worse) disrespect.

Identification and imitation

Additional principles like *imitation* and *identification* have also been introduced by theorists of different schools of thought to account for some of the subtleties of moral awareness and action. In the psychoanalytic (Freudian) concept of identification the child 'incorporates' his or her parents and their values as an ego-ideal. They form the basis of his or her moral standards. These events are thought to occur on the resolution of the Oedipus complex, at around the age of five (see Recommended Reading for further details).

Lawrence Kohlberg's account is similar in its timing. But in the case of *cognitive developmental theory*, identification is not a fixed, rigid personality structure which depends on a special relationship with the parents. Kohlberg suggests that children's behaviour is motivated by an intrinsic need to master the environment; adult approval for their behaviour is an indication that a satisfactory level of competence has been reached. Children seek and are increasingly dependent on adult approval; or rather, it is more correct to say that they wish to secure rewards or approval as a sign that they have performed the task competently rather than that they want to perform competently in order to obtain rewards and approval.

Before the age of two, children largely fail to differentiate what *they* do, from what an *adult* does. The cognitive development of the ability to differentiate between *self* and *other* leads to a recognition of how causal relationships work. This transforms their assimilation of what is merely interesting into a desire to control things and people. It is suggested that this differentiation is the prerequisite for the imitation of modelled behaviour. When the adult does something interesting, children want to see if they can do it too. After the age of five there is a decline in their tendency to imitate.

JEAN PIAGET

Fundamental questions about the nature of the person are central to investigations in the area of moral and social development. A key assumption of Kohlberg's theory of moral development (and also the work of Jean Piaget) is that there is a direct correspondence between moral reasoning and moral action. Maturing moral awareness leads not only to a judgement of right and wrong (deontic judgement) but also to a commitment to behave accordingly (judgement of responsibility). Jean Piaget devoted a considerable part of his seminal work *The Moral Judgement of the Child* to a discussion of the relative value for society of behaviour based on reciprocal relations of affection, trust and respect, and behaviour based on obedience to authority, arguing the superiority of the former and asserting the importance of an education which fosters mutual respect.

Piaget has demonstrated how the logic of children's moral reasoning changes radically from the age of four until adolescence. During the early stages of moral development (the first is called heteronomous morality or moral realism) the rules are felt to be absolute; morality is a unilateral system based, essentially, upon authority and, as such, external to the child. Duty is seen as allegiance and total submission to authority.

There is reason to think with regard to cognitive, moral and social development that the age of five or six is something of a watershed. According to Piaget there is a transition from preoperational thinking to operational thinking, and hence the decline in social as well as perceptual and cognitive 'egocentricity'. The child is being exposed to wider cultural influences through the mass media, visiting friends' homes and attending a school.

From the age of about six or seven years onwards (Piaget called this second stage autonomous morality or the morality of reciprocity), children increasingly experience relationships which involve mutual respect. They are involved in relationships between peers of equal status, thus they inevitably meet other children who do not always share their views. There is a growing awareness of different perspectives.

By the age of ten the system of morality has undergone considerable change so that children now perceive rules to be made by people. Morality is very much a matter of negotiation and compromise; the rules are seen to be flexible, capable of being changed if agreement can be obtained. Duty is seen as equality or a concern for the welfare of others. Piaget believed that the mature understanding of rules goes with an ability to keep them.

LAWRENCE KOHLBERG

On this point Lawrence Kohlberg would be in wholehearted agreement. He maintains that the person who understands justice is more likely to practise it. In order to explore a child's or young person's reasoning about difficult moral issues, such as the value of human life or the reasons for doing 'right' things, he devised a series of dilemmas. One of the stories is that of Heinz (see *Exercise 10.2* on page 181).

Moral reasoning

Kohlberg argues that moral development progresses through a number of levels, with different stages at each level (see *Table 10.1*). At the lower stages moral reasoning is characterized by its concrete nature and egocentricity; at the high stages moral reasoning is guided by abstract notions such as 'justice' and 'rights' and is much more social in orientation.

ADOLESCENT MORALITY

With adolescence the young person enters the final phase of moral development when morality is seen as a matter of individual principles. Most young adults begin to appreciate that without certain basic principles there would be no morality at all. They usually understand that although there may be endless debates and arguments over how these principles should be applied in particular circumstances, their existence *as principles* is vital to a civilized social existence. At this stage notions of right and wrong based on adult authority have been replaced by internalized principles of conscience.

Social cognition

This is a term used to describe a fairly new area of research and theory related to the area of moral development, which focuses on the child's

TABLE 10.1: *Kohlberg's stages of moral reasoning*

(1) *Orientation towards punishment and obedience*	(1) *Preconventional morality* The child judges what is wrong on the basis of what is punished. Obedience is respected for its own sake. One obeys because adults have superior power.
(2) *Indivudualism, instrumental purpose and exchange*	
(3) *Mutual interpersonal expectations, relationships and interpersonal conformity*	(2) *Conventional morality* The family or small group to which the child belongs becomes important. Moral actions are those that live up to what is expected of you. Being good is now important for its own sake. The child tends to value trust, loyalty, respect, gratitude and keeping mutual relationships.
(4) *Orientation toward the social system, conscience and law and order*	Here there is a shift in focus from the young person's family and close groups to the larger society. Good means fulfilling duties one has agreed to. Laws are to be upheld except in extreme cases. Contributing to society is also seen as desirable.
(5) *Social contract or utility and individual rights*	(3) *Postconventional or principled morality* This involves acting so as to achieve the greatest good for the greatest number. The child is aware that there are different views and values, and that values are relative. Laws and rules should be upheld in order to preserve the social order, but they can be changed. Some basic nonrelative values are accepted (e.g. the right to life and liberty).
(6) *Universal ethical principles*	The young person develops and is loyal to his or her own chosen ethical principles in deciding what is right. Because laws usually conform to those principles, laws should be obeyed; but when there is a difference between law and conscience, conscience dominates.

[Based on ideas from Kohlberg, 1976; Colby and Kohlberg, 1987.]

understanding of social relationships. Some of the elements of this social cognition are:

- *Empathy and role taking.* This is the ability to see things from the other person's point of view, i.e. to empathize with them, to feel *for* them.

- *Self-control.* Low self-control is characterized by impulsive behaviour, the apparent absence of thought between impulse and action. It is manifested by a failure to stop and think, a failure to learn effective ways of thinking about social situations, and a failure to generate alternative courses of action.

- *Social problem solving.* Social problem solving refers to the process, in a given social situation, of generating feasible courses of action, considering the various outcomes that might follow, and planning how to achieve the preferred outcome.

Robert Selman, author of *The Growth of Interpersonal Under-standing*, is one of the most influential thinkers in this field. He devised a series of stories that describe relationships and dilemmas within relationships. Children hear (or read) these stories and are then asked to say what the characters in the story should do or would do. *Exercise 10.3* on page 183 illustrates one example which you may like to try out. Based on their comments Selman proposed five stages or levels in children's ability to adopt a social point of view or perspective taking (see *Table 10.2*). These levels of social understanding are loosely related to particular ages, but there is a good deal of individual variation in the time it takes a child to move through each level.

Social understanding and moral judgement

Evidence suggests that cognitive understanding forms the underpin-ning of social understanding and that both underlie moral judgement. Moral behaviour or more skilful social behaviour appears to be at least partially linked to the child's level of social understanding. Socially skilful or effective children typically show somewhat higher levels of social understanding than those who lack social skills. The beginning of formal operations and a level three social understanding may be necessary, but not sufficient, conditions for the *conventional* level of moral reasoning.

Morality in delinquents

Kohlberg believes that the majority of adolescent offenders are preconventional (with attitudes of the four to ten year old) in their

TABLE 10.2 *Selman's five levels of social understanding*

Approximate age	Level of social understanding	Characteristics of child's social understanding
3–6	0	The child is capable of taking only an egocentric perspective. He or she may realize that other people experience things differently in a physical sense, but cannot yet appreciate that other people feel or think in a different manner from him or herself.
5–9	1	The child is now capable of taking a subjective differentiated perspective. He or she appreciates that other people feel and think differently and is aware that people may act differently from how they feel but does not yet realize that other people also perceive the same things about him or her.
7–12	2	The child is now capable of adopting a self-reflective and reciprocal perspective. He or she appreciates that there is two-way traffic in social relationships/interactions – that each member of a pair knows the other may think differently (I know that you know that I know). Relationships are perceived as being truly reciprocal.
10–15	3	The child is capable of adopting a third-person and mutual perspective. At this stage (early formal operations) he or she is able to stand apart from a relationship (i.e. outside it), and view it as if he or she were a third person. Relationships involve mutual coordinations, mutual satisfactions.
12–adult	4	The child is now capable of adopting an in-depth and societal-symbolic perspective. The young person understands that other people's actions are influenced by their upbringing, by their personalities, and by social forces. He or she is able to take these factors into account.

[Adapted from Selman, 1980]

moral reasoning, as compared with the mainly conventional reasoning of nonoffending adolescents. However, a review of structural-developmental studies of moral immaturity in juvenile delinquents indicates that preconventional reasoning does not represent a necessary component in the development of delinquency. Nor does conventional morality innoculate the individual against delinquency. On the most general level, it appears that adolescents who have failed to relinquish a preconventional moral orientation in Kohlberg's framework, at a time when their peers are moving to higher stages, are at risk of behaviour problems, whereas those performing along more conventional lines may or may not be at similar risk.

As was pointed out earlier, moral judgement and moral behaviour intercorrelate in a complex manner; nowhere is this fact more apparent than in the conduct disorders (see Chapter 11) and juvenile delinquency, where a plethora of variables to do with the adolescent's circumstances as well as his or her personality can be found in the causation (aetiology) of the disorders. To the extent that low-level moral reasoning is conducive to delinquent actions, it is not clear whether preconventional delinquents are 'fixated' in their moral development or are progressing at slower rates.

Advice on moral and social training

On the other hand, when it comes to parents and teachers and advice on everyday moral and social training, there are factors that facilitate the development of moral and social awareness, and which are therefore of potential value to caregivers. These include:

- strong ties of affection between parents and children;
- firm moral demands made by parents on their offspring;
- the consistent use of sanctions;
- techniques of punishment that are psychological rather than physical (i.e. methods that signify or threaten withdrawal of approval), thus provoking apprehension rather than anger;
- an intensive use of reasoning and explanations (inductive methods);
- giving responsibility to the youngster;
- helping the child to take other people's roles;
- encouraging the child to see the other person's point of view (empathy);
- increasing the child's level of moral reasoning by discussion.

Whilst it may be clear to parents and teachers that they do not always achieve the standard set in the above guidelines these represent an ideal towards which they may wish to strive.

Critique

There have been several criticisms of Piaget's and Kohlberg's work ranging from concerns about the psychological measurement (psychometric) and data-gathering methods used, to the philosophical assumptions underlying their approach. One such criticism concerns the assumption that morality implies a category of understanding ـnat develops with age and experience and applies equally to personal, social and moral issues. According to some theorists it is necessary to distinguish between *conventional* or *social rules* and *moral norms*. The first (for example sex roles) are arbitrary and culture specific. In contrast moral norms are neither arbitrary nor culture specific. Furthermore, the two types of norm can be distinguished by children from an early age. Preschool children and elementary school children are able to see that certain forbidden behaviour at school (for example transgressions concerning clothes) could be acceptable if there was a change in the school rules, while other behaviours are unacceptable regardless of the presence or absence of a rule (for example attacking or threatening another child). Children's understanding of these two types of rule follows different paths or stages. Stages (well differentiated from Kohlberg's and Piaget's stages of moral development) have been reported for children's understanding of social or conventional norms.

Another criticism has focused on Piaget's claim that very young children are unable to base their moral judgement on intentions, focusing almost exclusively on the consequences of transgressions. More recent studies suggest that children are capable of using such information as early as the age of three. It has also been reported that, as early as the age of six or seven, they are able to use, simultaneously, information regarding intentions, consequences and justifications of behaviour.

Then again, the assumption of an objective morality based on reason as opposed to experience, and the emphasis on justice as the ideal form of good (central to Kohlberg's theory) have been questioned. This latter emphasis on justice is said to be a masculine predilection or characteristic. It is suggested that the development of an ethic of caring would better represent the point of view and experience of women. Similarly, this principle of justice is not the only universal moral principle. Others based on different philosophical traditions are universal benevolence (that is, a principle of caring about the well-being of others) and a universal principle of maintaining social order.

In spite of these criticisms, Piaget's and Kohlberg's theories of moral development have received much empirical support from several cross-cultural studies and have provided a very useful framework for further research not only into moral behaviour but also broad issues of social awareness and antisocial activities (for example delinquency).

Recommended reading

Bee, H. (1985) *The Developing Child*, 4th edn. New York: Harper & Row. [Clear and critical account of facts and theories of child development.]

Colby, A. & Kohlberg, L. (1987) *The Measurement of Moral Judgement*. [2 volumes] New York: Cambridge University Press. [Methods for measuring moral judgement.]

Damon, W. (1977) *The Social World of the Child*. San Francisco: Jossey-Bass. [How the child interprets and is influenced by his or her social environment.]

Goodnow, J.J. & Collins, W.A. (1990) *Development According to Parents: The nature, sources, and consequences of parents' ideas*. London: Lawrence Erlbaum Associates. [A superb account of children's moral, social and other aspects of development as seen by parents.]

Harre, R. (1979) *Social Being*. Oxford: Blackwell. [A fascinating account of what it means to be social creatures.]

Herbert, M. (1991) *Clinical Child Psychology: Social learning, development and behaviour*. Chichester: John Wiley. [An account of moral and other aspects of children's behaviour and their clinical implications.]

Lickona, T. (1978) Moral development and moral education: Piaget, Kohlberg, and beyond. In J.M. Gallagher and J.A. Easley, Jr. (Eds) *Piaget and Education*. New York: Plenum Press. [Various ways of looking at moral development.]

Rubin, K.H. & Everett, B. (Eds) (1982) *The Young Child: Reviews of Research, Vol. 3*. Washington, DC.: National Association for the Education of Young Children. [Guide to available research.]

Schaffer, H.R. (1984) *The Child's Entry into a Social World*. London: Academic Press. [A masterly introduction to the psychology of socialization.]

References

Aronfreed, J. (1968) *Conduct and Conscience*. New York: Academic Press. [Studies of conscience development and action.]

Asch, S.E. (1956) Studies of independence and conformity: I. A minority of one against a unanimous majority. *Psychological Monographs*, 70, (9), No. 416. [Classic studies of the pressures to conform.]

Berenda, R.W. (1950) *The Influence of the Group in Judgements of Children*. New York: King's Crown Press. [As above, applied to childhood.]

Hartshorne, H. & May, M.A. (1928–30) *Studies in the Nature of Character*. New York: Macmillan. [Seminal work on honesty.]

Hoffman, M.L. (1970) Moral development. In P.H. Mussen (Ed.) *Carmichael's Manual of Child Psychology, Vol. II*. 3rd edn. Chichester: John Wiley. [Invaluable review of moral development issues.]

Hoffman, M.L. (1986) Affect, cognition and motivation. In R.M. Sorrentino and E.T. Higgins (Eds) *Handbook of Motivation and Cognition*. New York: Guilford. [Attempt to integrate emotion, thinking and motivation.]

Jurkovic, G.J. (1980) The juvenile delinquent as moral philosopher: A structural–developmental approach. *Psychological Bulletin*, 88, 709–727 [A look at the cognitive-moral basis of delinquency.]

Children's Behaviour at Home

QUESTIONNAIRE

(Interviewee answers to be tape-recorded)

(1a)   *Do you have rules about behaviour which you want your child to follow at home?*
       If 'yes' go to question (2).
       If 'no' or 'what do you mean?', go to question (1b).

(1b)   *Are there certain behaviours you expect from your child at home?*
       If 'yes' go to question (2).
       If 'no', probe further to make sure parent understands.

(2)   *What are they?*
       If only requirements are stated, probe about prohibitions and vice versa. Note where probe was made. If many are mentioned ask only for the most important. Stop when parent reaches ten. If parent only gives a few, probe at least twice but stop at ten.

(3)   *List in order the five most important rules to be followed.*
       Interviewer may need to 'remind' parent of listed rules.

(4)   *How is the existence of these rules or expectations conveyed to your child?*
       If the answer is that they are conveyed verbally, probe to see if this occurs only when the rule is broken.

(5)   *Taking each of the five most important rules in turn, ask why it is important for the child to follow that rule.*

(6)   *Does . . . have the same rules for your child?*
       In turn, insert the name of each other adult living in the home.

(7)   *How often is each rule broken?*
       For each of the five important rules, obtain estimate in terms of average number of times per week. (If low frequency behaviour, ask average number of times per month or year.)

(8)   *What happens when the child breaks these rules?*
       Take each of the five important rules in turn and probe for:
         (i) consequences,
        (ii) consistency across time,
       (iii) consistency across adults,
        (iv) whether or not a rationale is given.

(9)   *What happens when the child follows the rules?*

(10)   *Do you have the same rules for all children in the family?*
       If only child, ask what parent would do if there were more than one child.

(11)   *Ask the reason for the answer given to question (10).*

(12)   *Have you ever sought help from anyone for the management of any of your children's behaviour?*
       If the answer is yes, ask about whom was consulted, for which child, and get a brief account of what happened.

Moral Judgement Interview

Try this exercise for yourself and then on children you know well. Relate the answers to Kohlberg's stages of moral reasoning outlined in *Table 10.1* on page 174.

A woman was near death from a special kind of cancer. There was one drug that the doctors thought might save her. It was a form of radium that a chemist in the same town had recently discovered. The drug was expensive to make, but the chemist was charging ten times what the drug cost him to make – he paid £200 for the radium and charged £2,000 for a small dose of the drug.

The sick woman's husband, Heinz, went to everyone he knew to borrow the money, but he could only get together about £1,000, which is half of what it cost. He told the chemist that his wife was dying and asked him to sell it cheaper or let him pay later. But the chemist said, 'No, I discovered the drug and I'm going to make money from it'. So Heinz became desperate and considered breaking into the chemist's store to steal the drug for his wife.

(1) Should Heinz steal the drug? Why or why not?

(2) If Heinz doesn't love his wife, should he steal the drug for her? Why or why not?

(3) Suppose the person dying is not his wife but a stranger. Should Heinz steal the drug for the stranger? Why or why not?

(4) [If you could consider stealing a drug for a friend how would you feel in the following situation?] Suppose it's a pet animal he loves; should Heinz steal to save the pet animal? Why or why not?

(5) Why should people do everything they can to save another's life?

(6) It is against the law for Heinz to steal. Does that make it morally wrong? Why or why not?

(7a) Why should people generally do everything they can to avoid breaking the law anyhow?

(7b) How does this relate to Heinz's case?

continued . . .

Moral Judgement Interview cont.

Heinz did break into the store. He stole the drug and gave it to his wife. In the newspapers the next day there was an account of the robbery. Mr Brown, a police officer who knew Heinz, read the account. He remembered seeing Heinz running away from the store and realized that it was Heinz who stole the drug. Mr Brown wonders whether he should report that Heinz was the robber.

(1) Should Officer Brown report Heinz for stealing? Why or why not?

(2) Officer Brown finds and arrests Heinz. Heinz is brought to court, and a jury is selected. The jury's job is to find whether a person is innocent or guilty of committing a crime. The jury finds Heinz guilty. It is up to the judge to determine the sentence. Should the judge give Heinz some sentence, or should he suspend the sentence and let Heinz go free? Why or why not?

(3a) Thinking in terms of society, why should people who break the law be punished?

(3b) How does this relate to Heinz's case?

(4) Heinz was acting out of conscience when he stole the drug. What reasons are there for not punishing a lawbreaker if he is acting out of conscience?

(5) What does the word conscience mean to you? If you were Heinz, how would your conscience enter into the decision?

(6) Heinz has to make a moral decision. Should a moral decision be based on one's feelings or on one's thinking and reasoning about right and wrong?

(7) Is Heinz's problem a moral problem? Why or why not? In general, what makes something a moral problem or what does the word morality mean to you?

(8) If Heinz is going to decide what to do by thinking about what's really right, there must be some answer, some right solution. Is there really some correct solution to moral problems like Heinz's or, when people disagree, is everybody's opinion equally right? Why?

(9) How do you know when you've come up with a good moral decision? Is there a way of thinking or method by which one can reach a good or adequate decision?

(10) Most people believe that thinking and reasoning in science can lead to a correct answer. Is the same thing true in moral decisions or are they different?

A Moral Dilemma

Robert Selman has investigated children's ability to take other's perspectives (also called role-taking ability) by presenting story dilemmas designed to elicit reasoning about social or moral situations. Here is an example of a dilemma presented to children aged four to ten, together with some probing questions. Why not try this out on children at various ages and see how they answer the questions given below.

Holly is an eight-year-old girl who likes to climb trees. She is the best tree climber in the neighbourhood. One day while climbing down from a tall tree she falls off the bottom branch but does not hurt herself. Her father sees her fall. He is upset and asks her to promise not to climb trees any more. Holly promises.

Later that day, Holly and her friends meet Shawn. Shawn's kitten is caught up in a tree and can't get down. Something has to be done right away or the kitten may fall. Holly is the only one who climbs trees well enough to reach the kitten and get it down, but she remembers her promise to her father.

Does Holly know how Shawn feels about the kitten? Why? How will Holly's father feel if he finds out she climbed the tree? What does Holly think her father will think of her if he finds out?

You might try taping children's answers to your questions. Then see if you can categorize them according to the five levels of social understanding in *Table 10.2* on page 176. Categorize each child's explanation of the thoughts and feelings of each individual referred to in the dilemma and the relationships among their various perspectives. (For comments on this exercise see page 184.)

Kohlberg, L. (1970) *Moral Development*. New York: Holt, Rinehart & Winston. [A seminal work on moral development.]

Kohlberg, L. (1976) Moral stages and moralization. In T. Lickona (Ed.) *Moral Development and Behaviour: Theory, research and social issues*. New York: Holt, Rinehart & Winston. [A synoptic account of a major theory of moral development.]

Lickona, T. (Ed.) *Moral Development and Behaviour: Theory, research and social issues*. New York: Holt, Rinehart & Winston. [Comprehensive review of research and findings.]

Piaget, J. (1932) *The Moral Judgement of the Child*. New York: Harcourt & Brace. [Early classical study of moral behaviour in childhood.]

Selman, R.L. (1980) *The Growth of Interpersonal Understanding*. New York: Academic Press. [How people understand one another (person perceptions, social relationships).]

Turiel, E. (1974) Conflict and transition in adolescent moral development. *Child Development*, 45, 14–29. [Important journal article on the development of moral behaviour.]

Wright, D. (1971) *The Psychology of Moral Behaviour*. Harmondsworth: Penguin. [Highly readable account of moral behaviour.]

──────────────── COMMENTS ON EXERCISE 10.3 ────────────────

To be scored *nonegocentric* on this measure, children must be able to consider a hypothetical situation and verbalize their thoughts about the situation. Answering questions about people in a hypothetical situation may be more difficult for a child than assuming the point of view of a real person that a child knows.

11. *Childhood Problems*

What sort of childish actions should alert us to the presence of some abnormality of behaviour that merits serious concern? Are there any tell-tale signs or symptoms which point to a psychological problem requiring expert advice? To answer these questions we must find out what is meant by the term 'problem' as applied to children's behaviour. As we shall see, it turns out that there are no simple answers, no clear-cut formulae. The word 'problem' proves to be a vague and elusive term which is applied to different children for many different reasons and, only too often, for apparently no sound reason at all.

When is a problem a problem?

Let us look at two cases (very much simplified for our purposes) of children who were referred to a child and family guidance centre.

❝ *Wayne, aged 11, the only child of rather elderly parents, refused to go to school, and would speak to no one but his parents. These problems (together with bouts of bed-wetting) had begun after episodes of bullying at school, coinciding with the serious illness of his grandmother, who lived in the same house. Always a solitary and timid boy at school, Wayne became noticeably more shy and preoccupied. At home, where he had previously been a precocious,* *domineering child – 'a lovable tyrant', in his mother's words – he was sickly and weepy, and morbidly concerned about his mother's health. In the mornings he would complain of various ailments, and express a dread of going to school. His mother was at her wits' end and couldn't cope with his fears and physical symptoms, which seemed to get worse with each succeeding day. No entreaties, blandishments or threats would persuade him to return to school.* **"**

" *Ayesha, aged 11, was suffering from restless sleep and nightmares. Displays of temper and repetitive arguments with her father, who thought she was idle at school, were the reasons for her being called aggressive and rebellious. Apart from her poor achievement at school, the father complained of Ayesha's habit of biting her nails – 'a baby's habit', as he called it. The teachers at Ayesha's school (who were consulted by the Centre) had few complaints. In their words, Ayesha was 'a pleasant, sociable and conscientious girl, but inclined to be a bit erratic'. They added that her father seemed unyielding and ambitious – 'a self-made man with unrealistically high aspirations for his daughter'.* **"**

Parents and teachers naturally become concerned when a child in their care behaves in a persistently difficult manner and in a way that doesn't seem normal. But what precisely is, or is not, normal? Children are frequently troubled and they can also be troublesome.

Parents' and teachers' perceptions

Problem behaviour does tend to be annoying behaviour, but this does not necessarily mean that all behaviour which annoys and creates problems for parents is to be equated with maladjustment. Parents vary in what they can tolerate in the way of 'difficult' behaviour. The eminent child psychiatrist Leo Kanner observed that the high annoyance threshold of many fond and highly resourceful parents keeps away from the clinics a multitude of early breath-holders, nail-biters, face 'twitchers' and casual masturbators who, largely because of this kind of parental attitude, develop into reasonably happy and well-adjusted adults.

Indeed, there is evidence that parents' definition of 'problems', and referral of their children to clinics, may reflect problems in themselves (for example, they may be overanxious, or easily upset) rather than in their offspring. And it is important to bear in mind just how threatening to adult self-esteem the unruly, unmanageable behaviour of a son or daughter can be. Research has shown that dissatisfaction with oneself as a parent is at its highest when a child's behaviour is susceptible to influence by others but – for one reason or another – not susceptible to influence stemming from one's own efforts. In effect, the unhappiness springs both from not meeting one's own standards, and from explanations for one's adequacy or inadequacy that provide little comfort for not doing so. Experience may mitigate harsh expectations of oneself and the children in one's care. Teachers with only a few years' experience tend to view undesirable acts as being more serious than do teachers with ten or more years' experience.

THE POPULAR VIEW

The designation 'problem child' is most readily attached to a youngster whose actions are puzzling, if not incomprehensible ('I just cannot understand him any more'); whose acts are unpredictable and inconsistent ('It's a case of Jekyll and Hyde. . .I never know what she's going to be like from one day to the next'); or notably when his or her acts are uncontrollable ('I can't control him; he can't control himself. . .even the teachers at school can't do anything with the so and so'). In the popular view of normality, behaviour should be intelligible, consistent and capable of being controlled; in other words, it should conform to certain limits of meaning, predictability and self-discipline. If it doesn't it is not normal, and parents and teachers tend to get anxious if such patterns persist.

Lay persons (and some professionals) tend to treat normality and abnormality as clear cut and easily definable concepts. Some see them as mutually exclusive, representing opposites like hard and soft, clean and dirty. In this view, normal children are clearly marked off from other, allegedly abnormal children; and the abnormal children are thought to deviate, in some general sense, from normal children. But in fact, children with emotional and behavioural difficulties are not all 'problem'; they are simply children with *some* problems.

Situation specificity

Children, and, indeed, adults too, vary their actions to some extent according to the situations – and their perceptions of the settings and circumstances – in which they find themselves. The term *situation specificity* refers to the fact that behaviour is not usually manifested on a random basis. The probability of a specific action occurring varies according to contingencies (circumstances) in the surrounding environment. Thus a child whc is troublesome may display his or her unacceptable behaviour in the home, the classroom, the playground, or perhaps on the streets of his or her neighbourhood. Furthermore, there may be refinements of such specific situations in which the problem behaviour occurs. For example, the child with severe temper tantrums solely at home may have them only at bedtime and at mealtimes, and be quite co-operative and pleasant at other times of the day when at home.

The findings of several studies (notably those of Michael Rutter and his colleagues) suggest that maternal and teacher accounts of child behaviour are only slightly correlated, which is to say that they do not always agree. This is possibly due to the effects of situational factors.

Since mothers and teachers see children in different contexts governed by different rules and sanctions, there is no strong reason to expect that their ratings of behaviour should be identical. This discrepancy often comes as a surprise to parents who may hardly recognize the teacher's description of their son's or daughter's behaviour at school.

Although maternal and teacher ratings of particular children are only slightly correlated, there is quite marked stability in their ratings over time; in other words their individual judgements tend to be broadly consistent, even if they do differ somewhat. There is evidence to suggest that factors specific to the person doing the rating as well as factors related to the situation being rated may influence behaviour ratings. In particular, the mother's mood and notably depression appear to influence how she rates her child's behaviour at a particular time.

Emotional and behavioural problems are not like illnesses

Minor variations of emotional and behavioural problems can be identified in most 'well-adjusted' children. For example, the majority of children are shy at one time or another. Some, however, display a constant anxious avoidance of social situations. In other words, normality and abnormality are the extremes of a continuum; normality merges almost imperceptibly into abnormality.

The fact is that there is no clear distinction between the characteristics of problem children and other children; there are no absolute symptoms of psychological maladjustment in children, no recourse to the laboratory tests or X-rays which are so helpful in making a definitive medical diagnosis. We are not dealing with disease as medical persons understand it. Emotional or behaviour problems, signs of psychological maladjustment are, by and large, exaggerations of, deficiencies in, or handicapping combinations of behaviour patterns that are common to all children. Typical examples might be aggressiveness, social ineptitude and the awkward combination of poor concentration and underachievement. *Figure 11.1* shows the three classes of problematic behaviour.

There are, broadly speaking, three classes of problematic behaviour:

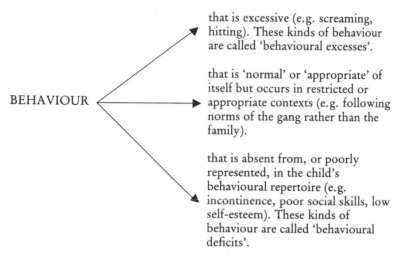

that is excessive (e.g. screaming, hitting). These kinds of behaviour are called 'behavioural excesses'.

that is 'normal' or 'appropriate' of itself but occurs in restricted or appropriate contexts (e.g. following norms of the gang rather than the family).

BEHAVIOUR

that is absent from, or poorly represented, in the child's behavioural repertoire (e.g. incontinence, poor social skills, low self-esteem). These kinds of behaviour are called 'behavioural deficits'.

FIGURE 11.1:   *Problematic behaviour*

Not surprisingly, so called 'abnormal' behaviour in children is not very different from normal behaviour in the way it develops (that is to say following the same laws and principles), and the manner in which it can eventually be changed. As we shall see there are advantages in this finding when it comes to the treatment or training of children with behavioural difficulties. It seems more profitable to ask how children develop behaviour in general, rather than to restrict the question to how they develop problem behaviour as such.

Returning to Ayesha and Wayne: after intensive investigations and discussions, the Centre staff concluded that Ayesha's problems were those of a normal girl of her age, and were part and parcel of growing up. To use their clinical jargon, these were the 'transient adjustment problems' of a girl going through a difficult patch at home. Her reactions to a rather difficult father and to a phase of life (early adolescence) notorious in some youngsters for its turbulence were 'well within normal limits' (see Chapter 12 for a discussion of adolescence). The Centre's staff felt that Ayesha did not require treatment, although advice was offered to her parents about the expectations they had of their daughter and their general style of management.

Wayne, on the other hand, was felt to have a persistent problem, and one serious enough to require treatment for himself, continuing guidance for his parents and consultations with the school. The clinicians concluded that his problems indicated a deep-seated pattern of 'maladjustment'.

NORMS AND NORMALITY

It is no accident that two of the most common synonyms for problem behaviour in childhood are *maladjusted* and *abnormal* behaviour. Let us examine both these terms. The family and the school are the most important representatives of society encountered by children during their formative years. Together they have the task of transforming a totally dependent, asocial and egocentric infant into a more or less self-supporting, sophisticated and responsible member of the community. This 'civilizing' process (as we saw in Chapter 10) is called *socialization*. Parents and teachers see themselves as having certain obligations, not only to the immature child him or herself, but also to the society in which he or she is growing up. They have a set of expectations with which the child's progress and present behaviour are compared. The child becomes a 'problem' when he or she fails to conform to certain guidelines of intellectual, social and moral behaviour.

The nature of norms

The criteria to which they are being asked to adjust in the name of social life are called *norms*. The judgements underlying these criteria constitute a potential Pandora's box of personal and cultural (not to mention theoretical) bias and prejudice. After all, the word 'norm' from its Latin root means a standard, rule or pattern. Thus 'abnormal' applied to children's behaviour implies (with the prefix 'ab' meaning 'away from') a deviation from a standard. An analysis of these standards, as used by professionals and public alike in referring to normality and abnormality, makes it clear that they are *social standards* (rules, expectations, codes, conventions, laws). To most people, behaviour is normal and acceptable if it is usual – if it conforms to the behaviour of the majority. If, say, children cannot or will not adjust to the norms, they are thought to be maladjusted. Judgements of problem behaviour are value judgements, and it is important to remember that criteria are not universal.

According to social anthropologists, judgement of what behaviour is abnormal or deviant varies from society to society. The occurrence and/or frequency of overt aggression, masturbation, crying and bedwetting are all examples of patterns which societies may view in very different ways in relation to the age of the child displaying them. Margaret Mead's early work among preliterate South Sea Islanders, for example, demonstrated huge variations in what are judged to be desirable attributes and attitudes. Even within one and the same society there are subcultures, for example a neighbourhood with different norms from those of the wider community, where shoplifting and truancy may well be considered 'fair game'. The standards of such a subculture may be 'antisocial' and a 'normally socialized' child in this setting will be very different from the 'normal' child, as normality is conceived in the wider community.

Our basic ideas of normality can also change with time. A hundred years ago standards were very different and the present-day preoccupation with the 'generation gap' is witness to the rift (as some would see it) between the values of young and old.

A statistical criterion

In essence, society's criterion of normality is *quantitative* in the sense that only what is relatively rare in the population is regarded as abnormal. All is well if the child conforms to what is generally done. Described baldly like this, normality suggests a very grey world where a child must be more or less indistinguishable from his or her peers, where to strive to be adjusted is to strive to be average. Distasteful as this may sound, society often claims to venerate individuality, but at another level does fear the manifestations of individualism.

It is important not to turn the statement, 'problem behaviour is rare' upside down! Not all children who display rare qualities – idiosyncracies and eccentricities – are necessarily maladjusted. Far from it. Child prodigies, for example, are gifted children who possess what most people would think of as very favourable psychological and physical attributes.

Developmental norms are essentially about how often certain behaviours and other attributes are manifested by children of different ages. In an American long-term, longitudinal study by Jean Macfarlane and colleagues of the development of children at large, problematic behaviours were fairly common and were found to shift over the years. For most children, problems manifested themselves briefly at certain periods and then became minimal or disappeared completely. One could speculate as to the reasons; doubtless sensitive and sensible parental management would be a significant factor. Problems such as moodiness, overdependence, sombreness and irritability showed the greatest persistence. Among the problems which declined in frequency with age were toilet-training problems, speech problems, fears and thumb sucking. Difficulties which declined at a rather later stage, and at a slower rate, were overactivity, destructiveness and tempers. In fact, one third of the boys were still having temper explosions at 13. Problems such as insufficient appetite and lying reached a peak early and then subsided. Many personality problems showed high frequencies around about or just before school-starting age, then declined in prevalence, and later rose again in puberty. Among these were restless sleep, disturbing dreams, physical timidity, irritability, attention-demanding, overdependence, sombreness, jealousy and, in boys, food-finickiness. Only one problem increased systematically with age – nail biting, reached a peak and began to subside only near the end of adolescence. Among the problems which showed little or no relationship to age was oversensitiveness.

It is obviously very useful to know about these 'norms' when trying to evaluate a child's difficulties, be it as parent, teacher or psychologist. (Turning back to our two 'problem' children for a minute, Ayesha's problems were not unusual for her age and circumstances, but Wayne's were unusual.)

Some working criteria

Psychological problems are seen as having unfavourable social and personal consequences for the child him or herself (for example phobic anxiety), for the family (for example truancy), and sometimes, the wider community (for example vandalism). It is necessary to distinguish between *antisocial* acts, the adverse repercussions of which are felt primarily by others, and *antiascetic* acts, forms of pleasurable self-indulgence judged by others to be harmful to those who engage in them.

Ultimately, the professional judgement of a child's psychological well-being is made in individual terms, taking into account the child's unique personality, his or her particular circumstances and all the opportunities, disappointments and stresses associated with them. It is the task of the psychologist, when called upon to carry out an assessment, to ascertain where children stand on the developmental 'scale', whether their progress and mental and physical status are appropriate to their age, retarded or advanced. In the light of this background information, the psychologist has to decide whether or not the child requires help. They may do this by applying several criteria to the facts gleaned about the child and his or her circumstances. This involves asking themselves a series of questions:

(1) Is the child's adjustive (adaptive, coping) behaviour appropriate to his or her age, intelligence and social situation?

(2) Is the environment making reasonable *demands* of the child?

(3) Is the environment satisfying the crucial *needs* of the child – that is to say, the needs that are vital at his or her particular stage of development?

Remember that Ayesha's father, among other things, was demanding academic brilliance beyond his daughter's capacity; while Wayne's parents, anxious and overprotective, were not allowing their child to learn to stand on his own feet – their cosseting was hindering his need for independence.

Parents and teachers may make excessive or conflicting demands on the youngsters in their care; unhappy parents, for example, can make children the emotional battle ground upon which to wage marital warfare. Society uses the family to act as its main agent in the socialization of the child, and it is precisely here that the child is most vulnerable. Generally, the process of socializing the infant and producing an independent and constructive member of the community is carried out well. But occasionally the basic unit of the community – the family – is itself, to a greater or lesser degree, psychologically disturbed. Thus, if the child's behaviour is abnormal (unusual) or troublesome and the answers to the second and third questions listed above are 'no', then we are still faced with a problem – but rather more of a 'problem situation' than 'problem child' as such.

Family therapy

Mention of the family is our cue for introducing another major strand of this chapter: the development and dynamics of family life. The perspective, influenced by a general systems or cybernetic paradigm was originally conceived by Ludwig von Bertalanffy in the late 1920s in an attempt to understand living organisms in a holistic way; and it was many years later that researchers in the 1970s applied it to work with families. The *systems approach* embraces the concept of circular/reciprocal causation in which each action can be considered as the consequence of the action preceding it and the cause of the action following it. No single element in the sequence controls the operation of the sequence as a whole because it is itself governed by the operation of the other elements in the system.

Translating these ideas to family life, it is suggested that any individual in a family system is affected by the activities of other members of the family, activities which his or her actions or decisions (in turn) determine. An individual's behaviour is *both* stimulus and response. Such considerations have influenced the way in which casework is conceptualized by many contemporary clinicians.

Systems theorists in contemporary practice focus not only on individuals but also on the system of relationships in which they act out their life. Thus the focus of help is not necessarily prejudged as only the child (say) who was referred to the clinic but will extend to their whole family. *Family therapy* is the name of the form of treatment to which this perspective gives rise.

The importance of self-image

For all the importance of the family and other social contexts within which children proactively shape their lives, and/or are reactively moulded, we should not lose sight of the *person*, and notably the intimate core of the personality known as 'self'. Psychological problems are very much bound up with the child's favourable or unfavourable self-perceptions (i.e. *self-image*) and his or her perception of, and relationship with, other people. So many of the difficulties which children have to cope with are social ones – the problems of getting on with brothers and sisters, or with other children of the same age, with teachers, their own parents, and, by no means least, getting on with themselves. Children need to rely on themselves, get to know themselves, understand their own limitations and make the most of their capabilities. In a nutshell, they must see themselves in a realistic manner.

Classifying childhood problems

Before leaving the subject of what is meant by the term 'abnormal', it is useful to see how professionals have tried to bring some order to the multiplicity of behaviours that people (mainly adults) think of as 'problematic'. Statistical methods are used in the search for clusters, patterns or syndromes of problems. These mathematical analyses endeavour to tease out, from masses of data culled from clinic records and epidemiological surveys, dimensions of disturbed behaviour which are explicit and operational (i.e. capable of measurement). An example of the search for common denominators to childhood problems is Herbert Quay's review of 55 factor analytic investigations which has elicited seven behavioural dimensions each with its cluster of associated characteristics. Essentially they are refinements of two major categories called conduct and emotional disorders.

Conduct and emotional disorders

Conduct disorders include a constellation of problems involving physical and verbal aggressiveness, disruptiveness, irresponsibility, non-compliance, and poor personal relationships. Youngsters with conduct disorders demonstrate a fundamental inability or unwillingness to adhere to the rules and codes of conduct, prescribed by society at its various levels. Such failures may be related to the failure to learn controls or to the fact that the behavioural standards a child has absorbed do not coincide with the norms of that section of society which enacts and enforces the rules. Because of the provocative and confrontational nature of these youngsters' actions (not infrequently a consequence – in part – of harsh life experiences) they tend to appear quite frequently and disproportionately among those children who are physically abused by their parents or other caregivers.

Emotional problems include childhood fears and phobias, depression, social inhibition (shyness), and tend (although there are sometimes exceptions) to be more benign and transient in nature than the conduct disorders. In practice, a sizeable proportion of children have behaviour problems which, to an important extent, share characteristics of both emotional and conduct disorders.

Continuity and discontinuity of behaviour

We have seen that certain behaviours correlate, that is they form clusters of associated activities. But what of associations between behaviour patterns over time – in other words, continuities? Do children who are seriously antisocial at, say, six or seven years of age tend to be so at adolescence or even as far forward as adulthood? Several studies have investigated the intercorrelations among behavioural or personality ratings over the years – an exercise fraught with methodological and interpretive problems.

The view that emerges from long-term, longitudinal (prospective) studies is that many individuals retain a great capacity for change; the outcomes of the events of early childhood are continually transformed by later experiences, making the course of human development more open than many theorists in the past ever believed possible.

For normal children, personal characteristics do not begin to crystallize or stabilize until the age of five to seven. And even then, only modest correlations with adult behaviours emerge. The view commonly held by workers in the mental health field that early characteristics remain relatively unchanged seems to be true only of a specially vulnerable section of the population.

Certainly, the emotional problems – fears, phobias, inhibitions of childhood – tend to be relatively short-lived, a matter of months to a year, although there are certainly exceptions to this generalization. Nevertheless, children who attend clinics for such problems are impossible to distinguish as adults from persons who were not referred in their youth for such problems. There is general agreement that it is those disorders involving disruptive, aggressive, or antisocial behaviour that are most likely to persist into adolescence (often involving law-breaking), and even adulthood, probably because adverse environmental influences tend to be reinforced time and time again, year in and year out. This is seen notably in sexual abuse where the abuser, so often, is a member of the family.

Delinquent behaviour

This mention of law-breaking introduces the concept of *delinquency*. It is not possible to draw a clear-cut line between delinquents and non-delinquents. Surveys have shown that it is not only, or even usually, children known to the police who have broken the law. A large number of English grammar-school boys were asked about their delinquencies. About one half of them admitted committing some sort of antisocial act. A large proportion of them, moreover, said that they had committed an act which could have landed them in a juvenile court had they been found out. Over half of the boys had stolen money, two thirds had shoplifted and nine out of ten had stolen something from school. In a survey of 1,000 school children aged 9–14 carried out in Norway and Sweden, 89 per cent confessed to petty illegal offences, 39 per cent to ordinary theft, 17 per cent to burglary and 14 per cent to wilful damage to property.

The term 'delinquent' is a very flexible one, being in part a function of a particular set of laws *and* law enforcement policies. Although many children commit 'delinquent' acts at one time or another, certain children (particularly those from privileged homes and schools) are more likely than others to avoid detection. The concept of a 'delinquent' is essentially an administrative rather than a clinical one. It is important to bear in mind that not all children with conduct disorders become delinquent, nor do all delinquent youngsters display clinical features of a conduct disorder. Although a large number of young people commit crimes, few develop into adult offenders. After a steady increase in the frequency of delinquent acts during childhood, reaching a peak in later adolescence, there is a fairly sharp decline in the delinquency rates in the early twenties. The large majority of 'delinquents' gradually merge with the more-or-less law-abiding population, settled down perhaps by leaving school, the source often (for some) of unremitting criticism and irrelevance, and by the responsibilities and rewards of a job, marriage and family life.

THE VULNERABLE CHILD: CAUSES AND EFFECTS

Why do only certain children develop serious emotional problems when faced with difficulties? Why, for example, did Emma refuse to go to school following an incident of bullying (the event which she blamed for her fears), while Fiona, another viction of the same persecutor, resolutely dried her tears and managed to soldier on? To put the question another way: why are some children emotionally vulnerable? It would be helpful if we could list factors X, Y or Z (for example inconsistent discipline, maternal rejection or being an only child) as invariable causes of A, B and C (say, disobedience, juvenile delinquency or shyness). Unfortunately, life is not that simple.

Multiple causation

Human actions – whether simple or elaborate, normal or abnormal – are produced by different combinations and permutations of influences which have somewhat unpredictable consequences.

Let us illustrate this, taking first of all the pattern of causation in which quite *dissimilar* causes can produce the *same* results.

“ *Mel – sensitive and highly strung from birth – had parents both of whom were shy and introspective. Unable to learn social skills from them, she developed an acute sensitivity to 'social rebuffs' from her playmates (who, in fact, mistook her shyness for aloofness). Eventually Mel became convinced of her personal inferiority, which in turn increased her fear of other people.* **”**

Yet another pattern of causation was present in the case of Pravin:

❝ *Pravin's parents were indifferent to him and made their rejection of him quite plain in many humiliating and frightening ways. Inevitably this sort of treatment led to feelings of hostility in the child which he could not tolerate in himself. He was anxious when he felt hostile, as he had been severely punished by his parents for displaying aggression. He began to fear social mixing because he found that social situations increased the unacceptable feelings of hostility within him.* **❞**

When considering problem behaviour, we have to bear in mind the irksome fact that not only can a particular environmental background or type of child-rearing philosophy produce a certain kind of emotional problem in one child and another kind of emotional problem in another child, but that it may result in no exceptional behaviour at all in yet a third child. The fact is that this level of 'explanation' is far too global.

Fortunately, there is an answer to this: the vast majority of children's behaviours are learned, and this includes their abnormal behaviours. In asking *how* a child becomes a problem child, clinical psychologists are able to capitalize on their understanding of the laws of learning (in particular) and those of behaviour (in general). Each case requires an individual and detailed assessment, called a *functional analysis*. This is based on the concept of a functional relationship with the environment in which changes in individual behaviour produce changes in the environment and vice versa. So if parents make a fuss and attend to their daughter's tantrums, such tantrums will persist and even increase in frequency because they give rise to a 'pay off' (positive reinforcement).

All forms of learning which are generally functional in their effects in that they help the child to adapt to life's demands can, under certain circumstances, contribute to maladjustment. In that sense learning is maladaptive or dysfunctional (self-defeating) in its effects. Thus a youngster who learns usefully on the basis of classical and operant 'conditioning' processes (see Glossary) to avoid dangerous situations, can also learn in the same way (maladaptively) to fear and avoid school or social gatherings. A parent may unwittingly reinforce immature behaviour by attending to it. Here is a rule-of-thumb:

acceptable behaviour + reinforcement = more acceptable behaviour

acceptable behaviour + no reinforcement = less acceptable behaviour

unacceptable behaviour + reinforcement = more unacceptable behaviour

unacceptable behaviour + no reinforcement = less unacceptable behaviour

In the light of the above you may wish to work out the likely consequences of some examples of parental behaviour shown in *Exercise 11.1* on page 200.

Behaviour therapy

Contemporary *behaviour therapy* (or behaviour modification) seems to offer what is both a useful theoretical and practical approach to the treatment of a very wide range of childhood and adolescent disorders. The traditional view of 'psychopathology' is associated with the belief that therapeutic activities must *only* be engaged in by very highly trained professional experts to the exclusion of other people in the patient's immediate environment.

In this so-called *dyadic model* the expert 'treats the patient', usually in a clinic. But therapists are unable to see parent–child (or teacher–child) interactions in their natural settings, and, given the artificiality of their consulting rooms, they may not even observe directly the problem behaviours for which the child is referred. Much of the information they get is hearsay and there can be a startling discrepancy between what parents say the child (and they themselves) are doing and what actually happens.

By contrast the *triadic model* embodied in the family-orientated behavioural approach is anchored in the natural environment; it uses to the full the goodwill and powerful influence of those involved in close everyday contact with the client. Indeed, there is growing evidence that effective assessment and treatment of many childhood disorders (particularly conduct problems) requires observation and intervention in the natural environment of the child. Furthermore, the systematic and successful training of parents, individually and in groups, in the management of children has increased considerably.

A case illustration

" *Gary was six and a half years old at referral and was described as a very unlovable child. He constantly screamed and shouted abuse at his parents, and had violent temper tantrums when he would indulge in physical aggression, hitting and punching people and furniture and screaming at the top of his voice until he got his own way. He was also persistently defiant and disobedient and seemed to enjoy provoking confrontations with his parents. Observation and assessment in Gary's home revealed that his behaviours were being massively reinforced by attention from his parents and by the fact that shouting and temper tantrums usually resulted in Gary getting his own way. Although his actions*

Predicting the Consequences of Parental Behaviour

Can you anticipate, in the light of the 'equations' described on page 198, the likely *longer-term* consequences of parental behaviour on the child's behaviour in the following situations?

Antecedents (A)	Behaviour (B)	Consequences (C)*
(1) Marjorie was asked to put away her toys.	She did so.	Her mum gave her a big hug and said thank you.
(2) James asked Dennis his brother for a turn on his new bike.	Dennis got off and helped James on to the bike.	Nil! Mother made no comment. James rode off without a word of thanks.
(3) David was told to leave the TV off.	He kept turning it on.	It was eventually left on – to give people a bit of peace.
(4) Anna was having breakfast.	She kept getting down from her place	Mum followed her round with a bowl of cereal, feeding her with a spoonful whenever she could.
(5) Hitesh wanted to go to the park; Dad said there wasn't time.	He kicked and shouted, lay on floor and screamed.	Dad ignored his tantrum; eventually Hitesh calmed down and began to play.

*Note: This 'equation' dealing with the effects of reinforcement upon behaviour is sometimes referred to as the ABC analysis.)

ANSWERS on page 202.

were socially 'dysfunctional' they were highly 'functional' for him. **”**

Not surprisingly, family relationships were very strained and Gary was so unpopular that on the rare occasions when he did behave appropriately he went unnoticed, which meant he was only getting attention for antisocial behaviour. In partnership the psychologist and parents successfully instituted a programme to deal with the shouting and temper tantrums. It involved discussing the household rules, deciding to 'set limits' by removing Gary from the room as soon as he started to shout, a procedure known as 'time out from positive reinforcement' and designed to eliminate the possibility of his receiving reinforcing attention for antisocial behaviour. At the same time great emphasis was placed on rewarding Gary for prosocial behaviour with tokens which he could then exchange for a privilege (such as staying up late) or a treat (such as a favourite play activity with his parents).

This programme (very much simplified here for illustration) was designed to improve the parents' relationship with Gary by setting limits, and by providing opportunities for mutually enjoyable (reinforcing) activities. These, and other aspects of their attitudes about child-rearing, were discussed with Gary's parents. By the end of the programme Gary was much calmer and happier, showing much more prosocial behaviour and getting on a good deal better with his parents who could now report 'enjoying' him again.

This relatively brief account of children's problems has, of necessity, been restricted in its coverage of other theoretical and therapeutic perspectives – of which there are many (see Herbert, 1988, in the Recommended Reading section for a review of a variety of approaches). The choice of the two major theoretical perspectives, behavioural (social learning theory) and family process (therapy) is based upon their adherence to psychological theories which are supported by fairly substantial empirical evidence. But this is not to deny that there is much of value in other ways (for example, psychoanalytic, cognitive, humanistic) of studying child development and the problems associated with growing up.

Recommended reading

Bandura, A. (1977) *Social Learning Theory*. Englewood Cliffs, New Jersey: Prentice-Hall. [An essential introduction to the theory.]

Gross, J. (1989) *Psychology and Parenthood*. Milton Keynes: Open University Press. [A highly readable review of the relevant literature.]

Herbert, M. (1988) *Working with Children and their Families*. Leicester: The British Psychological Society & Routledge. [The what, why and how of working with children and their families in problematic situations.]

Patterson, G.R. (1982) *Coercive Family Process*. Eugene, Oreg.: Castalia. [Exploration of coercion theory in practice.]

Richman, N. & Lansdown, R. (Eds) (1988) *Problems of Preschool Children*. Chichester: John Wiley. [Packed with useful survey and clinical information.]

Rutter, M. & Hersov, L. (Eds) (1985) *Child and Adolescent Psychiatry: Modern approaches*. 2nd edn. Oxford: Blackwell Sciences Publications. [Major text on child psychiatry.]

References

von Bertalanffy, L. (1968) *General Systems Theory*. Harmondsworth: Penguin. [The seminal work on systems theory; a major influence on family theory and therapy.]

Coopersmith, S. (1967) *The Antecedents of Self-Esteem*. San Francisco: Freeman. [The precursors and influences on high and low self-esteem.]

Douglas, J. & Richman, N. (1984) *Coping with Young Children*. Harmondsworth: Penguin. [Readable book with practical advice for caregivers.]

Elmhorn, K. (1965) Study in self-reported delinquency among schoolchildren. In *Scandinavian Studies in Criminology*. London: Tavistock. [High rates of 'delinquent' acts among 'ordinary' youngsters.]

Ferguson, D.M. & Horwood, L.J. (1987) The trait and method components of ratings of conduct disorder. Part 1: Maternal and teacher evaluations of conduct disorders in young children. *Journal of Child Psychology and Psychiatry*, 28, 249–260. [Similarities and differences in the ways parents and teachers evaluate problem behaviour.]

Forehand, R.L. & McMahon, R.J. (1981) *Helping the Noncompliant Child: A Clinician's guide to parent training*. New York: Guilford Press. [One of the foremost texts on training parents to manage disobedience in children.]

Gibson, H.B. (1967) Self-reported delinquency among schoolboys and their attitudes to the police. *British Journal of Social and Clinical Psychology*, 6, 168–173. [Survey findings.]

Herbert, M. (1987) *Behavioural Treatment of Children with Problems: A practice manual*. London: Academic Press. [A practical guide to the 'nuts and bolts' of doing behavioural work with children.]

Kanner, L. (1953) *Child Psychiatry*. Springfield, Ill.: C.C. Thomas. [Famous, but now somewhat dated, text on child psychiatry.]

McFarlane, J.W., Allen, L. & Honzik, M.P.A. (1954) *A Developmental Study of the Behavior Problems of Normal Children Between Twenty-one Months and Fourteen Years.*. Berkeley, Calif.: University of California Press. [Classic longitudinal study of children and their normal problems.]

Mead, M. (1935) *Sex and Temperament in Three Primitive Societies*. London: Routledge & Kegan Paul. [Fascinating early study of preliterate people by an eminent anthropologist.]

Quay, H.C., Routh, D.K. & Shapiro, S.K. (1987) Psychopathology of childhood: From descripiton to validation. *Annual Review of Psychology*, 38, 491–532. [Useful account of the emotional and behavioural disorders of childhood.]

Rutter, M., Tizard, J. & Whitmore, Y. (Eds) (1987) *Education, Health and Behaviour*. London: Longman. [Survey of health and behaviour of cohort of Isle of Wight children.]

-----------------------------ANSWERS TO EXERCISE 11.1-----------------------------

(1) Marjorie is even more likely in future to put her toys away when requested.

(2) Dennis is less likely in future (perhaps unlikely) to share his bike on future occasions is if asked.

(3) David is more likely to disobey instructions on future occasions when given them.
(4) Anna is unlikely in the future to sit properly at the table having her breakfast.
(5) Hitesh is more likely on future occasions to comply with his father's instructions.

12. Puberty and Adolescence

▽ The nature of adolescence
▽ The changes of puberty
▽ Discovering personal identity
▽ Problems of adolescence
▽ Parent–child relationships
▽ Adoption and its effects
▽ Parental prejudice

Lousy stinking school on Thursday. I tried my old uniform on, but I have outgrown it so badly that my father is being forced to buy me a new one tomorrow. He is going up the wall but I can't help it if my body is in a growth period can I? I am only five centimetres shorter than Pandora now. My thing remains static at twelve centimetres.
      (Sue Townsend, *The Secret Diary of Adrian Mole Aged 13¾*)

Somewhere between the immaturity of childhood and the hoped-for maturity of adulthood lie the years we refer to as adolescence. Young Adrian Mole, long-suffering 'offspring' of author Sue Townsend's imagination, manifests in this fragment from his diary several common adolescent preoccupations: bodily changes, sex, school, relationships with parents and, not least, himself and the opposite sex. But what is adolescence?

THE NATURE OF ADOLESCENCE

Adolescence is usually thought of as a stage of *transition* – lasting some seven or so years – from the irresponsibility enjoyed by children to the responsibility of adulthood. Children are wholly dependent upon their parents for love, nurturance and guidance; adults are required to be independent and able to care for themselves. Seven years is far too long to reify adolescence into a homogeneous 'entity'. For this reason it would seem sensible to distinguish between early, middle and late adolescence: the first (from about 11 to 13 years of age) being closer to childhood in its ramifications, the third, the late teens (18 or 19), overlapping with young adulthood.

The term *adolescence* refers to the *psychological* developments which are related (loosely) to the physical growth processes defined by the term *puberty*. To put it another way, adolescence begins in biology and ends in culture – at that point determined, in large part by one's culture or society, where the boy and girl have attained a reasonable degree of psychological independence from their parents. Small wonder that there is a lack of precision in the definition and timetabling of adolescence; there is no clear endpoint. Even the beginning point – puberty itself – varies according to climatic and hereditary factors, and can be triggered or delayed by many external influences.

Parental worries: the turbulent years

Having referred to the preoccupations of adolescent boys and girls, it is worth asking what are the concerns of their parents and other caregivers. By and large, they are apprehensive about the risks and unforeseen 'transformations' in their loved ones during this period of life. They tend to see the teens as years of 'storm and stress', to be endured rather than enjoyed as parents. Why, it must be asked, has adolescence been 'isolated' from the rest of development and given – relative to other stages – such a bad name? The popular (and professional) notion that adolescence is different from the whole of development which precedes it, and the whole of development which follows it, is of relatively recent origin. Among the early proponents of this view was G. Stanley Hall in his 1904 treatise on the subject: *Adolescence: Its psychology and its relationship to physiology, anthropology, sociology, sex, crime, religion and education.* As the title suggests, this was a weighty, and indeed, influential work.

Hall's belief that adolescence is necessarily a stage of development associated with emotional turmoil and psychic disturbance was to become so deeply rooted, reinforced by a succession of psychoanalytically orientated writers, that it persists to this day. The 'storm and stress' story (built on eagerly by journalists in sensational items about feckless teenage hooligans and vandals) has filtered down to street level as a veritable 'demonological' theory of adolescence. Small wonder that so many parents await their child's adolescence with foreboding, and given the potency of self-fulfilling prophecies, the 'confirmation' of some of their worst predictions.

Certainly, professionals – not surprisingly given the biased *clinical* sample they see – have taken a jaundiced view of adolescence and have noted its neurotic- or psychotic-like features: hysteria, regression, mood swings and disintegration. A psychiatrist in the 1930s described adolescence in Alice in Wonderland terms as a period of development in which 'normally abnormalities so often happen it is abnormal that everything passes normally'. Anna Freud, writing much later about adolescence in *Psychoanalytic Study of the Child*, said it was 'abnormal' if a child kept a 'steady equilibrium during the adolescent period. . . . The adolescent manifestations come close to symptom formation of the neurotic, psychotic or dissocial order and merge almost imperceptibly into. . .almost all the mental illnesses'.

While adolescence is not without its very real difficulties, as one would expect of a period of rapid and dramatic change, the negatives have been much exaggerated as we hope to show.

The ambiguity of adolescence

The period between childhood and adulthood devoted to adolescent development varies from culture to culture. In the past half-century or so, within Western societies, adolescence has been reduced in some ways (in the UK the age of majority is down from 21 to 18) but has become in other ways a longer span of years, in the sense that much sought-after higher education prolongs the youngster's dependence on parents. It is sociological phenomena, such as status, duties, privileges, the end of education, the right to marry and enjoy economic independence, which are most frequently cited as the termination of adolescence. Not surprisingly, ambiguity over these matters leads to conflict between parents and their 'grown-up' (as the adolescent sees it) child, when it comes to their freedom of choice and action. This has a bearing on the youngster's search for an identity of his or her own – an image of self that could last, with minor modifications, for a lifetime.

Life tasks

The major *life task* of the adolescent stage – according to contemporary psychologists like Erik Erikson – is the individual's need to discover, shape and consolidate his or her own *self-identity*. This refers to the core of an individual's character or personality and is thought to be a vital precursor to true intimacy and depth in personal relationships.

At the very foundations of adolescent self-awareness, the self-image is a representation of their body, what it is like, and how it looks to others. It is the radical nature of the growth which occurs at this time – the physical, physiological and mental changes – that transform children into adults.

THE CHANGES OF PUBERTY

Puberty may bring about a certain self-centredness in children. The very ground of familiarity on which the young person has been standing so securely up to now begins to shift. The body the child has taken for granted becomes the focus of attention, with a lot of mirror-gazing and minute scrutiny of blemishes and 'good points'. The end of childhood, for the boy, is signposted by an increase in the size of testes, scrotum and penis; in the girl there is an increase in the growth rates of breasts, ovaries and uterus (womb). The physical and physiological changes that take place (on average) at 12 in girls and 14 in boys, are due to the action of hormones. Growth in virtually all parts of the body is sharply accelerated. For both sexes there is an increase in the size of shoulders and hips, arms and legs, height and total body weight. Growth tends to be most rapid at the periphery and to move in towards the trunk, so the young adolescent appears to be 'all hands and feet'. Of course, size eventually gets back into proportion.

The growth spurt

All of these events are referred to as the adolescent *growth spurt*. Because the peak in growth rate occurs at different times for different parts of the body, the basic balance of the body is temporarily disturbed, producing, for some, a disconcerting sense of disequilibrium. Because teenagers have more social awareness now than they had before, the feeling of being out of synchrony can be intolerable at times. Adolescents are very much the victims of biological forces they cannot always comprehend. The feeling of events being out of one's control can be decidedly uncomfortable. The sense of having reasonable direction over one's life as opposed to little or no control over events (i.e. one's behaviour doesn't really work) is referred to as *internal* versus *external locus of control*. A shift from internal to external is a temporary feature of this stage of development for some adolescents.

Puberty is not just a matter of changes in the size and shape of the body. Physiological developments in glandular secretions, particularly those affecting sexual function, occur. Up until puberty, males and females have similar quantities of both sex hormones in the blood stream, with only a slightly greater proportion of the sex-relevant hormone. Thus boys have nearly as much oestrogen (the female sex hormone) as androgen. At puberty, however, there is a sharp increase in the secretion of the sex-related hormone. Hormonal changes bring, in their wake, psychological changes. Youngsters will have to manage their increased sexual arousal; parents will have to deal with their offsprings' increased (and, in fact, hormone-driven) assertiveness.

In normal boys there is roughly a five-year variation in the age at which puberty is reached. One of the main indicators is ejaculation or emission. By the age of 16, the average boy is fully developed sexually and is capable of becoming a father. The word 'testes' comes from the Latin for 'witness' – the presence of testicles was a witness to a man's virility and his potential as a father. Breast development, beginning between 8 and 13, is often the first sign of pubescence and early womanhood. But it is important to remember the considerable variation between individuals in the timing and ordering of these physical changes. Menstruation is generally a signal that a girl is producing ova and is capable of becoming a mother; a girl's first period is therefore a notable landmark in her life. Surveys suggest that a very small proportion of girls (about ten per cent) when asked about their reactions to the onset of their menses demonstrate enthusiasm; most report that they are indifferent; a significant proportion feel worry or anxiety and a few are panic-stricken. Girls' development is about two years ahead of boys, and it tends to continue to be so throughout the developmental timetable.

DISCOVERING PERSONAL IDENTITY

In Western culture the importance of *body image* is evident in the considerable expenditure of time and effort that is spent altering the body's appearance. Individuals of all ages are constantly seeking – by means of clothes, bleaches, skin preparations, cosmetics, tattooing and even plastic surgery – to change their appearance and to make themselves look like some fashionable ideal, and this preoccupation is particularly evident in 'teenagers'. Adolescents develop a set of feelings and attitudes towards their bodies which contribute significantly to their evolving sense of personal identity. These subjective impressions (referred to as the body image) are made up, in large part, of the attitudes that young persons imagine others have towards their own body and its parts. The resulting body concept may be pleasing and satisfying or it may lead to a view of the body as offputting, dirty

'*I know it's a bit late, but looking at our Nigel, I think I'm starting a post-natal depression.*'

or shameful. Clearly, the latter has an adverse effect on the individual's self-esteem.

Answering the question 'Who am I?'

Much of the self-absorption associated with this period of life has its origins, not only in the immense physical changes taking place at puberty, but also in the discovery of identity. There are sometimes disconcerting swings from total narcissism to self-hatred and self-depreciation. When there is a large discrepancy between teenagers' self-concept ('myself as I am') and their idealized self ('myself as I would like to be') there is also likely to be anxiety and over-sensitiveness in close attendance.

There is a popular belief that a crisis over personal identity in adolescence, producing all or some of the symptoms of stress (anxiety, depression, a sense of frustration, conflict and defeatism) is inevitable. Erik Erikson sees adolescence as one of a sequence of stages in the life cycle which (like the earlier and later ones) contains a particular life challenge to be resolved or *developmental task* to be confronted. For the teenager it is the challenge between 'identity' and 'identity diffusion'. In leaving behind their childish roles adolescents are thought to become preoccupied with finding for themselves a satisfactory answer to the question 'Who am I?' They may 'try out' a variety of identities in their search for answers; they seek experience in different roles and through a variety of relationships. It is self-exploration through experimentation. Some settle for an immature self too soon ('foreclosure'); others are too late. Thus it is suggested that if boys and girls fail to clarify and give substance to their personal identity they are likely to experience depression and even despair. These feelings, plus a sense of meaninglessness and self-depreciation, are the indications of what Erikson calls 'identity diffusion'. Of course, many of us never cease questioning our identity and elaborating or reshaping our personalities, but we enjoy the security of a clear sense of who we are at the core or centre of our being.

The development of identity doesn't always proceed smoothly, but evidence calls into question Erikson's belief that adolescents *usually* suffer a crisis over their identity. Most teenagers actually have a positive but not unrealistically inflated self-image, according to several studies. This view of themselves also tends to be fairly stable over the years.

Early and late developers

Early maturing boys tend to cope better than early maturing girls; their early maturity puts them on a par with girls of the same age. Girls, in particular, may find that their early maturity is perceived as sexually provocative by some. They are often self-conscious about their precocious sexual development, especially their body image and the fact of menstruation which is frequently viewed in negative terms (the 'curse'). Premature sexual development seldom means premature sexual outlets of an adult kind. In general, premature puberty leads to an increase in sexual arousal, but sexual behaviour tends to remain roughly in line with the child's actual age and social experience.

Late maturers look childlike for their age. They are more likely to be teased by their peers and thus beset by feelings of inferiority and a sense of social isolation. Girls are likely to suffer less than boys because they are on a par with most boys of their own age, but they may worry about late breast development and the late onset of their periods, particularly if under pressure from their more physically advanced peers. Boys who are late developers seem to feel the most pressure and lack most in self-confidence and research shows that such feelings may last well into adult life – long after physical maturity is achieved.

PROBLEMS OF ADOLESCENCE

As a major period of transition and change it would be surprising if there were not more serious problems than the ones just referred to during adolescence. There are, but contrary to popular opinion adolescence does not, in fact, appear to be a *markedly* more vulnerable stage of development than others. Nevertheless, about one in five adolescents do experience significant psychological problems. Among these problems are:

- *depression* (and suicide attempts, a phenomenon with a peak at 15–19 years)
- *anxieties* (particularly fears about school and social situations)
- *conduct problems and delinquency* (see Chapter 11)
- *eating disorders* (anorexia nervosa, bulimia nervosa)
- *substance misuse*

What *is* different is that because adolescents are experimenting with, and rehearsing, adult roles, the implications of errors of judgement or inexperience can be more serious.

Drug use and misuse

For example, drug use is now relatively common among adolescents, and drug misuse is a growing problem. But what are drugs? The term can be applied to many things from alcohol and cigarettes to cannabis and heroin; their use and misuse can exact awful penalties in the lives and well-being of individuals. It is natural for parents to feel hurt and angry, and then desperate, when they discover that their child is taking drugs. Teenagers do not know a world without cannabis and amphetamines, and it is not surprising if they are tempted to experiment. This does not make them addicts any more than getting drunk made their parents alcoholics when they were the same age.

Most young people are fairly sensible and not as unaware of the risks of excessive drug use as they are of excessive drinking. However, adolescence can be a difficult time for some young people who are under pressure at school, those who are on bad terms with their parents, or on no terms at all with their peers. For some, work, or the lack of work, is frustrating and boring. All of this means temptation when an acquaintance offers an unhappy youngster something which is 'exciting' or 'fun', something which everyone else is taking. Many children say no; a growing number appease their curiosity or give in to the social pressure. But not all of those who use alcohol or other drugs can be said to be unhappy, emotionally disturbed or psychiatrically vulnerable. Most youngsters will outgrow drugs and the drug scene.

The risk for some is that of becoming addicted accidentally because the dangers have not been fully assessed; hence the importance of education about drugs. What may begin as a fairly harmless experimenting with various substances for pleasure may, when the drug is addictive (i.e. when tolerance increases rapidly with time), become a dependency. Such a person's unwitting slide into dependency is rather different from that of the depressed youngster, who feels inadequate, and who eagerly embraces the 'lift' or 'anaesthetic' quality of drugs.

The school environment and its influence

The secondary school phase of a child's life is not without its problems; the demands of school seem to highlight, indeed exacerbate, the difficulties of vulnerable youngsters. School introduces boys and girls to social and working relationships and to various forms of authority. The areas of academic success, social behaviour, moral values and occupational choice represent major spheres of influence by teachers as well as parents, in the socialization of young people. Michael Rutter and a team of researchers, in their study of London secondary schools, found that children and adolescents are more likely to show socially acceptable behaviour and good scholastic attainment if they attend certain schools rather than others, irrespective of their catchment area.

The strong 'message' to emerge from this research was that school values and norms appear to be more effective if it is clear to all that they have widespread support. Discipline is easier to maintain if the pupils appreciate that it relates to a generally accepted approach and does not simply represent the whims of the individual teacher. The particular rules which are set and the specific disciplinary techniques which are used, are probably much less important than the establishment of some principles and guidelines which are clearly recognizable, and accepted by the school as a whole.

Cognitive development

It is during roughly the years from 11 or 12 to 15 that children begin to free their thinking from its roots in their own *particular* experience. They become capable of *general* propositional thinking, in other words they can propose hypotheses and deduce consequences, as we saw in Chapter 7. Language is now fast, versatile, and extensive in its use. It is public, so that adolescents not only gain from their own thoughts but also from the articulated thoughts of others. Their world has become larger and richer, socially, intellectually and conceptually. Logical thinking or rationality is an important requirement for adjusting to life's demands; it is also a vital criterion of mental health. It can also constitute a 'trial' for parents as teenagers flex their intellectual 'muscles' by asking 'why?' or 'why not?', thereby questioning parental social and moral values.

PARENT–CHILD RELATIONSHIPS

The relationship between parents and teenagers is often a greater problem for the former than the latter. For those parents who are unwilling (or unable) to let their offspring break away from them, or those who, in unhappy or broken marriages, invest all their devotion in their children, adolescence may prove an ordeal. Many families become worried about conflicts over the granting of autonomy to adolescents. Typically, the adolescents want independence to do things such as smoke, select their own clothes, go to bed and stay out when it suits them at a younger age than the parents are prepared to accept. Parents will often ask psychologists to give some indication of what are appropriate ages for the granting of autonomy to adolescents. Since these questions involve personal values rather than 'scientific facts' (which is to say that there are no 'right' or 'wrong' answers) we suggest you try *Exercise 12.1* on page 214. You might compare persons of different ages, sexes, ethnic membership, and so on (i.e. group comparisons).

Is the generation gap a problem?

The much beloved (by the media) and feared (by parents) 'generation gap' is not as pervasive in adolescence as is generally thought. 'Distancing' is not a typical pattern. Most adolescents are still attached to their homes in a positive way, and they continue to depend upon their parents for emotional support, goodwill and approval. The family continues to be of critical importance to them as it was in earlier years of childhood. Indeed, concern and supervision (as long as it is not oppressive, or too intrusive) can be demonstrated to be vital during a phase when youngsters are experimenting with life by 'trying on' different personae.

It is exceptional for teenagers to feel torn between their two 'worlds' of parents and peers, certainly on the more important issues of life. There are more likely to be differences of opinion on minor issues such as hairstyle, fashion, social habits and privileges, where parental views are likely to be rejected in favour of the standards of their offspring's

Questionnaire on Adolescent Autonomy

Fill in this questionnaire, and if you are part of a group, compare and discuss your answers. It would be interesting to see whether there are differences between generations in the replies given to the questionnaire below.

In the two righthand columns indicate at what age you think boys and girls should be allowed to:

		Boys	*Girls*
(1)	Go shopping to a large complex without their parents.	....	....
(2)	Decide when they should leave school.	....	....
(3)	Decide what food they eat.	....	....
(4)	Decide what time they go to bed.	....	....
(5)	Drink alcohol if they want it.	....	....
(6)	Decide which television programmes they watch.	....	....
(7)	Go out with boyfriend/girlfriend if they want to (dating).	....	....
(8)	Decide what school they will go to.	....	....
(9)	Decide which clothes they will wear.	....	....
(10)	Decide which films they can go to see.	....	....
(11)	Decide what time they should come home at night.	....	....
(12)	Smoke if they want to.	....	....

friends. Where major issues are concerned, it seems that only a minority of adolescents radically depart from their parents' views.

A majority of adolescents share their parents' attitudes (although they may not always admit it to them) toward moral and political issues, and are prepared (by and large) to accept their parents' guidance on academic, career and personal issues. If anything, it could be said that the generations are drawing together rather than apart. Teenagers and their parents tend to agree on the important issues more than do parents and *their* parents (grandparents). Although the evidence is meagre, it does appear that rebelliousness and alienation are more likely in young persons who, in spite of considerable maturity, remain economically or in other ways dependent on their parents, thus prolonging adolescence. Typical of this would be students in higher education.

Sexual behaviour

Another popular belief about adolescence is that teenagers are sexually rampant and promiscuous. Although adolescents have become more accepting in their attitudes toward premarital sex, this does not imply a massive rise in casual sexual relationships. Young people, and particularly girls, continue to emphasize the importance of love and stable emotional attachment in premarital sex, although intended marriage or an engagement is not so often seen as a prerequisite of such relationships. The emphasis on a stable relationship with one sexual partner at a time is referred to as 'serial monogamy'. Girls do, however, display more conservative attitudes to these issues than boys.

Most youngsters wish to get married and have children. Certainly, a committed relationship is generally thought to be essential for the rearing of children, and, although a majority would wish such a long-standing commitment to take the form of marriage, a substantial minority reject such a view. An American study indicated that a majority of teenagers expect sexual fidelity after marriage, even though they do not always expect it before then.

ADOPTION AND ITS EFFECTS

Adolescence can be a critical time for children who have been adopted and their adoptive parents. Curiosity about one's birth parents, what they are like, where they are and questions about who I 'really' am, often come to a head when adopted teenagers (like their peers) 'sort out' their identity. And adoptive parents often reflect on the young person they have reared. Has it all worked out well? Has *their* influence prevailed whatever the biological inheritance of their child? Were their fears about adopting – especially where it was an older child – justified?

As we saw in Chapter 3, adoption is widely viewed as never achieving such positive outcomes for children as 'home' rearing. Indeed there is a belief that children reared in institutions in the early years and adopted beyond infancy are so damaged by their experience that they are incapable of subsequently establishing attachments to anyone. One investigation followed up late-adopted children into adulthood. A sample of 44 individuals, all of whom had been adopted between the ages of two and eight, were traced when in their mid-twenties. They were compared with a group of 40 who had been institutionally reared for a major part of their childhood and adolescence. Most of the adoptees had been removed from their family of birth in their first year and admitted into public care. They came mostly from highly deprived backgrounds, and the delay in placing them for adoption was mainly due to doubts as to whether these 'high risk' children should be adopted at all. During their period in care all experienced a number of moves between institutions and foster homes, and according to the agency records nearly half were said to have had moderate to severe emotional problems at that time.

The authors of this report were able to conclude that 'the good adjustment achieved by the vast majority of adoptees, indicates that, given a new and caring environment, children can form fresh attachments and overcome deprivations and deficits'.

When interviewed as adults, the adoptees took a largely positive view of their childhood. Well over 80 per cent expressed fair or considerable satisfaction with the adoption experience (as compared with 55 per cent of the residential group's view of their childhood). Asked for their feelings about the quality of their relationship with their adoptive parents, 45 per cent rated it as very good, 41 per cent as good, 9 per cent as mixed and 5 per cent as poor. In the great majority of cases they considered themselves to have been emotionally close or very close to the parents, to have also had warm relationships with siblings and members of the extended family, and to have regarded the adoptive family as 'theirs'.

PARENTAL PREJUDICE

Why have parents been so prepared to believe the worst of teenagers? While the reasons are many and varied, the context of raising teenagers is an important factor; parents are facing shifts at this time in their own personal development, from youthful maturity to early middle-age. We cannot consider adolescents and their problems without considering the manner in which they interact with their parents, who are not without their own preoccupations and anxieties. Some examples of how we may explore the family are shown in *Exercise 12.2:* A Family Life Map on page 218. Here we can see the kinds of life tasks and life events that may affect family members at different stages in life.

Most parents are over 30 years old when their first child reaches puberty. Indeed, there are many parents whose children reach their teens when they are in their forties or even fifties. Parents sometimes feel vulnerable as they survey their own bodily changes, reappraise their identity and achievements and look forward, with some apprehension, to the future. To some extent their preoccupation with self- and body-image, their changing, sometimes disturbing, thoughts about the meaning of life, the directions they have taken, and the choices put upon them, converge with those of their teenage children. This may well contribute to the ambivalence of parent–adolescent relationships.

Recommended reading

Baldwin, D. (1981) *Know Your Body*. Harmondsworth: Penguin. [Filled with useful information about the human body and its workings.]
Coleman, J. (1980) *Nature of Adolescence*. London: Methuen. [A useful introduction.
Conger, J. (1979) *Adolescence: Generation under pressure*. London: Harper & Row. [The stresses and strains of being a teenager.]
Herbert, M. (1987) *Living With Teenagers*. Oxford: Basil Blackwell. [An unjaundiced account of adolescents. Debunks some of the myths of stereotypes.]
Irwin, E. (1979) *Growing Pains: A study of teenage distress*. London: MacDonald & Evans. [The problems of being adolescent.]
Laufer, M. (1975) *Adolescent Disturbance and Breakdown*. Harmondsworth: Penguin. [Adolescence and disorders associated with it.]
Rubin, M. (1981) *Women of a Certain Age: The midlife search for self*. London: Harper Colophon Books. [A neglected stage of development (midlife) and its preoccupations.]

References

Coleman, J.C. (1974) *Relationships in Adolescence*. London: Routledge & Kegan Paul. [Relationships with parents, friends, the opposite sex.]
Conger, J.J. (1973) *Adolescence and Youth*. London: Harper & Row. [Theories and facts about adolescence.]
Coopersmith, S. (1967) *The Antecedents of Self-esteem*. London: W.H. Freeman. [Influences leading to high and low self-esteem.]
Elkind, D. (1980) Strategic interactions in early adolescence. In J. Adelson (Ed.) *Handbook of Adolescent Psychology*. New York: Wiley. [Coping with puberty and early adolescence.]
Erikson, E.H. (1965) *Childhood and Society*. London: Chatto & Windus: The Hogarth Press. [Stages of development and life tasks; identity formation and crisis.]

A Family Life Map

This is an example of a family system at work (a family life map). Draw a similar outline for a family you know well (or an imaginary family) and work out the numbers of life tasks and life events. How do these affect the family members as they interact so as to facilitate relationships or create potential tension?

TIM: 22 months	*ANNE: 10 years*	*PETER: 14 years*
LIFE TASKS	*LIFE TASKS*	*LIFE TASKS*
• develop motor skills	• cope with academic demands at school (underachieving)	• adjust to physical changes of puberty
• develop self-control	• developing her sense of self	• and to sexual awareness
• elaborate vocabulary	• learn to be part of a team	• cope with the opposite sex
• explore his world – make 'discoveries'		• deepen friendships (intimacy)
LIFE EVENTS	*LIFE EVENTS*	*LIFE EVENTS*
• parents insist on obedience now	• afraid to go to school (cannot manage maths)	• worried about his skin (acne) and size of his penis
• adjust to temporary separations when mother works	• bullied by a girl in her class	• has a girlfriend – his first
• not the centre of attention and 'uncritical' deference	• jealous of attention Tim gets (calls him a spoilt brat)	• upset by his parents' quarrels
	• worried about father's health	• complains that his mother is always watching him

A Family Life Map cont.

MOTHER: 38 years	FATHER: 45 years	GRANNY: 66 years
LIFE TASKS • review her life and commitments • adjust to loss of youth and (in her perception) 'looks' • cope with an adolescent as a patient and caring parent	*LIFE TASKS* • review commitments in mid-life • develop new phase in relationship with wife • face physical changes – some limitation on athletic/sexual activity	*LIFE TASKS* • deal with increasing dependence on others • come to terms with old age/death • cope with loss of peers
LIFE EVENTS • coping with late child – an active toddler • has taken part-time job to relieve feeling trapped • feels guilty • bouts of depression • no longer enjoys sex	*LIFE EVENTS* • threat of redundancy • high blood pressure • worried about drifting apart from his wife • had a brief affair • feels unattractive	*LIFE EVENTS* • poor health • gave up home when bereaved (may have made a mistake!) • enjoys the little one, but • feels 'claustrophobic' with all the activity/squabbles

Erikson, E.H. (1968) *Youth, Identity and Crisis.* New York: Norton. [Adolescent crises of self-image and identity.]

Freud, A. (1958) *Adolescence: Psychoanalytic study of the child.* New York: International Universities Press. [A psychoanalytic view of adolescence.]

Hall, G. Stanley (1904) *Adolescence: Its psychology and its relationship to physiology, anthropology, sociology, sex, crime, religion and education.* New York: Appleton (2 volumes). [An early classic.]

Herbert, M. (1987) *Living With Teenagers.* Oxford: Basil Blackwell. [Demythologizes the more negative stereotypes of adolescence.]

Herbert, M. (1987) *Conduct Disorders of Childhood and Adolescence.* Chichester: Wiley. [The antisocial, sometimes delinquent problems of young persons.]

Hudson, A. *Personal Communication.*

Hutter, A. (1938) Endegene en functionelle ber kindern in den pubertatsjahren. *A Kinderpsychiat,* 5, 97–102. [An early psychiatric account of adolescence.]

Institute for the Study of Drug Dependence (1982) *Drug Abuse Briefing.* London: ISDD. [All about drugs and drug use, and misuse.]

Josselson, R. (1980) Ego development in adolescence. In J. Adelson (Ed.) *Handbook of Adolescent Psychology.* New York: Wiley. [Development of the self or ego – a central facet of personality.]

Mothner, I. & Weitz, A. (1986) *How to get off Drugs.* Harmondsworth: Penguin. [A valuable, practical guide for drug-users.]

Open University Course Organizers (1982) *Parents and Teenagers.* London: Harper & Row. [Practical course work; exercises and readable text.]

Rutter, M. (1971) *Normal psychosexual development. Journal of Child Psychology and Psychiatry,* 11, 259–83. [Invaluable review of the literature.]

Rutter, M. (1979) *Changing Youth in a Changing Society.* London: The Nuffield Provincial Hospitals Trust. [Packed with data, findings about adolescents and their social context.]

Rutter, M. et al. (1979) *Fifteen Thousand Hours.* London: Open Books. [A study of London schools, their attributes and influence on pupils.]

Schofield, M. (1965) *The Sexual Behaviour of Young People.* London: Longmans Green. [Survey of attitudes to sex and sexual activities of early and later adolescence.]

Schofield, M. (1973) *The Sexual Behaviour of Young Adults: A follow-up study.* London: Allen Lane. [Follow-up study described above: some years on.]

Sorenson, R.C. (1973) *Adolescent Sexuality in Contemporary America.* New York: World Publishing. [American survey of early sexuality.]

Tattum, T.P. (1982) *Disruptive Pupils in Schools and Units.* Chichester: Wiley. [Why's and wherefore's of classroom disruption.]

Triseliotis, J. & Russell, J. (1984) *Hard to Place: The outcome of adoption and residential care.* London: Heinemann. [What happens to youngsters who are adopted or placed in residential institutions.]

Wellings, K. (1986) *First Love, First Sex: A practical guide to relationships.* Wellingborough: Thorsons. [Useful manual and coursebook.]

Youniss, J. (1980) *Parents and Peers in Social Development.* Chicago: University of Chicago Press. [Role of the family in socializing the child.]

13. *Growing Older*

▽ *Work and leisure*
▽ *Marriage and parenting*
▽ *Cognitive changes in adulthood and old age*
▽ *Attitudes and personality*
▽ *Old age and 'ageism'*

'Growing older' is both a biological and a social matter. It is biological in that humans, like members of other species, inherit a genetically fixed life span. Although improvements in health care and in occupational safety mean that life expectancy at birth is now much greater than it was 100 or even 50 years ago, the biblical account of the 'years of man' as three score and ten is still a reasonable approximation to our life span, barring accidents, today. Comparatively few of us will live beyond 80 and very few past 90. There are family differences and sex differences in life span, even when differences in life circumstances between the sexes and among families are allowed for.

However, growing older is also socially defined and determined. Any society has socially defined life stages and expectations about age-appropriate behaviour, and it is often life stage rather than age which determines our attitudes and our behaviour. In our own society, for example, it is expected that men should earn their living, that people should marry at an appropriate age and should have children; that women should probably have paid work before they marry, unless they marry very young, but that they should probably withdraw from full-time employment when their children are young and (an increasing expectation) return to at least part-time work when the children are older or adult; that people should retire at an appropriate age, and that their behaviour should be tailored to their life stage. It is age-appropriate to travel cheaply round the world when you are 21, but not when you are 35, or 55, or 65; age-appropriate to live an independent life in your twenties, but to 'settle down' with a steady job and children when you are a man of 30; all right for a woman of 20 to wear a miniskirt and sunbathe in a bikini, but less so for a woman of 50 and certainly not for a woman of 70. Ageing is much influenced by stereotypes of age-appropriate behaviour and conditions, and the stereotypes are not only occasionally irritating to older people but also sometimes actually harmful. We shall return to the question of stereotypes and age discrimination later.

In this chapter we shall consider some life events which characterize and help to define adulthood, concentrating on aspects of work and leisure, marriage and parenting. We shall also consider the evidence concerning adult age changes in cognition – intelligence, learning and memory, for example – which may be at least partly biological rather than social in their origin; and we shall consider changes in attitudes, social engagement and personality.

WORK AND LEISURE

For most people 'work' means employment for money, whether on an employed or self-employed basis. Work, by this definition, is different from leisure activity, which is carried out for enjoyment rather than for economic reward. But the distinction is not as clear cut as it seems. For one thing, are housework and child care which are not paid for but carried out in the domestic context to be regarded as 'work'? Most people, if not all, would class housework as work, while the classification of child care might be more varied and, probably, judged to have elements of both. One not infrequent complaint about fathers who are 'good with the children' is that they share the aspects of child care which are usually thought to be intrinsically enjoyable, such as playing with the children or taking them out, but are less likely to take their turn at changing dirty nappies or the sheets after a child has wet the bed.

Paid employment often means considerably more to the employee than simply a way of earning a living. Robert Havighurst, for example, pointed out that work, for many workers, provides new experiences and variety of activity. It may offer the opportunity for creativity and the use of an individual's skills; it may provide a source of self-respect, prestige and status. It is also a means of making, and maintaining contact with friends. Of course these are characteristics of leisure activity too, and satisfaction with both work and leisure, and with life in general, depends partly on how well activity fulfils these conditions. For more discussion of Havighurst's views, and those of others, see Kabanoff (1980).

However, this is not to say that in every person's life work and leisure have the same characteristics and fulfil the same needs; the relation between work and leisure can take several forms. Leisure activity may be a 'spillover' from work, sharing similar characteristics and functions; or it may be complementary, serving the needs work doesn't fulfil and providing a change from it; or it may be quite different and 'segregated' from work activity. Some attributes of activity which are important for job satisfaction, such as variety of work and the chance to use skills, are not reliable indicators of life satisfaction in retirement, where the most important ingredient of non-work activity seems to be social interaction. The relation between work and leisure is different for different people and also, of course, for different types of work and of leisure activity.

'Working' women

One of the most striking changes in the nature of the labour force in industrialized countries in recent years has been the increasing number of women in paid employment. It is now the norm for women to have a paid job before they marry, and, if they marry, to continue in their paid work until the first child is expected; and the number of employed mothers has increased dramatically in recent years, although many of them, particularly those with preschool-age children, are in part-time employment. There are many possible reasons for these trends. For one thing, technological advances and economic recessions in industrialized societies have led to a decline in some traditionally male industrial jobs and an increase in some traditionally female jobs, such as health care and other service occupations. Rising costs of living have more or less obliged some women to become second earners to keep the family going, and unemployment rates among men and rising divorce and separation rates have turned others into primary breadwinners.

However, women's earnings are consistently lower than those of men. Traditionally female-dominated jobs are generally worse paid than male-dominated jobs, and women working in male-dominated jobs tend not to advance as rapidly, or at all, to higher pay levels. They are more likely to have an interrupted career pattern; family commitments, if they have partners and children, may make it impossible for them to accept promotion which will involve them in longer hours away from home and mobility; and negative stereotypes of women's low commitment (which are, incidently, not borne out in research studies) affect their access to further training and promotion.

Older workers

In virtually all Western industrialized societies the percentage of elderly men in the labour force has declined, over perhaps the last 100 years in the case of men aged 65 or more and the last 50 in the case of 55 to 65 year olds. The decline is partly due to the comparatively recent phenomenon of retirement, and to the provision of state and occupational pensions; but it is also due to age-related problems of employment for the older worker. These problems are particularly acute in industrialized societies, and much less evident in developing, primarily agricultural societies. In industrialized societies workers typically have to adjust quickly to new methods and techniques, and perhaps to work at a fast pace. Middle-aged and older employees may be less well equipped to work in this way, and their skills and training are more likely to be obsolete than are those of younger workers. Moreover, even if they are not in fact at any significant disadvantage, employers, other employees and they themselves may believe them to be. They may be seen as out-of-date, untrainable and less productive than younger workers. They are less likely to be offered a place on a retraining programme, and if they become unemployed they are less likely to be re-employed.

Are these negative views of the older worker justified? It is remarkably difficult to answer this question, since quality of work may be defined in various ways, different types of work produce different age effects and a number of methodological problems make studies difficult to interpret. To take an example, a study might find no difference in performance between older and younger workers, but this might simply be because the older workers who could no longer cope well with their work had either left voluntarily or been 'eased out' into other work or out of the work force, leaving only the most able of the older workers to compare with a cross-section of younger ones. On the whole, however, there is very little evidence that older workers are less competent than younger ones, except in jobs requiring considerable physical strength, fast reactions or close attention to visual detail. Older workers are not noticably more prone to accidents at work, and their job satisfaction and commitment to work may be higher. The empirical evidence does not convincingly support the stereotype.

Unemployment

In recent years the number of unemployed people, above all of unemployed men, has risen sharply in the UK and other Western countries, and the number of *long-term* unemployed, both in absolute and proportional terms, has risen sharply. Unemployment is greatest for men in unskilled and semi-skilled manual occupations, least for those in managerial and professional work, and both older and younger men are more at risk of long-term unemployment than are men of, say 25 to 50. Since most research has been concerned with male unemployment, this is the area we propose to consider.

The most obvious consequence of unemployment is loss of income, and often poverty, for the unemployed and their families. There are also psychological costs, related and unrelated to loss of income, which have been investigated in a number of studies from the 1930s onwards. This work has recently been reviewed by one of the authors: Julia Berryman. Studies of long-term unemployment and adaptation suggest that difficulties of adjustment arise fairly early in unemployment, after an initial feeling, sometimes, of 'being on holiday'. With time people do seem to adjust to unemployment although they may not return to the psychological well-being of their employed days. A large number of studies comparing employed with unemployed men have found that the unemployed are less happy and less satisfied with life, have lower self-esteem and are more likely to experience physical and psychiatric health problems. Obvious reasons for poorer morale and health are low income and financial worry. Another is that, partly because of lower income, the amount and variety of activities and social contacts are restricted. Unemployed men take on more child care and meal preparation, but they also spend more time sitting about, sleeping and watching television; and there is some evidence that men who cope best with unemployment are those who stay active and maintain membership of religious, political or community groups. Uncertainty and insecurity about the future also constitute a major problem for the unemployed at all occupational levels.

Perhaps the worst aspect of unemployment is lowered self-esteem. An unemployed man is apt to feel he has failed as a breadwinner and even disgraced his family; and low self-esteem is encouraged and aggravated by unfavourable, and even hostile, social attitudes towards him. The unemployed are often regarded as being to blame for their unemployment, and even if they are not seen as 'guilty' it is often, apparently, felt that unemployment benefits should be kept punitively low to encourage them to look for work rather than to remain idle.

Retirement

In theory retirement should have both positive and negative aspects: positive because it should be a stage of life free from the demands of work and of parenting, but negative because it may represent loss of income, social role and identity. In practice the common stereotype of retirement is as a 'bad thing', causally associated with lowered morale, life satisfaction and health and perhaps with increased mortality.

There is some evidence for poorer morale and health in retired as compared with still-working people, and for greater death rates; but retired people on average are poorer and older than those still in work. Robert Atchley, for example, found that about 30 per cent of retirees interviewed in the USA reported problems of adjustment, but very few said that this was because they 'missed the work' – rather, they quoted money and health problems and bereavement. Where retirement is associated with poor health, it is often because ill health leads to retirement, rather than the other way around.

It has also been suggested that the effect of retirement depends on occupation and on attitude to work – the nastier the job, the more favourable one's attitude to retirement, while the more we enjoy our work the less we wish to give it up. In fact studies of work attitude and retirement attitude find little or no relation between the two. The hypothesis may hold for a particular type of 'workaholic' – for

"Grimsby has opted for phased retirement."

Drawing by Stevenson; © 1979 The New Yorker Magazine, Inc.

example, self-employed businessmen for whom work is a central and dominating part of life, but there is little evidence even for that. Most of the studies look at the relation between attitudes to work and attitudes to *anticipated* retirement, among people still at work; we still know little about the relation between work attitude and the *experience* of retirement.

When people retire, they may experience a number of *stages* in adjustment. Robert Atchley, for example, suggested that there is typically a 'honeymoon' phase, followed, six to 12 months after retirement, by disenchantment. This in its turn is followed by a period of reorientation and stability. There is some empirical evidence for stages of retirement, and adjustment to it, along roughly these lines, although findings are not very consistent and the timing of 'stages' appears to vary widely even when they are consistently reported.

Most studies of retirement have been concerned with men, while a few have dealt with wives' adjustment to their husbands' retirement. Retirement has often been thought less crucial for women than for men, because women's domestic role continues after retirement from work and because they are more used to 'role inconstancy' throughout adult life. But the few existing studies of retired women tend to find that retirement can be just as traumatic for women as it is for men, more problematic in some cases, in fact, since women's lower rates of pay and often interrupted work history may result in appreciably lower retirement income. However, most women and men adjust satisfactorily to retirement, at least in the comparatively short term, and many actively look forward to and enjoy it. The psychological impact of retirement, good or bad or a bit of both, is principally related to income level, health status and the existence of substitute activity – social, leisure, and familial – both during working life and after retirement.

MARRIAGE AND PARENTING

Marriage and parenthood are still the norm in our society, but they take many forms and their nature is changing. The traditional view is that a family consists of a single, male, breadwinner, a dependent wife, and children; but this pattern applies to only a small minority of Western families. The majority of couples are now *dual-earner* couples, and the majority of mothers, including nearly half of mothers with preschool-age children, also work, though many of them work part-time. The difference in pattern is not that wives and mothers work, since they have always done so, either outside the home or within it in home-based industries, but that increasingly they work independently of the family and are paid for their work.

Another change in family structure results from rapidly increasing divorce rates. A growing number of families with children are now headed by a single parent, more often than not the mother (about 25 per cent of children under 18 in the USA live in single-parent households). About 10 per cent of children live in 'reconstituted' families in which divorce (or occasionally bereavement) has been followed by marriage and step-parenting. There are also, of course, families with one or more child in which the parents are not married. These families vary considerably, but in many cases are virtually indistinguishable from those of the conventionally married, and may lead to the marriage of the partners.

The number of multigenerational households, in which three or more generations of the family live together, is comparatively low in the UK and other Western European countries and in the white population of the USA (it is higher for other ethnic groups in the USA and in some other nations, such as Japan and Italy). This is sometimes quoted as an example of social change, and more often than not as a change for the worse, indicating the breakdown of family relationships and a lack of caring on the part of adult children. But this seems a misguided opinion. In Western societies multigenerational households appear, from census data, always to have been fairly uncommon except in times of hardship or family emergency; and although adult members of different generations may not live together they are quite likely to live near one another and to offer frequent, and mutual, support.

Stages of marriage

All marriages follow their own pattern, but in most there are clearly identifiable stages which are milestones, not only in the marriage but also in the lives of its partners. In most cases the early months or years of marriage end at the birth of the first child, when parenting begins and marital roles and priorities often have to be renegotiated. After the birth of the last child the pattern of the marriage may again change as the emphasis shifts from child-bearing to child-rearing, and may change again when the children go to school and when they reach adolescence. Active parenting is concluded with what is colourfully called a 'launching' period, in which the children, one by one, leave home; and then couples reach the post-parental stage, which can involve both preretirement and postretirement phases, and, at some stage, grandparenting. All of these stages involve transition and stress.

Happiness in marriage

How does happiness, or marital satisfaction, vary over the stages of marriage and parenting? Our answers are not very reliable, because they involve introspective reports from marriage partners which may not be reliable and because different elements of satisfaction – with the spouse, with the children, with work, income, living arrangements – are difficult to untangle. But a number of studies have reported that marital satisfaction (concerning love, companionship, children, understanding of spouses, and standard of living) *declines* steadily through the early and middle years of marriage. One reason for the decline is likely to be the arrival of children, which is apt to produce a heavy workload, a renegotiation of relationships, a problematic division of labour, extra expenditure and a loss of income. This is not the whole answer (satisfying though it seems!) since childless marriages also show declining satisfaction, though it is less marked.

What happens to marital satisfaction in later years is less clear: some studies report that it stays low, others that it shows an upswing after children have left home, though not, on the whole, returning to the high spot of the earliest years. One possible explanation for the upswing, of course, may be that when the divorce rate is high it is the most happily married who are still married and willing to complete satisfaction ratings. Another likelihood is that the loss of children from the home, which has sometimes been described as the 'empty nest' stage and held to be traumatic, especially for women, is in fact more pleasant than unpleasant, representing increased disposable income and greatly increased freedom. Although many mothers and fathers have mixed feelings when the last of their children leave home, it is principally the so-called 'super mothers', who have devoted their lives to their children and seem to have no other interests and activities to fall back on, who find themselves living in an empty nest rather than a child-free home.

Maternal employment

How does the paid employment of wives and mothers affect families? The most obvious effect, and in most cases the motive for maternal employment in the first place, is that family income goes up, and the material standard of living is improved; but the improvement is usually achieved at a cost. In addition to their paid work, most employed wives and mothers also shoulder the bulk of the responsibility for housework and child care (including making child-minding arrangements) and are likely to experience 'overload', stress and conflict between the demands of their paid work and their domestic responsibilities. Yet most studies find that employed mothers report higher morale than unemployed mothers, particularly where there is also a more egalitarian relationship between husband and wife and, unsurprisingly, when employment, and the nature of the paid work, are the woman's choice and are not forced upon her by economic necessity. The effect of wives' employment on husbands' morale is less clear, and seems to be unfavourable rather than favourable in spite of the increased income which it brings. Although we might guess that this is the result of greater domestic burdens and less emotional support from busy wives, the explanation most favoured by evidence is that husbands of employed wives feel less adequate as breadwinners.

There has been a great deal of concern about the effects of maternal employment on children, partly prompted by the common assumption that the children of such mothers are likely to be emotionally deprived and ill-cared for (this topic was discussed in Chapter 3 in relation to infants in daycare). Obviously the quality of substitute care is important, but on the whole research indicates that children of employed mothers may well be advantaged rather than disadvantaged. Although employed mothers spend less time with their children, the *quality* of mother– child interaction is not poorer than for mothers who stay at home, and may be better. Children of mothers in paid work are generally more independent, both practically and emotionally, and on the whole do better in school. (A possible exception to this is in the case of preadolescent sons, who have been reported to do worse when the mother is employed than when she is not.) Finally, dual-earner families provide a model for their children of higher female status and independence and of a more equal economic and domestic partnership between the sexes which is appropriate for the roles which they themselves will almost certainly take on in adult life. Maternal employment is now the rule rather than the exception, and is likely to remain so.

Divorce

It goes without saying that divorce is usually a fairly traumatic affair for the divorcing partners and, if there are children, for them too. It involves the breakdown of a relationship, the renegotiation of financial and domestic affairs with a rejected or rejecting partner and often with little goodwill, and the establishment of new ways of life, new relationships and old relationships on a different footing. Divorced people are emotionally worse off, at least for a time, than those who have never married, and for older people the emotional difficulties are more acute. Perhaps most vulnerable are so-called 'displaced homemakers' – older women who married in the expectation that their marriage would be for life and that their place was in the marital home.

It is not easy to generalize about the effects of divorce on children. It has been argued, using children's reports as evidence, both that they are better off, and that they are worse off undergoing parental divorce rather than continuing to live in a two-parent family with marital discord.

The enduring problems of divorce are both emotional and financial. It is usually the mother who retains custody of any children after divorce, and the role of a single parent is a difficult one. Even when maintenance payments have been ordered, or agreed, fathers not uncommonly fail to pay, and the single parent may either live in poverty or take on the burdens of often low-paid maternal employment with little or no support from other adults. Fathers too may suffer drastic reduction in income if they pay maintenance, and may also suffer 'paternal deprivation' when they no longer live with their children and have limited access to them. Financial problems don't necessarily end when, as is often the case, divorce ends in the remarriage of one or both partners. Fresh emotional problems can arise as the partners, old and new, establish or re-establish relations with each other and with new extended families.

Bereavement

If marriages do not end in divorce they end in the death of a spouse, most often the husband. Bereavement almost invariably brings emotional distress: shock, sorrow, sometimes anger, and often loneliness. It is also associated with mental health problems, notably depression, and with physical ill health and even increased mortality. These effects are stronger when the death was sudden, unexpected, or 'off-time': for example, widowhood appears to be more distressing and harder to adjust to for younger than for older widows. Some studies have reported that widowhood is harder for women than for men, while others come to the opposite conclusion; it depends on what aspects and measures of adjustment are being considered.

Most studies have found that the acute stage of widowhood lasts for about six months, and that distress has abated (though not disappeared) and health risks returned to age-normal levels by about a year after bereavement. But other difficulties follow bereavement and are more long-lasting: one is reduced income, which can be particularly severe for elderly widows. Social activity may also be drastically reduced, both because of lack of money and because social conventions sometimes make 'joining in' more difficult for single people than for couples. Another factor may be *relocation*, or moving house, which is not necessarily associated with bereavement but is made more likely by it. Relocation – to an adult child's home, to a retirement home, sheltered housing or an institution – is not necessarily unfavourable, and sometimes means an improved standard of living, increased social interaction and the chance of useful and rewarding 'grandparenting', but it does have emotional and perhaps health risks of its own.

COGNITIVE CHANGES IN ADULTHOOD AND OLD AGE

It is a common stereotype that advancing age is associated with a decline in intellectual ability, learning capacity and memory performance. The earliest studies of intelligence testing, for example, examined test scores of people at ages ranging from early or mid-childhood to 60 years or more, and commonly reported a decline in performance from the late teens or early twenties. It is often argued that 'you can't teach an old dog new tricks', and that old people tend to 'live in the past' but to be forgetful over more recent events. However, there is abundant evidence to show that these views are exaggerated if not totally inaccurate. There does seem to be some decline in cognitive capacity in older adulthood, but the decline is later and smaller than the stereotype suggests. Some aspects of performance are more sensitive than others to the effects of age, and where performance is worse in older people there may be other reasons than poorer cognitive capacity.

Age differences or age changes?

Studies of cognitive change in adulthood are nearly all *cross-sectional* in design: groups of adults of different ages are tested at one point in time, and their results compared. While this design may tell us something about age *differences*, it does not tell us about age *changes* – that is, changes within individuals as they grow older. People of different ages differ not only in age but also in *birth cohort* (the historical time in which they were born), and people of different birth cohorts grow up in different circumstances. They experience different standards of nutrition and health care, different access to education and different educational methods, different styles of socialization, and different social conditions – style of government, war or peace, economic boom or recession.

Age differences, then, may not truly represent the effects of age itself, but rather the effects of cohort. This is particularly true of intelligence-test performance: members of earlier birth cohorts have on average had appreciably fewer years in formal education, and at any age there is a clear correlation between years in formal education and IQ scores. Of course it could be argued that the cleverest people spend more time in formal education, hence the relation between education and IQ scores, but this is not the whole story. It is also true that formal education teaches people the 'tricks' that are needed for successful IQ test performance, and other people are less likely to have learned these tricks. Cohort differences may also be important for studies of learning and memory, and are certainly important for studies of attitudes and personality, which we shall discuss later. The problems of cross-sectional studies are considered further in the next chapter.

Intelligence

Generally speaking, recent studies of intelligence-test performance have found that scores tend to rise through early childhood, and then to drop again; the drop may begin at 40 years of age, but it becomes substantial only when the adults tested are 50, 60 or even 70 years old. Since nearly all these studies are cross-sectional, much of the age difference is likely to be a matter of cohort differences rather than of age changes, and when older and younger adults are matched with respect to education levels much of the later decline disappears. *Longitudinal* studies, in which the same participants are tested repeatedly over a matter of years, and so-called *cohort-sequential* studies, which combine the features of longitudinal and cross-sectional studies (discussed further on page 237) produce very little evidence of age-related decline. But these designs, too, have their problems, including *selective participant attrition*: when people have to be retested over periods of years they don't all remain available for retesting, and the ones who do remain available tend to be those who were more able, healthier and more motivated in the first place. This means that longitudinal studies and cohort-sequential studies may *underestimate* age changes, while cross-sectional studies overestimate them.

Some IQ tests show greater age differences than others. Generally speaking, *verbal* subtests, such as vocabulary or 'similarities' tests, show very little decline with advancing age, while *performance* tests, such as picture arrangement, certain kinds of pictorial reasoning tests, and digit-symbol substitution, show much more marked disadvantage for older adults. One possible reason for this is that performance tests depend very much on *speed* for successful performance, so older adults, who perform more slowly in just about every respect, are at a disadvantage. But even if performance tests are scored for quality of performance rather than speed, the age difference persists.

A more likely reason for the unequal decline pattern is that some tests depend more than others on experience and knowledge (or, as Raymond Cattell termed it, 'crystalized intelligence'), and older people perform well on such tests. They may well be less good at tests which don't depend on knowledge but more directly on the capacity to perceive 'new' relations, on reasoning and abstraction and which are not greatly helped by previous experience. This is termed 'fluid intelligence' by Cattell. It is thought to depend on the efficiency of physiological functioning, and so it is likely to decline in older age. Elderly adults may not do very well at abstract problem-solving tasks, but are often at least as good as younger people at practical, everyday problems. Although there are some difficulties with this explanation too, it does help to show that there may be 'real' decline in intellectual capacity at advanced ages, but that the decline is not very substantial in healthy people, that it may not pose problems in everyday situations, and that elderly people are on the whole well able to use experience, knowledge and common sense in getting round any theoretical differences which they may face.

Attention, learning and memory

Like studies of intelligence, studies of attention, learning and memory in older adults are nearly all cross-sectional, so where a poorer performance is found in older adults it needs to be interpreted carefully. None the less, there is evidence that old age does bring some problems. Older people often find it harder to divide attention between two or more tasks or sources of information (although it is not always clear whether this is because they find the division of attention harder or simply because two tasks make heavier demands than one, and older people have less processing capacity), and they may be less able to attend selectively and to ignore distractions. Older adults are also worse at most learning tasks in the psychology laboratory, and while there is some (though not much) evidence that their short-term memory is impaired, there is plenty of evidence that long-term memory may be poorer. This is partly a matter of poor learning – if you don't learn material very well you cannot be expected to recall it perfectly – but also a matter of memory difficulties in their own right.

One reason for poor performance, as in the case of intelligence, is response speed. Most divided-attention tasks, many learning tasks and some memory tasks are strictly paced: older participants don't perform well under paced conditions and do better when tasks are slower or self-paced. Another factor is that older people are often *overcautious* and may not produce correct responses even when they know them, because they are more afraid than younger people of making errors. Their performance is often improved, in learning and memory tasks, by giving financial incentives to respond (five points for a correct answer, two for a wrong answer, nothing for no answer at all; exchange your points for money at the end of the experiment). This technique also produces improvement in intelligence-test performance.

Response speed and cautiousness in responding affect how well older people produce what they know, but they clearly have problems at input as well as output. They are less likely than young adults to use *active* learning strategies (for example, working at learning by the use of verbal elaborations or visual images or mnemonics, or even parrot repetitions) and more likely to go through the learning task passively. In memory experiments they may have greater difficulty in retrieving what they have learned, so that age deficits often appear in 'recall' experiments, in which the task is to fish out what has been stored without help from the experimenter, but not in 'recognition' experiments, in which the learned material is presented along with other irrelevant material, and the task is to pick out the learned items from the rest. The lack of effort may be partly a matter of reduced resources, but not entirely, since older people can be encouraged to adopt active strategies and to improve their learning performance, if not always to the level of young adults.

Extraneous variables and 'age fairness'

Many of the difficulties which elderly people may face with psychologists' tests of cognitive ability are not really 'cognitive' difficulties at all. We have already mentioned problems of slower responses and cautiousness which may depress their performance. Health, income level, home circumstances and access to social and other activities may be comparatively unfavourable, and all these factors have been shown to relate to test performance. Fatigue may be more likely to depress their performance when testing sessions are fairly long, and they may be more anxious in test situations (although the evidence for this is rather poor: it's more likely that older people are anxious when – and because – they feel they are doing badly, rather than that they do badly because they are too anxious).

It has also been suggested that older participants are less motivated to do well at laboratory tasks because they view them as irrelevant and silly. Learning to associate pairs of words, to arrange pictures to tell a story, or to suggest the missing item in a display of nonsense symbols may be reasonable tests for people in, or recently out of, school, but they may have little relevance to what most 70 year olds have been doing with their lives for the past 50 or more years. Such items may not be 'age-fair' and the same may be true of general knowledge and vocabulary items, which may well favour one age group (not necessarily the young). Warner Schaie has argued that we need to devise intelligence tests which have *ecological validity* for older as well as younger people: that is, tests which are relevant to the ways in which we cope with everyday problems. Some attempts along these lines have produced smaller age differences than on standard tests, and sometimes age *increments*, rather than decrements, in performance. But we are still a long way from devising standardized versions of ecologically valid tests which can be applied over a wide age range, and the problems of age-fairness will not be easily solved.

ATTITUDES AND PERSONALITY

Do personality and attitudes change as we grow older? It is often thought that they do. In particular, older people are said to be 'set in their ways': inflexible, cautious, conservative and resistant to change. There is some support for this picture, not only from studies of personality and attitudes but also from studies of intelligence test performance and problem solving, where, as we have already seen, older people are likely to have problems with abstract reasoning and to be overcautious in response. But inflexibility in cognitive tasks is not necessarily the same thing as rigidity and conservatism in a wider context.

Attitude changes

Several studies have shown that elderly people are more *conservative* in attitude, with respect to political, economic and social issues, than middle-aged people, who in turn are more conservative than young adults. For example, older people may be more consistent in their voting behaviour; they may be less liberal in their attitudes to abortion, divorce and equality between the sexes, and less approving of state intervention in child care and other 'welfare' issues. But is this evidence of changing attitudes with age? Nearly all the studies are cross-sectional, so they may well be reflecting *cohort differences* in political attitudes and political socialization, rather than attitude change. Longitudinal studies tend to show stability of attitude as people grow older; in some cases there is evidence of change in a 'liberal'

"That was back then. I now espouse gerontocracy."

Drawing by Ed Fisher; © 1983 The New Yorker Magazine, Inc.

direction with respect to issues such as abortion or sex equality. These studies, though, are as hard to interpret as cross-sectional studies are, since they confound age changes with *secular* changes – changes in the climate of opinion over the years. Secular changes are almost certain to affect the attitudes of individuals, unless of course older people are too set in their ways to take any notice of them.

Probably the best evidence we have comes from studies which combine the features of cross-sectional and longitudinal designs. Stephen Cutler for example, examined attitudes to abortion as recorded in a series of government surveys in the USA between 1965 and 1977. He separated out different birth cohorts of respondents, ranging from birth dates before 1911 to a cohort of 1936–1947, and compared the change in attitude in time for each cohort separately. Cutler found that, over all, attitudes to abortion became more favourable between 1965 and 1972, and changed very little thereafter; and this change was shown for *all* cohorts. Older cohorts may have started from a rather less favourable attitude to abortion than younger cohorts, but they showed a change in attitude in the same direction, and at the same rate over time.

This study, then, found no age differences in people's readiness to change their attitudes in line with secular changes. Some other studies with similar designs, though, have reported that older cohorts show a slower rate of change than younger ones. This has sometimes been interpreted as showing that older people do have an underlying resistance to change, although they are still affected by secular trends. Another important possibility is that older people are less swayed by secular changes in attitudes because they are less efficient at receiving and assimilating new ideas and knowledge, and there is some evidence for this interpretation.

Finally, age differences in attitude and in attitude change, may depend on the particular issue being examined. Older people may be more 'conservative' than younger ones on some issues, more 'liberal' on others. It is likely that some differences at least come from the differences in the relevance of certain issues to individuals at different life stages: older people, for example, may be less in favour of additional funding for state education than are younger adults in the active parenting stage, but more in favour of extra funding on hospitals and medical services. Self-interest, at all ages, is a more likely explanation than a 'theoretical' attitude change with age.

Personality in later life

Although cross-sectional studies sometimes show age differences in personality characteristics, on the whole personality does not change substantially as we grow older. When marked personality change does occur it is likely to be evidence of ill health or pathological senility. Indeed, Bernice Neugarten suggested that with advancing age people become more like themselves: essential characteristics become more salient, and, perhaps because social pressures and expectations ease up after retirement and the end of active parenting, underlying features, needs and wishes which have been muted in earlier life are more fully expressed. One example of this may be the *diminished sex-typing* which is often said to occur in later life, when the demands of employment, parenting and the division of labour within the family no longer impose fairly rigid gender-appropriate behaviour. For most personality traits, then, stability rather than change is associated with age, particularly when cohort differences arising from different socialization experiences can be allowed for.

However, some studies do suggest that there may be some modification of personality with age. The change most consistently reported is that older people become more introverted and less sociable. The most famous statement of this change is in the theory of *disengagement*, which was proposed in the early 1960s by Elaine Cumming and William Henry.

Activity and disengagement

Cumming and Henry defined disengagement as a mutual withdrawal of the individual from social interaction, and of society from the individual. Disengagement, in their view may be social (representing a reduction in the amount of physical and social interaction with the environment and other people) and it may be psychological (representing a reduction of emotional commitment with outside events). The two aspects of disengagement do not necessarily, but may, occur together. Disengagement can come about for various reasons. Changes in work and family roles, illness, reduced fitness and energy, communication difficulties and forgetfulness may all encourage withdrawal from social interaction and make it more difficult. It may also be that detachment and inner-directedness arise as part of a general tendency for some elderly people at least to spend time looking back, reviewing and making sense of their lives.

Cumming and Henry argued that disengagement was a natural and inevitable feature of later life. They also argued that disengagement helps people to adjust to old age, and leads to greater life satisfaction and higher morale. But research by Bernice Neugarten, Robert Havighurst, Robert Atchley and others has found that on the whole the relation between disengagement and life satisfaction is negative, rather than positive. This has led to an opposing argument, so-called *activity theory*, that maintenance of activity and social interaction are desirable and necessary to preserve self-esteem and morale in later life.

What should we make of these opposing views? There is rather more evidence in favour of activity as a predictor of happiness than in favour of disengagement. But it is likely that this is at least partly because factors making for happiness, such as good health and adequate income, also make social interaction and leisure activities possible. There is no guarantee that being active will make you happy, and if anything it is likely that being happy will make you more active. As we have already mentioned in the context of work and leisure, only certain kinds of activity, particularly social interaction, are reliably related to life satisfaction. Finally, it is probable that the relation between activity level, or disengagement, and morale will depend on pre-existing personality, the individual's activity level at younger ages, and their modes of adjustment to the events of ageing.

OLD AGE AND 'AGEISM'

Throughout this chapter we have referred to common views and stereotypes about older people and in pretty well every case the stereotype is an unfavourable one, portraying the elderly as 'worse' than the young, to an extent which is not justified by the research evidence about age changes and age differences. In preliterate societies the old have often been valued, respected and even feared as sources of knowledge and wisdom. In contemporary industrialized societies like our own, in contrast, they appear often to be negatively valued, regarded as senile, 'past it', and a worthless drain on the nation's economic and social resources. While it is an exaggeration to regard this attitude as complete and universal, our society is to some extent *ageist*, just as it is, sometimes, sexist and racist, but with the bizarre distinction that while men are unlikely to become women, or whites to become blacks, we are all – barring accidents – likely to become old.

Ageism, or negative discrimination against the elderly, is seen in attitudes, common descriptions of the aged, and jokes about them. It can be particularly striking in the case of women, who are disadvantaged more than men by the premium placed by our society on youthfulness in standards of attractiveness. Compare, for example, the average age and age range of movie heroes with those of movie heroines. Discrimination can occur not only in attitudes but also in practice: mandatory retirement at 60 or 65 is an example of discrimination and, as we have already mentioned, older workers may be first in line for redundancy or encouraged to take early retirement, and may have less access to promotion or retraining. It is commonplace for job advertisements to quote acceptable age ranges which exclude applicants over, say, 35 or 40, and age discrimination is likely to apply when not officially stated. Senile and elderly patients are most at risk when health service cuts are implemented, and minor health problems are less likely to be taken seriously in elderly than in younger people, and more likely to be regarded as inevitable ('we're none of us getting any younger') and left untreated. Perhaps worst of all, elderly people themselves often share these stereotypes: older workers are less likely to *apply* for retraining and promotion, and the old tend to view the old as a tedious lot (although perhaps viewing themselves as exceptions). 'I wouldn't want to live with a lot of old people' is a common response when elderly people discuss retirement homes with their friends and families.

How can ageism be counteracted? For a start, it is not all-pervasive, and not all elderly people occupy disadvantaged places in society. There are increasing numbers of well-off elderly, and as birth rate declines reach the labour force, elderly people will begin to be in demand for employment, although not always in 'desirable' jobs; and growing numbers of the elderly, many of them with considerable spending power, are now beginning to be wooed as consumers. We do not become passive recipients of society's attitudes when we grow old; many, perhaps most, of us remain as satisfied as we ever were with our lives, as sure of our own worth and our usefulness to others. Adequate *income* to make continued independence and activity possible is an essential antidote to ageism; so is appropriate *legislation*. Most important of all is *education*, to teach us all, from childhood, that the old have equal rights with the young; that the disadvantages of age are real, but remedial, and that they should not be exaggerated; and that old age, like youth, can be a time of happiness and growth.

Recommended reading

Bromley, D.B. (1988) *Human Ageing: An introduction to gerontology*, 3rd edn. Harmondsworth: Penguin. [A multidisciplinary, more than purely 'psychological' account of ageing.]

Carver, V. & Liddiard, P. (1978) *An Ageing Population*. Sevenoaks: Hodder & Stoughton. [Useful source chapter on various social aspects of ageing, predominantly in a British context.]

Kimmel, D.C. (1990) *Adult Development and Ageing*. Dubuque: Brown. [Two good introductory accounts of adult development, both predominantly American in cultural emphasis.]

References

Atchley, R. (1976) *Sociology of Retirement*. New York: Halstead. [A classic discussion of the social and psychological impact of retirement.]

Berryman, J.C. (Ed.) (1985) *The Psychological Effects of Unemployment*. University of Leicester: Department of Adult Education. [Reviews effects of unemployment, including its links with higher rates of anxiety, depression and attempted suicide.]

Birren, J.E. & Schaie, K.W. (Eds) (1985) *Handbook of the Psychology of Aging*. 2nd edn. New York: Van Nostrand. [Authoritative and detailed accounts of theory and evidence in most areas of the psychology of ageing, including intelligence, learning, memory and personality.]

Butler, R.N. (1975) *Why Survive? Being Old in America*. New York: Basic Books. [A powerful discussion of 'ageism', by the author who is generally credited with having coined the term.]

Cumming, E. & Henry, W. (1961) *Growing Old*. New York: Basic Books. [The classic statement of the 'disengagement' theory of ageing.]

Cutler, S.J., Lentz, S.A., Muha, M.J. & Ritter, R.N. (1980) Aging and conservatism: Cohort changes in attitudes about legalized abortion. *Journal of Gerontology*, *35*, 115–123. [A critical, and methodologically ingenious, examination of the notion that the elderly are more conservative and resistant to change of attitude than the young.]

Davies, D.R. & Sparrow, P.R. (1985) Age and work behaviour. In N. Charness (Ed.) *Aging and Human Performance*. Chichester: Wiley. [A comprehensive account of research concerned with the older worker.]

Hoffman, L.W. (1986) Work, family, and the child. In M.S. Pallak & R. Perloff (Eds) *Psychology and Work: Productivity, change and employment*. Washington, DC: American Psychological Association. [A review of the psychological characteristics and consequences of 'working' wives and mothers.]

Kabanoff, B. (1980) Work and non-work: A review of models, methods, and findings. *Psychological Bulletin*, *88*, 60–77. [A classic review of the relations between work and leisure.]

Neugarten, B.L., Havighurst, R.J. & Tobin, S.S. (1968) Personality and patterns of aging. In B.L. Neugarten (Ed.) *Middle Age and Aging*. Chicago: University of Chicago Press.

O'Brien, G.E. (1981) Leisure attributes and retirement satisfaction. *Journal of Applied Psychology*, *66*, 371–384. [An examination of the contribution of different types of leisure activity to life satisfaction in later life.]

Palmore, E., Cleveland, W.P., Nowlin, J.B., Ramm, D. & Siegler, I.C. (1979) Stress and adaptation in later life. *Journal of Gerontology*, *34*, 841–851. [An examination of the impact of different 'life events' upon physical, social and psychological well-being.]

Research and Statistics Units (1989) *Women and Men in Britain* Equal Opportunities Commission. London: HMSO. [Statistics on women, including details of those with children, in employment.]

Schaie, K.W. (1978) External validity in the assessment of intellectual development in adulthood. *Journal of Gerontology*, *33*, 695–701. [Discussion of the inadequacy of intelligence tests as predictors of 'real world' competence, particularly for older people.]

Taylor, A. (1986) Sex roles and ageing. In D.J. Hargreaves & A.M. Colley (Eds) *The Psychology of Sex Roles*. London: Harper & Row. [A review of theories and evidence concerning sex roles in late adulthood and old age.]

The Meanings of Work and Leisure

▶ Enlist as participants people who are, or who have been, in paid employment. Ask each participant to tell you his or her job (or previous job) and to list three leisure activities in which they are engaged on a regular basis (just about anything is acceptable – hang-gliding, stamp collecting, watching television, sex . . . .)

▶ Then ask your participant to rate each of the four activities on the check list below, giving:

5 to a statement which is *very true* for that activity

4 to a statement which is *quite true*

3 to one that is *so-so*

2 to a statement which is *quite untrue*

1 to a statement which is *very untrue*.

ACTIVITY (job or leisure)   RATING

A source of income
Intellectually stimulating
Earns me recognition and respect from others
Allows me to relax or 'let off steam'
Makes a change from other activities
A chance to meet other people
A chance to be useful to others
A chance to express myself
A chance to use my skills
A way of passing the time

What are the 'meanings' which your participants most often, and most strongly, associate with their work and with their leisure activities? How far are the meanings of work and of leisure alike or different?

If your participants have represented you with a wide range of jobs and leisure activities, do there seem to be differences in the 'meanings' of different occupations and interests?

Compare your conclusions with the discussion in this chapter and in the references given.

Beliefs about Age

Do we tend to have beliefs and expectations about the 'typical' characteristics of young, middle-aged and elderly people?

Ask as many people as possible to rate 'typical' members of three age groups. Try to enlist people of different ages and with varying experience of age groups other than their own – for example, some young people who have little contact with elderly people as well as some who are in close contact with one or more older person, such as a grandparent.

Ask each participant to complete three rating sheets, one relating to each of three age groups: 20–39, 45–55, 70 and over. Each sheet lists a number of characteristics; ask each participant to place a tick in the column alongside each statement to show the extent to which he or she agrees with it. The first rating sheet is given below.

	(1) *Very* *true*	(2) *Quite* *true*	(3) *Don't* *know*	(4) *Quite* *untrue*	(5) *Very* *untrue*
PEOPLE AGED 20–39 ARE **LIKELY TO BE:**					

– creative
– serene
– lonely and isolated
– forgetful
– cranky
– good at learning new things
– happy
– opinionated
– independent
– boring
– selfish
– competent

The second and third sheets are identical, except that the second is headed 'People aged 45-55 are likely to be:' and the third is headed 'People aged 70 or over are likely to be:'.

Beliefs about Age cont.

Give a tick in column 1 a score of 5; column 2 scores 4, column 3 scores 3, column 4 scores 2 and column 5 scores 1. Work out the average score, or measure of agreement, for each of your statements for each age group separately. Are the scores different for different age groups? What do the differences tell you about your participants' views about young, elderly and middle-aged people? Do their views seem to be justified by what you have read in this chapter and in other sources?

Do people who have plenty of contact with members of other age groups show a rather different pattern of age-related beliefs from people with little present experience of age groups other than their own?

Some of the characteristics listed could be seen as 'favourable', others as 'unfavourable' (most people would probably agree that characteristics 1, 2, 6, 7, 9 and 12 are favourable and the rest unfavourable). Try reversing the scores for the 'undesirable' items, so that strong agreement gains a score of 1 rather than 5, strong disagreement a score of 5 rather than 1, and so on. Totalling the scores over all 12 items will now give you an overall 'favourability' rating, for each rater and for each age group. Are people in any one age range seen as possessing more favourable characteristics than people in another?

The characteristics listed on the rating sheet are not very precise. Some of your participants may object that they don't know what some items mean; others, or the same ones, may argue that there are too many exceptions to the rule for any general rating of 'people' to make sense. Discuss these objections with your participants. Does the discussion give you more information about people's beliefs about age, or suggest better definitions of characteristics which might be seen as age-related?

14. *Studying Development*

— Can a baby make any sense of its world before birth?
— What is the role of love in human development?
— How does personality develop?
— Why do children play?
— How do children learn language?
— Is children's thinking different from that of adults?
— Can we measure intelligence successfully?
— How do children acquire aesthetic appreciation?
— Do children have a sense of right and wrong?
— Is adolescence always a time of storm and stress?
— In what ways does ageing change the person?

Psychologists have tried to answer all these questions, and, of course, many more. Just a few of the methods that they used have been outlined in Chapter 1 and you, the reader, will have gleaned something about methodology as each study was described. Let's look at the current state of this developing 'science'.

John Watson was a highly influential figure in the early years of research in developmental psychology. Watsonian *behaviourism* emphasized the influence of experience on shaping the individual. There was an emphasis on learning. What do children learn? When? How? In recent years the methods of the *ethologists* (those who emphasize the importance of research on animals in their natural habitat) have begun to have considerable impact on developmental psychology. Ethologists have traditionally emphasized the innate qualities of the organism. In studying animal behaviour they looked for 'species-specific' patterns. Behaviour just as much as structure (morphology) was seen as something that evolved and behaviour patterns could be seen as just as characteristic of a particular species as its shape, size or colour. The notion that many animals were preprogrammed to behave in quite specific ways may seem highly inappropriate when applied to humans. We see ourselves as infinitely flexible creatures. Instinctive patterns are for the birds and bees, human responses are more subtle, highly tuned by experience to fit each situation. It is easy to get into this *nature–nurture* debate and assume that one side or the other is more influential, but as we shall see this dichotomy is, in itself, a valueless one for each depends on the other and the interaction between them is crucial in shaping the organism.

Undoubtedly some human qualities are inherited, although establishing this is far from easy. Rudolph Schaffer, for example, discusses a range of possible 'intrinsic' patterns in babies in his book *Mothering*, and he suggests that the quality of 'cuddliness' in babies may be such a characteristic. Schaffer found that some babies are 'non-cuddlers' resisting close physical contact, and he observed that this characteristic appeared not to stem from the mother's behaviour towards her infant.

Although the methods used by the ethologists grew out of a concern with the 'innateness' of behaviour patterns, it is their techniques of observation that have been important in psychological methodology. Modern ethology places its emphasis on careful initial observation of a species prior to any form of experimentation and this has added an important dimension to methodology in developmental psychology.

Niko Tinbergen argues that when we ask questions about behaviour we are actually looking at four different levels of question:

- *Why does the animal behave in this way now?* [Immediate causation]
- *How did this particular individual grow up to respond this way?* [Development and learning]
- *What use is this (response) to the animal?* [Survival value]
- *Why does this kind of animal solve this problem in this particular way?* [Evolutionary origins]

Thus we can see that 'learning' has a place, but it is only one possible facet in a range of answers to the questions which we can ask of behaviour. Take the example of the behaviour called rooting (searching for the nipple) in babies. The immediate causation might be the touch of the mother's nipple on her baby's cheek. In terms of development we know that this is a reflex – an unlearned response, but it is not an enduring feature of humans. If you touch your own cheek you won't find yourself turning towards that finger for the reflex is lost early in development.

Its use in survival would seem to be to facilitate feeding, enabling the baby to locate its source of food more efficiently. Finally in evolutionary terms the questions here concern the nature of mammalian infant feeding systems and their evolution.

The rooting reflex is an innate response, but to the new parent this is not necessarily evident. A mother may try to help her newborn locate the nipple by nudging the infant's cheek towards her breast. In so doing she impedes the infant's progress to her nipple for the baby will move towards her fingers and away from the breast. Thus our everyday understanding of behaviour may not reveal the true causation of a given behaviour pattern.

As mentioned earlier, the important point about the ethological approach is that it emphasizes careful *naturalistic* observations prior to any form of controlled experimentation. Prolonged observation leads to the generation of more realistic hypotheses. Armchair speculation, or even speculation in the laboratory setting, can lead to ludicrous questions which have no bearing on what children or adults do in 'real life'.

Sit and watch

This first phase of research is to do just that. Observe your 'subjects' unobtrusively and see what they do. Make notes but avoid using major categories in classifying behaviour. 'The girl showed frequent bouts of aggression' tells us nothing for the observer has already classified the behaviour. Ethologists distrust major categories and prefer simple description of movements, facial expressions and so on. The advantage of using a method originally developed on non-human animals is that with humans it is difficult not to be too emotionally involved, and hence lacking in objectivity.

Events that we view as insignificant may be important in explaining subsequent behaviour. Yawning, in higher primates (including us), is an example here. This is a pattern which is not just something to do with being tired – it actually reveals a lot about the dynamics of the social situation and the status of individuals (their level of anxiety for instance) within it. Only careful analysis of sequences of behaviour in primates led to this conclusion. The same applies to humans – we must avoid making assumptions about which types of behaviour are important and which are not.

Nick Blurton Jones warns against the idea that if we want to study 'aggression' or 'attachment' we look for a 'good' measure of it. Counting movements of all kinds may be difficult, but if we decide what is meaningful before embarking on research then why bother with the research?

Because humans can talk, there is a tendency to short-circuit the time-consuming observation phase by asking questions. Indeed introspection was a major source of data to early psychologists, but it is only one facet of reality. Sigmund Freud relied heavily on what his patients said, or dreamt, or indeed left unsaid, but in formulating his ideas about psychosexual development he was not out in the 'field' observing babies and children. He constructed a view of the 'normal' child's psychosexual development not only via the preoccupations of his adult patients and the concerns of childhood elicited during psychoanalysis but his view of normality was also generated through his observation of those who might be viewed as abnormal. Had Freud been an ethologist of today it is unlikely that the notion of the Oedipus complex would have emerged.

The hypothesis

After the observation phase comes the posing of questions and the generation of a testable *hypothesis*. Whilst questions may be broad and general, hypotheses must be quite specific. For example: 'What factors foster the development of love in human babies?' is an important and interesting question but the psychologist needs to be precise about his or her choice of 'factors', the definitions of babies (the age range) and the expression of love by babies. The hypothesis can only take on one minute element of this question. It may be necessary to limit the study to infants aged 3–6 months and explore the impact of the amount of physical contact the infant receives from a specific caregiver. Now, the hypothesis, which is a statement of prediction, could be:

INCREASED PHYSICAL CONTACT BETWEEN THE MOTHER (OR MAIN CAREGIVER) AND BABY FACILITATES THE DEVELOPMENT OF ATTACHMENT BY THE BABY.

This statement is now testable and a study can be planned which can verify or refute it.

METHODS IN DEVELOPMENTAL PSYCHOLOGY

It is likely that the hypothesis generated above has been derived from the observational phase of research. The psychologist starts out with a hunch of some sort and then does some observations of babies and their caregivers before deciding how to proceed. In the example linking physical contact and more rapid attachment formation in infants one of the most obvious methods of proceeding might be the *correlational study*.

Correlational studies

In this we might select a group of babies and mothers and record the frequency of all forms of physical contact in a given period and then assess the development of the babies' attachment to the mother during that same period. How we did the latter would have to be settled and Chapter 3 describes some widely used measures of attachment behaviour.

Suppose that we find that the babies whose mothers classed as high on physical contact are also those babies that score high on measures of attachment behaviour, and those that score low on physical contact also score low on the latter measure – does this show clear support for our hypothesis?

It does not.

Undoubtedly we have found a *positive correlation* between the frequency of physical contact and our measures of attachment but we cannot conclude that one causes the other. Why not? Perhaps mothers who hold their babies more often also show other forms of maternal responsiveness more frequently than mothers who do not. Or perhaps Rudolph Schaffer's 'cuddliness' factor influences the baby's behaviour. Perhaps non-cuddler babies prefer talking to touching and hence we may need to take into account the infants' temperamental characteristics. It may be true that there is a *causal* relationship between these two factors – but this correlational study cannot reveal it. A carefully controlled experiment may bring us closer to the answer. Nevertheless absolute proof is an entirely different matter.

The experimental method

As we saw in the first chapter, the *experimental method* is designed so that the psychologist ideally controls all but one *variable* – the independent variable – and he or she varies the amount of this variable in two or more groups or conditions. In reality it is impossible to control all but one variable. All our participants are individual and unique and thus introduce variability into the study. Following the design as described in Chapter 1 we would select the participants from a particular population and randomly assign them to either the *experimental* or the *control* group. Since the independent variable is 'amount of physical contact between mother and baby', one way of testing the effect of this variable might be to ask mothers in the experimental group to adopt their normal daily regime with their baby but in addition to this 'pick up and hold the baby for an additional 60 minutes a day in not more than three separate sessions'.

An adequate control group would not be simply to give no instruction – mothers might be asked to spend at least 60 minutes closer to their child talking to it but not physically touching it. Alternatively there could be two controls, one to whom no instructions are given and one like that described above.

In each group, attachment behaviour (the dependent variable) would have to be recorded throughout the study period. Let us say that the duration of the study was to be six months from 3–9 months – since we know the time when attachments are typically formed we might expect to observe differences between the groups, should they occur, within this period.

Problems of experimental design

As you read this experiment it is probable that you are thinking: 'But what if . . .?' Let's look at some problems:

- How do we find participants?
- Do volunteers differ from non-volunteers?
- What do the participants think the experiment is about?
- How do the participants interpret the instructions?
- Do they try to please the experimenter?
- Do they behave differently because they are being studied?
- If subjects drop out do they differ from those who don't in some systematic way?
- If they cannot or will not carry out the instructions do they say so?
- How ethical is it to interfere with something as important as how often mothers cuddle their babies?
- Can the experimenter really be objective in recording the dependent variable?
- Can the experimenter be consistent in the methods of recording over the period of the study?

. . . and lots more.

Each of the questions above has to be considered carefully. It is unlikely that our participants will be a random sample of the population, so if volunteers are used the psychologist must be very cautious in generalizations he or she may wish to make about the findings. The view participants take of the study is important because it will undoubtedly influence their performance in the experiment.

If participants know 'too much' about what the experimenter's hypothesis is they are likely to be biased. Sometimes experimenters have to try a little subterfuge. But in our hypothetical study the experimenter is requiring a lot of the participants: to ask for 60 minutes contact a day is a tall order to request or impose on even willing participants. Eager-to-please mothers may go beyond the call of duty, and do more than the average mother might. Less eager mothers may drop out over the test period, or simply pretend they've carried out the instructions rather than disappoint the researcher. The ethics of this study are tricky. Would you be prepared to do it? Even if an ethical committee accepted this proposal individuals invited to participate may feel differently.

Experimenters are just as human as their participants. Quite often it is said that the area psychologists choose to research reveals a lot about their personal concerns. Is physical contact a particular problem area for the psychologist planning this study? Has he or she a bit of a 'touch taboo' and wants to understand more about the role of physical contact in child development? Has he or she a vested interest in showing that touch is not so important as people like Ashley Montagu believe? If so will it bias his or her attitude in running the study? One way round this is to use an additional researcher blind to each participant's diagnostic category who assesses the dependent variable. Thus in the example here the researcher would not know which babies being assessed were in the 'extra contact' experimental group or either of the control groups.

Experiments play an important role in examining causal relationships, but in exploring the whole of human psychological development we need to look at studies over a much longer time period, and as was outlined in Chapter 1. This is where cross-sectional and longitudinal studies have a role.

Longitudinal and cross-sectional studies

As we saw in Chapters 1 and 13, the major problem with these two methods is that they appear to give two different answers to the same question (see *Figure 14.1*).

Cross-sectional studies confound historical (or generational) changes with individual (or ontogenetic) changes. The generational differences may be so great that they account for most of the variation between different age groups, studied at one point in time. Thus to attribute the observed differences to age *per se* is quite inappropriate. *Longitudinal*

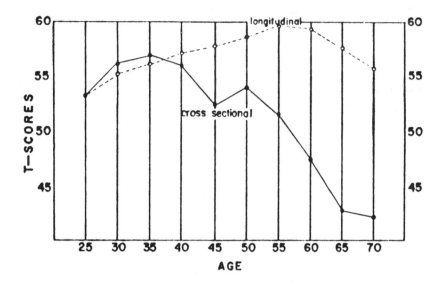

FIGURE 14.1: *Cross-sectional and longitudinal age gradients for tests of verbal meaning*

studies suffer from loss of participants, the problem associated with repeated testing, and the very practical problem for researchers – that funding for research rarely enables the psychologist to plan more than a few years ahead and hence undertake a really long study. Loss of participants is important because those who drop out may be very different from those who stay in a longitudinal study. Thus the sample we end up with is quite unlike the original participant population.

Warner Schaie's research

Warner Schaie and his colleagues were interested in exploring age-related changes in cognitive abilities and they devised an intriguing way of investigating the impact of both the cohort effect and the problem of loss of participants in these two methods of study.

Schaie decided he would convert a cross-sectional study into a longitudinal one. In 1956 he did a cross-sectional study of cognitive abilities, seven years later in 1963 a follow-up was conducted and he was able to re-test 60 per cent of the 1956 group. To deal with the problem of loss of participants a new sample of participants was also taken from the same population and age range in 1963, seven years after the first study and this group was tested just as the 1956 group had been. This gave one longitudinal study over seven years and three cross-sectional studies, one in 1956 and two in 1963.

Seven years later Schaie was able to re-test the same population for a third time. This time he now had data from some people for 14 years and data for many people for two distinct seven-year periods. *Figure 14.2* shows comparative cross-sectional and longitudinal data for the 'space test' (which is concerned with spatial visualization and is used as part of an intelligence test).

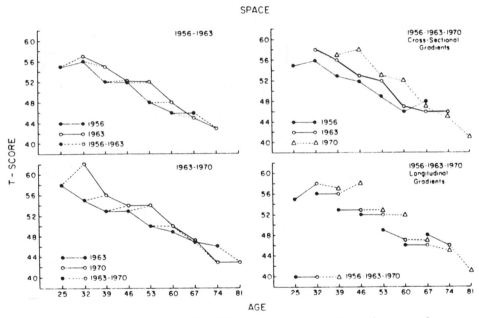

FIGURE 14.2: *Cross-sectional and longitudinal age gradients for tests of spatial ability*

The particularly interesting result of these studies was, as we might have predicted (see discussion in Chapter 13) that *later-born cohorts* performed at a higher level than earlier-born ones. Each generation appeared to be getting cleverer. Could this be true? Schaie's conclusion was rather different. He argued that in the areas of intellectual skills and abilities old people, in general (and if they are reasonably healthy) are not showing a decline, but their skills and abilities developed in youth have become obsolete. Thus the further they are from their youth, and their experience of full-time education, the more 'decline' they appear to show in a cross-sectional study. However the longitudinal studies, which examine change within the individual, produce something quite different. Here the 14-year period revealed little decline until quite late in life: participants showed either an improvement or little change, only the oldest cohort showed a significant drop.

In summary what these findings appear to show is that environmental change and ontogenetic change are *interdependent*. Age differences are not a guide to psychological change within the individual; what we need to look at is the interlinkage between individuals and life events.

Paul Baltes' approach

Paul Baltes and colleagues have developed this sort of idea further by identifying three major systems of influence on development. For each individual the basic determinants of the influences which Baltes proposes are biology, the environment and the interaction between these two. The extent to which any one of these may have impact on a single individual varies. For instance it is not possible to say that, at the level of the individual, intelligence is determined, say, 80 per cent by biological factors. In individual cases the balance varies and at present we cannot specify what that balance is.

The influences that shape development are in Paul Baltes' view 'normative age graded', 'normative history graded' and 'non-normative life events'. Age-graded events are said to be *normative* if they tend to occur in highly similar ways (their timing, and duration) for all individuals in a culture (or subculture). They may have been determined by biological, or environmental factors or an interaction between these. Examples include education and schooling, puberty, marriage, having children, the menopause, retirement and so on; each of these is not set at one specific age but 'biological' clocks and 'social clocks' play a greater or lesser part in determining when they occur. Thus the menopause is influenced more by the former and the age of retirement or marriage more by the latter.

Normative history-graded influences again have the same biological and/or environmental determinants, but these are influences to which most members of a generation or cohort are exposed. Wars, major epidemics, and economic depression would be examples here. 'Non-normative life events' are events that do not occur in either of the above ways for most people. They are highly individual. Before proceeding further turn to *Exercise 14.1* on page 265 which enables you to explore your own very personal ways of viewing the course of development. You may see that your own particular approach is reflected in the ideas of the researchers to be discussed next.

Baltes suggests that examples of 'non-normative life events' might be an accident, illness, career change, death of a loved one and so on.

If we consider the impact of these three types of influences it is easy to see, particularly in cross-sectional research, why age *per se* may be a totally inadequate concept to explain differences or similarities between people. A child who has lived through a famine in Ethiopia, compared to one reared in an aristocratic family in the UK, and one who lives in the black ghettos of New York have so little in common that age tells us nothing about their physical growth or psychological development.

Attempts to look at the life span in terms of developments beyond the purely biological time clock have produced some interesting findings.

Studying life-span development

Most people recognize that throughout the course of human life there are important stages or milestones. Shakespeare reflected this view in his cynical and poetical description of the 'seven stages' in human life. More recently there have been more systematic attempts to identify stages in life common to individuals in a given culture.

TABLE 14.1: *Buhler's biological and psychological phases of life*

Approximate age	Biological phase	Psychosocial phase
0–15	Progressive growth	Child at home, prior to self-determination of goals
16–25	Continued growth and ability to reproduce sexually	Preparatory expansion, experimental determination of goals.
26–45	Stability of growth	Culmination
46–65	Loss of reproductive ability	Self-assessment after striving for goals
Over 65	Regressive growth and biological decline	Experience of fulfilment or failure

[Adapted from Buhler, 1968.]

Charlotte Buhler and others studied 400 biographies and autobiographies and from these discovered that certain phases repeatedly appeared in the lives which they analysed. They identified five biological phases that could be linked to five stages in psychosocial development (see *Table 14.1*). Essentially psychosocial development was viewed in terms of goal setting. The theory views the peak period of life in the twenties, thirties and forties with the phase after 45 as one of contraction.

Life's problems and crises

Another approach to the life cycle has emerged from the clinical setting. Carl Jung, Alfred Adler and later Erik Erikson all formulated their views as a result of helping those with various types of psychological disorder.

For Jung life stages were concerned with how the individual dealt with problems of the psyche. In 'Youth', a period which he identifies as from puberty to the middle years (around the age of 40), the concerns are focused on overcoming inferiority and coping with the sexual drive. After this phase there are gradual changes which often involve an increase in rigidity and intolerance. Jung observed that in old age there may be a shift in psychological terms so that the older woman may become more masculine and the older man more feminine.

Adler saw three great problems in life, these were: social interest, occupation, and love and marriage. Whilst these problems are not specifically associated with ages in life it is obvious that they are almost the universal concerns of the adult years.

Erik Erikson identified eight 'ages of man' and saw the boundaries of each as a crucial turning point or crisis. As has already been noted, he, like many others, sees most change occurring in the first part of life (see *Table 14.2*) – five of his crucial turning points occur under the age of 20, with only three for the rest of life. In Erikson's view, how we, individually, cope with each stage influences subsequent coping. Each 'age' can be seen as a building block; if we cope successfully each block sits neatly on the one below, if not then we may have a rocky tower, one that is easily knocked down by the slightest turbulence in life. Clearly here the main foundations are laid in childhood and it is on these that later coping depends. However, Erikson's intriguing theory has been criticized on several grounds. It is hard to prove empirically; it recognizes little in the way of coping or change during the major part of adult life; and it seems sex-biased very much in the direction of male rather than female adult development.

These approaches towards studying life show very clearly that, in psychological terms, age *per se* is not a crucial factor in shaping the individual. It is what happens to the individual and the expectations imposed by his or her particular society and culture, in a given historical time that can have an overriding influence.

TABLE 14.2: *Erikson's eight 'ages of man'*

The 'ages'	Psychological crises or issues
1 Oral Up to 2 years*	Basic trust versus mistrust
2 Anal 2–4 years	Autonomy versus shame, doubt
3 Genital 5–7 years	Initiative versus guilt
4 Latency 6–12 years	Industry versus inferiority
5 Adolescence 13–19 years	Identity versus role confusion
6 Young adult 20–30 years	Intimacy versus isolation
7 Middle Adult 31–65 years	Generativity versus stagnation
8 Late adult Over 65 years	Integrity versus despair

*Approximate figures only

OTHER RESEARCH METHODS

Studying twins

The influence of environmental factors was stressed in the preceding section and yet all of us are aware that biology must play a key role too. At the start of this chapter, it was noted that the ethologists emphasize this view and these two approaches have sometimes given rise to the nature and nurture debate. Which is more important – biology or environment?

Nature versus nurture. One way of examining the biological components of behaviour is the study of twins. Identical twins are *monozygotic* (MZ): they come from a single egg and thus share *all* their genetic material. Fraternal twins are *dizygotic* (DZ): they arise from the fertilization of two separate eggs and thus genetically they are no more similar than 'ordinary' siblings. Of course they share the uterus and are born at the same time so if experience is to be more influential than biology we might predict that they should be just as similar as MZ twins at birth (on average). Sharing a uterus does not necessarily mean having identical environments, one twin may have a better position than the other. We are often particularly aware of this in the young of animals that have large litters. In a litter of piglets there is often a runt, one very small piglet who had the least advantageous part of the uterus.

If samples of MZ twins are compared with samples of DZ twins on any characteristic we know that whilst the former share 100 per cent of their genes, the latter only shares 50 per cent on average. By correlating our measure with the twin type we may well find that concordance rates (agreement between the correlations) between MZ twins and DZ twins differ. Hill Goldsmith and Irving Gottesman looked at the heritability of activity level in babies in this way and found a concordance rate of .57 for MZ twins compared with .35 for DZ twins (a significant difference) where 1.00 would be a perfect correlation. From this study we might conclude that biology plays a greater role in babies' activity levels than does environment. But there are problems in this argument.

Most babies are not twins, thus using twin babies to help us explain behaviour in general may be misleading.

Another way of examining *heritability* is to use MZ twins reared together compared with those who, through force of circumstance, have been reared apart. This is quite an appealing method initially because whilst holding the genetic component constant we can 'manipulate' the environmental component to a greater or lesser degree. Studies of the incidence of various psychological disorders, such as schizophrenia, have used these methods to try to assess the influence of these two components on the likelihood of suffering this disorder. The results of this work are not clear cut. Some studies find much higher concordance rates than others, thus suggesting that the influence of biology and environment is variable. Again there are problems with such research, the first problem, identified above – that most babies are not twins – still applies. Second, the families chosen to rear the separated twins are often fairly similar in terms of education, socioeconomic status and other characteristics, so that they do not represent the range of possible environments in which children can be reared.

Heritability is often misunderstood because some believe that it reveals the degree to which a characteristic is determined by the genetic component in an *individual*. However it can only ever be applied to populations. It is the extent to which a characteristic is determined by inherited components within a population, thus at the level of the individual it tells us nothing. What is important to remember is that genes and the environment are not separate components. Exactly how a given gene works, in terms of the way it shows itself in the individual, depends on the type of environment it is in. The genes and the environment *interact* together. A good example of this is seen in the Himalayan rabbit, guinea pig, or the Siamese cat.

In their infancy the young of these animals require a certain ambient temperature if they are to develop the light body with dark extremities (ears, nose, feet and tail) with which we are familiar. The expression of this genetic predisposition depends on the temperature of the skin during a critical period of postnatal development. Normally the extremities are cooler than the rest of the body and at normal rearing temperatures they turn browny-black. If our kittens or guinea pigs are raised in a very warm atmosphere they remain light in colour and if placed in an ice box they become uniformly dark.

So two individuals who are genetically identical may have different phenotypes as a result of very different environments, whilst two individuals who are genetically very different may, because they share an environment, emerge very similarly.

Measures of heritability can give us a rough guide to the influence of genetic factors for a given sample, but for individuals it is an entirely inappropriate concept. It is also a rather dangerous concept, for if we mistakenly attribute a given characteristic to our genetic programming then this prevents us from considering the possibility that anything can be done to alter that characteristic. For example 'boys are aggressive, it's in their nature' implies that we cannot change them so it's not worth trying. There may be genetic influences on aggression but these undoubtedly interact with environmental influences. Since we can influence someone's environment but not their genes then it is surely to the former that we should direct our attention.

Case studies

In relation to the nature–nuture debate it was noted that heritability refers to populations and not individuals. Many psychological methods deal with fairly large samples of people so that we can look for general rules governing behaviour, thought and emotion. Yet individually we all feel unique and often when we read about psychological studies our reaction may be 'That doesn't apply to me, I behaved quite differently in those circumstances'. Exceptions to rules usually arise because generalizations don't allow for individual variation. One way of capturing the uniqueness of a person is the *case study*.

This method, which has often been in the clinical setting, enables us to record a person's life in detail. It may involve interviews with the participant about his or her experiences, plus interviews with people close to them, family and friends for example. Memories concerning past events may be verified through historical records so that it is possible to reconstruct the participant's life as they and others see it. Case studies mentioned in this book include baby biographers such as Charles Darwin (in Chapter 1), 'Isabelle' who was described by Kingsley Davis and was the little girl who made astonishing progress after many years of deprivation, and the 'wild boy of Aveyron' (in Chapter 3). Case studies usually involve one person but they may use small groups. Anna Freud and Sophie Dann's study of the six young children persecuted by the Nazis is an example of the latter (see Chapter 3).

Whilst generalizations about people cannot be made from case studies they may often provide interesting hypotheses. Jean Piaget's detailed records, or case studies, of his children referred to in Chapter 7 led to his research on cognitive development. In the book *Living through the Blitz* Tom Harrison shows that individual memories of historical events differ quite dramatically from accounts documented at the time. Such work shows us that each of us interpret or construe the world in quite unique ways depending on our own particular experiences. The truth, as each of us sees it, is only one facet of reality, and yet trying to account for each individual's way of viewing events is an important area within psychology.

Surveys

When they want to make broad generalizations about people researchers often use the *survey* method. Surveys have been carried out on everything from opinions about tomato ketchup to sexual behaviour, or the way in which individuals are likely to vote at an election. You will probably have been stopped in the street and asked your opinion of consumer products.

Surveys often use very large samples that are selected so that they represent a given population. Audience research carried out for television and radio often involves samples of a thousand or more people who are chosen to represent the viewing or listening public. Thus the age, sex, educational background, socioeconomic status and many other variables have to be accurately identified in the whole population being researched and faithfully represented in the sample to be surveyed. If the sample is not *representative* then the results will be biased. Surveys are typically *correlational* studies. They tell us much about the associations between 'types' of people and behaviour patterns, but nothing about causes.

RELIABILITY AND VALIDITY

If one psychologist carries out an experiment and finds some exciting results these findings are not accepted until the research can be replicated by another researcher. *Reliability* in research is shown by the repeatability of research studies. If the method is followed by another investigator it should produce the same results if the method is reliable. If it does not then we may question the objectivity of the researcher and the care with which he or she has reported what was done. Research studies must always be reported in such a way that others can repeat the work. If methodology is glossed over then we are justified in questioning the findings. Cyril Burt is probably one of the most well-known psychologists whose *unreliability* in methodology eventually emerged.

Validity in research concerns whether it measures what we think it measures. Early studies of 'intelligence' in non-human animals involved setting numerous different species tasks such as maze learning. Some animals such as rats were found to be 'intelligent' and others (many fish species) were found to be unintelligent. If by 'intelligence' we mean 'ability to solve certain problems' the problem here was that the task set for a given species was often highly inappropriate for the species. Deep-sea fish are unused to mazes and they rarely encounter walls in their environments, whereas rats are used to living in holes and are well suited to solving maze learning tasks. To conclude that certain fish are 'unintelligent' on the basis of this sort of test is invalid. Such research merely tells us that these fish cannot learn mazes.

Laboratory work has often been criticized because researchers may claim that their findings represent what people or other animals do in 'real life'. If you took part in a psychology experiment in the laboratory it's unlikely that you would be your natural self in such a setting. You might be shy or awkward in the laboratory for instance. If the researcher was studying social skills and concluded that you were a shy and awkward person with others the conclusion is likely to be *invalid*. You might be exactly the opposite in 'real life'; it was the psychologist and the laboratory that produced a change in your behaviour. The essence of validity is: does the test or experiment *really* measure what the psychologist thinks it does? The method employed may be reliable – it can be replicated by other researchers – but are the results meaningful in the way that is claimed?

In conclusion

Psychologists have developed a variety of methods which enable them to investigate many facets of human behaviour. If the questions which are asked are generated from careful observation of people in naturalistic settings then the hypotheses which are formed are likely to be ones which will illuminate our understanding of people. However, even if the research methods are both reliable and valid there are many areas of human life that cannot be researched directly. Ethical issues may prevent us from being able to investigate experimentally, as we saw in Chapter 1. In other areas of life we may not be able to do more than correlational studies so that the causes of human behaviour will not be identified. However sophisticated the methodology we will never achieve all the answers. Each individual is unique and mysterious so that developmental psychology faces a continual challenge in its attempts to explain the development of behaviour, emotion and thought. One of the exciting, and sometimes maddening, features of this subject is that there are no simple answers. We cannot explain an individual's behaviour without reference to his or her unique biology and environment. The answers must always be prefaced by 'it depends' – because in psychological terms we are complex beings and the causes of our behaviour are generally complex too. The answers we come up with today may be inappropriate for future decades.

Nevertheless psychological research has provided guidelines for dealing with a host of human concerns: in the widest sense it has been used to shape social policy and it has also had impact on us all at a most personal level.

Do psychologists have an advantage in relationships?

This question is often asked of psychologists. Indeed developmental psychologists, perhaps more than those in other fields, are often asked 'how does your knowledge influence your behaviour as a parent?'. Very little research has addressed this question, although Peter Barnes has reported on the parenting styles of some well-known psychologists.

John B. Watson believed that independence in children was encouraged by a cool, unemotional approach by parents. Watson's biographer however believed that Watson's sons suffered. Indeed Billy Watson attributed many of his later personal problems to his treatment in childhood. Burrhus Skinner raised his younger daughter Deborah in a controlled environment – a kind of germ-free box or 'baby-tender'. Despite rumours to the contrary Deborah grew up to lead a normal life without any notable difficulties. Abraham Maslow observed 'Our first baby changed me as a psychologist. It made the behaviourism I had been so enthusiastic about look so foolish that I could not stomach it any more'. For him the experience of parenthood made him see the subject of psychology quite differently.

It would seem from these three examples that real life may make us question psychological research and theory, just as the latter may influence how we look at 'real life'. Most psychologists are rather wary about assessing their own competence as parents – but in the view of the authors of this text a knowledge of psychology does give us insights in our dealings with children. However, putting theories into practice is never easy, as all parents know. A knowledge of psychology in our experience can heighten both our understanding and enjoyment of others at any stage of development – but that is not to say that we are any better as parents (or caregivers). Indeed just how much a knowledge of psychology influences our behaviour as a parent is one of the many questions that still needs to be researched.

Recommended reading

Gardner, H. (1982) *Developmental Psychology*. Boston, Toronto: Little, Brown & Co. [A lengthy but very readable text on developmental psychology.]
Lipsitt, L.P. & Reese, H.W. (1979) *Child Development*. Glenview, Ill.: Scott, Foresman & Co. [Chapters 1–5 are particularly useful in explaining methods in psychology.]
Lisney, M. (1989) *Psychology: Experiments, investigations and practicals.* Oxford: Basil Blackwell. [A useful guide on how to run psychological experiments.]

References

Baltes, P.E., Reese, H.W. & Lipsitt, L.P. (1930) Life-span developmental psychology. *Annual Review of Psychology, 31,* 65–110. [Baltes' approach to life-span development.]
Barnes, P. (1987) A load of psychological cobblers. (A poster presented at The British Psychological Society Developmental Section Annual (September) Conference, in York.) [A review of the parenting skills of some famous psychologists.]
Blurton Jones, N. (1972) Characteristics of ethological studies of human behaviour. In N. Blurton Jones (Ed.) *Ethological Studies of Child Behaviour.* Cambridge: Cambridge University Press. [Discusses ethological research and Tinbergen's four questions about behaviour.]
Buhler, C. (1968) The developmental structure of goal setting in group and individual studies. In C. Buhler & F. Massarik (Eds) *The Course of Human Life.* New York: Springer. [Buhler's view of the life cycle.]
Goldsmith, H.H. & Cottesman, I.I. (1981) Origin of variation in behavioural style: a longitudinal study of temperament in young twins. *Child Development, 52,* 91–103. [Activity levels in twins.]
Harrison, T. (1976) *Living through the Blitz.* London: Collins. [Memories of historical events.]
Hofer, M.A. (1981) *The Roots of Human Behaviour: An introduction to the psychology of early*

Life Cycle Questionnaire

Please answer questions as fully as possible.

(1) Do you see life as a series of milestones/stages?   YES/NO
     If yes, what are the key stages for you (include those in the past, present and future)?

(2) Have there been any important turning points in your life?   YES/NO
     If yes, please list the turning points which you have experienced or expect to experience.

(3) Are there any things in life which are important to you for which you are now aware that you are too old?

(4) Are there any things in life which are important to you for which you feel you are still too young?

(5) At what time during the life cycle do you think that there is most learning and psychological change – please give your answers in terms of ages, for example, 0–5 years, 20–45 years.

(6) Do you think that there comes a time in everyone's life when he or she has a period of self-assessment, looking back at what has been achieved? If so, when is that period (or periods)? Please give your answer(s) in terms of ages.

(7) At what stage in life might you expect to experience noticeable signs of ageing in terms of the ability to learn and to adapt to new situations? Please give your answer in terms of age.

▶ **Comment:** There are no right answers to this questionnaire, it is a personal exploration of how you view life. Compare your answers with those of your family and/or friends. You may be surprised to see how differently people view life. Chapter 14 discusses different theories of the life cycle – compare your own views with those discussed.

development. San Francisco: W.H. Freeman. [Coat colour in kittens as a function of ambient temperature.]

Jung, C.G (1971) The Stages of Life. In J. Campbell *The Portable Jung*. New York: Viking. (Originally published in 1933.) [Jung's views of life.]

Kuhlen, P.G. & Johnson, G.H. (1952) Change in goals with increasing adult age. *Journal of Consulting Psychology*. *16*, 1–4. [Support for Buhler's view of life from a study of teachers.]

Maier, H.W. (1978) *Three Theories of Child Development*. London: Harper & Row. [Erik Erikson's theory.]

Montagu, M.F.A. (1971) *Touching: The human significance of the skin*. New York: Columbia University Press. [Detailed account of the significance of touching.]

Orgler, H. (1973) *Alfred Adler: The man and his work*. London: Sidgwick & Jackson. [Alfred Adler's 'three problems of life'.]

Peck, R.C. (1968) Psychological developments in the second half of life. In B.L. Neugarten (Ed.) *Middle Age and Ageing: A reader in social psychology*. London: University of Chicago Press. [Peck's refinement of Erikson's life stages.]

Schaffer, R. (1985) *Mothering*. Glasgow: Fontana. [Intrinsic behaviour patterns.]

Schaie, K. (1975) Age changes in adult intelligence. In D.S. Woodruff & J.E. Birren (Eds) *Aging: Scientific perspectives and social issues*. New York: Van Nostrand. [Longitudinal studies of aging and intelligence discussed.]

Schaie, K.W. & Labouvie-Vief, G. (1974) Generational versus ontogenetic components of change in adult cognitive behaviour: A fourteen-year cross-sequential study. *Developmental Psychology*, *10*, 305–320. [Details of the 14-year longitudinal study of aging and intelligence.]

Schaie, K.W. & Stromer, C.R. (1988) A cross-sequential study of age changes in cognitive behaviour. *Psychological Bulletin*, *70*, 671–680.

Stafford-Clark, D. (1965) *What Freud Really Said*. Harmondsworth: Penguin. [Freud's ideas and methods.]

Watson, J.B. (1913) Psychology as the behaviourist views it. *Psychological Review*, *20*, 158–177. [Watson's views on learning.]

GLOSSARY

Accommodation: Piagetian term which describes the changes which occur in thinking when new objects or experiences are encountered. When the infant discovers that some objects can be sucked but that others cannot, for example, his or her sucking scheme is said to be accommodated to those new objects (see also *assimilation*; *schemes*).

Activity theory: a theory which states that activity and social participation are positively related to well-being in later life.

Adolescence: the stage in development which begins at puberty and ends when physiological or psychological maturity is reached. However, the attainment of maturity is impossible to specify precisely.

Adult–child register: a form of speech, characterized by simplicity, clarity and repetition, typically used by adults talking to children; also called 'baby talk' or 'motherese'.

Age norms: the average scores obtained on psychological tests by people at given age levels.

Ageism: the existence of unfavourable stereotypes, expressed by attitudes, beliefs and discriminatory behaviour, concerning elderly people.

Androgens: a collective term for the hormones produced chiefly by the testes, the chief one of which is testosterone. Responsible for the maintenance and development of many male sexual characteristics.

Assimilation: Piagetian term which describes the process of incorporating new objects or experiences into thinking. When the infant learns by experience that some objects can be sucked and that others cannot, for example, the former are said to be assimilated to the sucking scheme (see also *accommodation*; *scheme*).

Attachment: a binding affection, an emotional tie between individuals

Attachment behaviour : behaviour which promotes proximity and physical contact with the object of the attachment.

Autonomous morality: Piaget's second stage of moral reasoning characterized by judgement of intent and emphasis on reciprocity.

Biological clock: an internal (physiological) mechanism that keeps time or rhythm so that the organism shows by its behaviour that many biological processes are timed. The cycles of such rhythms may vary widely: especially common are daily, tidal, monthly and annual rhythms.

Circular reaction: Piagetian term describing the infant's repetition of an action after it has produced some observable effect on the environment.

Classical (respondent) conditioning: the process whereby new stimuli gain the power to evoke respondents. In the language of learning theorists: if a stimulus, originally neutral with respect to a particular (and natural) response, is paired a number of times with a stimulus eliciting that response, the previously neutral stimulus itself will also come to elicit that response.

Cognition: a person's thoughts, knowledge and ideas about him or herself and the environment.

Cognitive processes: refers to mental activities involving evaluation and appraisal. They can sometimes be used as equivalent to thought.

Cohort: a group of people born at about the same time and thus passing through similar historical experiences as they move through the life span.

Cohort-sequential study: a study in which people of different ages (and thus birth cohorts) are repeatedly tested over time, and which thus combines features of *cross-sectional* and of *longitudinal* studies.

Compensation: Freudian term describing the process by which unconscious problems can be overcome by acting them out in a stress-free medium, such as play.

Cones: elements of the retina concerned with colour vision.

Conservation: a cognitive advance which Piaget proposed as a central feature of concrete operational thinking, acquired at around the age of seven.

Constancy: the fact that an object perceived from different points of view still looks like the same object.

Control group: a group in an experiment that is not given the treatment whose effect is being studied (see also *experimental group*).

Conventional morality: the second level of moral judgement proposed by Kohlberg, in which the person's judgements are dominated by considerations of group values and laws.

Correlational study: a study which is designed to find out the degree of correspondence or association between two sets of measures.

Cross-sectional study: a study in which groups of individuals differing in age (and thus birth cohort) are tested, and their performance compared, at a single point in time.

Cybernetics: the study of systems of control and communication applied by psychologists to animal and human behaviour, and notably to the ways family systems function.

Dependent variable: the behaviour or response measured in a psychological experiment which is believed to be changed by the independent variable.

Disengagement theory: a theory which states that withdrawal from social participation is a 'natural' concomitant of old age, and that the withdrawal is positively associated with well-being.

Dyadic model: one-to-one, face-to-face therapy.

Ecological validity: the appropriateness of a given test as an indicator of people's performance, or competence, in everyday situations.

Egocentrism: the tendency to see the world only from one's own point of view, which Piaget believed to be a central feature of early childhood.

Elaborated code: a mode of speaking which is sufficiently rich and varied as to be meaningful without reference to the immediate context (see also *restricted code*).

Empiricists: those who base their views on the fundamental assumption that all knowledge comes from experience (see also *nativists*).

Ethnocentric: tendency to see things from one's own ethnic/cultural perspective only.

Ethologist: one who researches the behaviour of animals, and who works primarily in their natural habitats rather than the laboratory.

Experimental group: a group in an experiment that is given the treatment whose effect is being studied (see also *control group*).

Figural strategy: an approach to drawing which captures the overall shape of the subject rather than its precise details (see also *metric strategy*).

Gene: the biological unit of inheritance for all living organisms. Genes are located on the chromosomes which are inside the cell nucleus. A gene, or a combination of many genes, is responsible for inherited characteristics, e.g. eye colour, personality, components of intellectual ability.

Genetic epistemology: literally the study of the origins of knowledge, which Piaget used as a description of his work with children.

Grammar: a model of language use, including the study of speech sounds, words and affixes, sentence structure and, in many cases, meaning.

Habituation: the reduction in the strength of a response to a repeated stimulus.

Heritability: the proportion of the variation of a trait within a population that is attributable to the genetic differences between individuals in that population.

Heteronomous morality: Piaget's first stage of moral reasoning, by moral absolutism and belief in immanent justice. Judgements are based on consequences rather than intent. Ends at six or seven years of age.

Holophrase: a single word which serves as, and many have the implicit grammar of, a complete sentence.

Hysteria: a form of neurosis often involving emotional outbursts and physical symptomatology (i.e. imaginary illnesses, paralysis, etc).

Ideational fluency: the ability to generate a number of different ideas from a given open-ended problem.

Imitation: Piaget used this as a technical term to describe children's adaptation of their thinking to copy the world around them.

Imprinting: learning that occurs within a limited period early in life (usually in relation to the mother and likened by Lorenz to a pathological fixation); and which is relatively unmodifiable.

Independent variable: the variable in a psychological experiment which is under the control of the psychologist, and is varied by him or her.

Inflections: endings (such as -ing, -s, -d) added to the stem of a word to modify its meaning, but not its grammatical class.

Intellectual realism: characteristic of young children's drawings according to which they draw 'what they know, and not what they see'.

IQ (Intelligence quotient): a person's age-referenced score on an intelligence test.

Life span: the genetically fixed life expectancy for members of a given species, barring accidents or major illness before old age.

Longitudinal study: a study in which a group of people of the same birth cohort are tested more than once over a period of time to measure age-related changes.

Mean length of utterance (MLU): a measure of sentence length, either in words or in *morphemes* (word stems plus inflections), averaged over a number of sentences.

Melodic contour: the 'shape', i.e. pattern of ups and downs, of a melody.

Metric strategy: an approach to drawing which incorporates the precise details of the subject (see also *figural strategy*).

Monotropism: the innate tendency of the infant to become attached to *one* particular individual with the implication that this attachment is different in kind from any subsequent attachments formed.

Morpheme: the smallest linguistic unit of meaning. It may be a word capable of standing alone (a free morpheme) or part of a word, such as an *inflection* (a bound morpheme).

Motherese: a popular term for an adult–child register.

Nativists: those who base their views on the assumption that genetic, inherited influences on behaviour, thought and emotion are of overriding importance (see also *empiricists*).

Object permanence: the concept that objects still exist when they are out of sight, which Piaget proposed was acquired in infancy.

Ontogenetic: pertaining to the development of an individual organism.

Operant conditioning: the strengthening of a response by presenting a reinforcer if, and only if, the response occurs.

Paradigm: a theoretical model or perspective; a very general conception of the nature of a scientific endeavour within which a given enquiry or psychological intervention is being undertaken.

Phonology: the study of recognizably different speech sounds and their patterning.

Polygenic inheritances: the action of several genes – the basic units of inheritance (applies to the genetic basis, inter alia, of personality and intelligence).

Preconventional morality: Kohlberg's first level of morality in which moral judgements are dominated by consideration of what will be punished and what feels good.

Principled morality: the third level of morality proposed by Kohlberg, in which considerations of justice, individual rights, and contracts dominate moral judgement.

Privation: a lacking of satisfaction, or the means to achieve satisfaction of one's needs (as opposed to deprivation which is the removal of such means).

Psychoanalysis: a method developed by Freud and his followers concerning the treatment of mental and nervous disorders in which the role of the unconscious is emphasized.

Psychology: the systematic study of cognition (thoughts), emotion (feelings) and behaviour.

Psychometrics: the theory and practice of psychological testing.

Psychotic: suffering from a mental illness involving symptoms such as hallucinations, thought disorders, delusions.

Puberty: the age at which the sex organs become reproductively functional. It is marked by the menarche in girls, but in boys it is less easy to specify; the growth and pigmentation of underarm hair is often taken as criterial.

Reflex: a physiological reaction, such as an eye-blink to a bright light, over which we have no control.

Regression: a return to immature activities and behaviours.

Reliability: a statistical index of the degree to which a test provides consistent measurements.

Restricted code: a mode of speaking which is not meaningful without reference to the immediate context (see also *elaborated code*).

Rods: elements of the retina concerned with black and white vision.

Role theory: the explanation of people's behaviour in terms of their acting out social roles.

Schemes: cognitive structures which are abstract representations of events, people and relationships in the outside world.

Semantics: the study of meaning.

Social clock: this is produced (according to Neugarten) by the interaction of age norms, age constraints, age status systems and age-related roles. It is by the social clock (or age norms, etc) that individuals set their own internal sense of social timing. Social clocks may differ in different societies.

Social learning theory: an explanation of behaviour which combines principles of reinforcement (reward and punishment) with those of cognition (thinking).

Somatic: to do with the body; somatic (i.e. physical) symptoms.

Stereotypes: generalized sets of beliefs or attitudes, often inaccurate, about identifiable groups of people.

Symbolic play: play in which children use their own bodies or objects as symbols for other people or objects, and in which they create make-believe or fantasy.

Syntax: the lawful patterning of words and 'parts of speech' into sentences.

Temperament: the constitutional (inherited) aspects of personality.

Time out: behavioural techniques; removing a child temporarily from a situation in which he or she is being reinforced for undesirable behaviour.

Triadic model: working therapeutically through a third person (mediator) to help a child. This may involve training a caregiver to work therapeutically.

Validity: a statistical index of the degree to which a test measures that which it is supposed to measure.

Visual realism: a characteristic of children's drawings after the age of 10 or so, whereby objects are represented as they actually appear.

ILLUSTRATION AND EXERCISE CREDITS